Reforging the Weakest Link
Global Political Economy and Post-Soviet Change in Russia, Ukraine and Belarus

Edited by
NEIL ROBINSON
University of Limerick

ASHGATE

Published by
Ashgate Publishing Limited
Gower House
Croft Road
Aldershot
Hants GU11 3HR
England

Ashgate Publishing Company
Suite 420
101 Cherry Street
Burlington, VT 05401-4405
USA

Ashgate website: http://www.ashgate.com

British Library Cataloguing in Publication Data
Reforging the weakest link : global political economy and
    post-Soviet change in Russia, Ukraine and Belarus. - (The
    international political economy of new regionalisms series)
    1.Russia (Federation) - Economic conditions - 1991-
    2.Ukraine - Economic conditions - 1991- 3.Belarus -
    Economic conditions - 1991- 4.Russia (Federation) - Foreign
    economic relations 5.Ukraine - Foreign economic relations
    6.Belarus - Foreign economic relations 7.Russia
    (Federation) - Economic policy - 1991- 8.Ukraine - Economic
    policy - 1991- 9.Belarus - Economic policy - 1991-
    I.Robinson, Neil
    330.9'47086

Library of Congress Cataloging-in-Publication Data
Reforging the weakest link : global political economy and post-Soviet change in
Russia, Ukraine and Belarus / Edited by Neil Robinson.
    p. cm. -- (The international political economy of new regionalisms
series)
    Includes bibliographical references and index.
    ISBN 0-7546-3494-9
    1. Former Soviet republics--Foreign economic relations. 2. Former Soviet
republics--Commercial policy. 3. Former Soviet republics--Economic policy. 4. Post-
communism--Former Soviet republics. I. Robinson, Neil, 1964- II. Series.

    HF1557.R44 2004
    337.47--dc22

                                                                    2004005861

ISBN 0 7546 3494 9

Printed and bound in Great Britain by MPG Books Ltd, Bodmin, Cornwall

90 0619524 9

REFORGING THE WEAKEST LINK

The International Political Economy of New Regionalisms Series

The International Political Economy of New Regionalisms Series presents innovative analyses of a range of novel relations and institutions. Going beyond established, formal, interstate economic organizations, this essential series provides informed interdisciplinary and international research and debate about myriad heterogeneous intermediate level interactions.

Reflective of its cosmopolitain and creative orientation, this series is developed by an international editorial team of established and emerging scholars in both the South and the North. It reinforces ongoing networks of analysts in both academia and think-tanks as well as international agencies concerned with micro-, meso- and macro-level regionalisms.

Contents

List of Tables

Glossary

CBR	Central Bank of Russia
CEE	Central and Eastern Europe
CEFTA	Central European Free Trade Area
CIS	Commonwealth of Independent States
CMEA	Council for Mutual Economic Assistance
CPE	Centrally planned economy
EBRD	European Bank for Reconstruction and Development
EU	European Union
FDI	Foreign Direct Investment
FIGs	Financial Industrial Groups
FR	Financial Repression
FSU	Former Soviet Union
GDP	Gross Domestic Product
GKOs	Short-term Russian government discount bills
Gosplan	Soviet central planning agency
G-7	Group of Seven (France, USA, United Kingdom, Germany, Japan, Italy and Canada)
G-8	Group of Eight (G-7 plus Russia)
HDI	United Nations Human Development Index
IFI	International financial institution
IMF	International Monetary Fund
IT	Inflation Tax
JV	Joint venture
NATO	North Atlantic Treaty Organization
NBB	National Bank of Belarus
NBU	National Bank of Ukraine
OFZs	Russian government fixed coupon bonds
QR	Quantitative Restriction
TACIS	Technical Assistance to the CIS programme (EU)
WTO	World Trade Organization

List of Contributors

Marko Bojcun, Senior Lecturer (Politics) and Director of the Ukraine Centre, University of North London. Co-author, *The Chernobyl Disaster* (1988); author, *Ukraine and Europe: a difficult reunion* (2001); editor, *Eastern Europe and European Integration: A Collection of Public Documents 1990-2000* (2001). Author of many papers on Ukrainian affairs, including recent papers in *Problems of Post-Communism, Visnyk Kharkivskoho natsional'noho Universytetu, Journal of Ukrainian Studies.*

Julia Korosteleva is currently completing a PhD at the Department of Economics and International Development, University of Bath. She has published on the role of banks in Belarus and on Belarusian economic policy.

Nadia Lisovskaya is currently completing a PhD at the University of Manchester on foreign trade and transition. Author of several book chapters on economic reform in the former Soviet Union in English and French, and on foreign trade and transition in *Mirovaya ekonomika i mezhdunarodnie otnosheniya.*

Anastasia Nesvetailova, Lecturer, School of International Relations and Politics, University of Sussex. She has written book chapters and articles on globalisation and Russia, the Asian and Russian financial crises of 1998, and Russo-Belarusian relations.

Neil Robinson teaches politics in the Department of Politics and Public Administration, University of Limerick, Ireland. Author, *Ideology and the collapse of the Soviet system* (1995) and *Russia: a state of uncertainty* (2002); co-author, *Post-communist politics* (1997); editor, *Institutions and political change in Russia* (2000).

For Sáoirse and Mancur

Chapter 1

Global Economy, the USSR and Post-Soviet Change

Neil Robinson

Introduction

The transition to market economy and democracy in the former Soviet Union is closely linked to the reintegration of post-Soviet states and their economies in to the global economy. The purpose of this chapter is to outline the circumstances that have shaped efforts towards, and opposition to, economic reintegration. We will begin by examining the relationship of the USSR to the global economy. We will see that the USSR exhibited a peculiar combination of economic backwardness alongside its well-developed industrial structure and society. This combination made the Soviet economy, and by implication those of its successor states too, uncompetitive in world markets. Being uncompetitive made the prospect of post-Soviet reintegration with the global market unattractive to many economic actors. Reintegration with the global economy has, however, been a key theme in thinking about reform. In theory, it offers a unique means of creating incentives for change amid the distortions of post-Soviet economy and reduces the risks of embarking on reform. In the absence of major social forces in favour of reintegration acting on theory depends on politicians. However, politicians have balanced the potential theoretical gains of reintegration against the prospects of opposition that would come from losers in economic reform and the uncertainty that economic openness might bring. This calculation generally went against reform, a fact will be confirmed in the case studies and other chapters of the book. This chapter ends by picking out the key themes in these chapters.

The USSR and the global economy: relative isolation and backwardness

The revolution of October 1917 and the subsequent formation of the Soviet Union were supposed to break world capitalism asunder permanently. For Lenin and the Bolsheviks, the spread of colonialism and the conflict of imperial powers in World War One demonstrated that capitalism had become 'moribund'. It was no longer able to reproduce itself except by external conquest and exploitation, a situation that was bound to cause conflict between imperial powers since the territory available to them for exploitation was finite. Lenin argued that the decay of capitalism in its imperialist stage meant that the world was ripe for social revolution. The spread of imperialism meant the spread of oppression, the growth of exploitation and the heightening of national struggles for liberation. However, the outbreak of social revolution was stymied in the most advanced imperialist powers. The wealth generated by imperialism enabled the bourgeoisie of the largest imperialist states to bribe their working classes and subvert their revolutionary movements (Lenin, 1916). To counter this, socialists had to take advantage of the crises thrown up by imperialist war and convert it into a civil war (Lenin, 1915, p.195).

Fortuitously for Lenin, this was to prove easiest in Russia, where the military incompetence of the Tsarist government and its inability to manage the economic demands of modern warfare combined to create the revolutionary opportunities of 1917. Since the crisis that led to social revolution and the creation of a new economic order took place in Russia, rather than in one of the more advanced capitalist powers, Lenin's assertion that were strong imperialism was able to divert the revolutionary movement looked prophetic to his followers. The implication that they drew from Lenin's thesis was that imperialism had not been able to subvert revolution where it was weakest, in Russia. Subsequently, and as a part of the creation of a cult of genius around Lenin, Lenin's complaints about the lack of revolutionary zeal in advanced capitalist states was elevated to the grander status of prophecy. By the mid-1920s, Stalin (1924, p.19) was claiming that Lenin's theory of imperialism had predicted that revolution follows 'the breaking of the chain of the world imperialist front at its weakest link ... In 1917 the chain of the imperialist world front proved to be weaker in Russia than in the other countries. It was there that the chain broke and provided an outlet for the proletarian revolution.' This claim in turn supported Stalin's assertion that the correct course of socialist development was to build 'socialism in one country', a call that by the end of the 1920s was to see the USSR embark on rapid industrialization based on the administrative allocation of resources through planning.

The belief that capitalism had been broken at its 'weakest link' and that it was possible to build socialism on the back of this fracture set the Soviet Union on a course of economic development that largely isolated it from trends in the global economy. Not being a part of the 'chain' of international capitalism, the USSR under Stalin tried to develop primarily on the basis of its own resources and in ways that did not make it dependent on a hostile outside world. This meant exploiting its labour force and reserves to extract the maximum amount out of them and utilizing the vast natural resources of the USSR (Kornai, 1992, pp.181-86; Olson, 2000, pp.111-34). The USSR's relative isolation from the international economy was thus ideological in origins. It should be stressed that the USSR was never totally autarkic in development; it traded with other states from very early on its existence, selling energy in particular (Considine and Kerr, 2002, pp.25-29). But the degree of control that the central leadership had over economic policy and trade made it a near-complete 'functional autarky' (Lavigne, 1990, pp.7-49). Little thought was given to how exports and imports might help to generate growth, except insofar as the West was a source of technology that could be imported and imitated, and a market that could be exported to in order to fund technology imports. Overall, foreign trade was a residual category in Soviet economic thinking, something that was used to make up for shortfalls in domestic economic activity, but which was not seen as fundamental to economic development (see also Chapter 5, pp.80-3). The trade with the capitalist world that did take place was very tightly controlled. The central state held a monopoly over foreign trade, administered by the Ministry for Foreign Trade, and the central planning system did not allow the international economy to affect the domestic economy through prices. The price paid by Soviet enterprises and consumers for imported goods, and the revenue that they earned from exports, did not necessarily reflect the foreign currency prices of goods traded. Firms produced goods for export at the same price as for the domestic market; where this price was less than the world market price, the central state retained the difference as a contribution to its budget; where it was more, the central state bore the cost of the difference in an indirect subsidy to the producer. The same was true for imports: where they were deemed necessary imported goods were either sold to consumers and enterprises at subsidized prices or else the state took the difference between world and domestic prices as a contribution to the central budget (Evangelista, 1996, pp.165-9).

Centralized control over foreign economic relations obviously impeded the extent to which the USSR traded with other states. However, it is arguable that the increasing relative backwardness of the Soviet economy as the USSR developed was equally important in restricting Soviet trade outside the CMEA. This relative backwardness was primarily the result of the planned economy, although its isolation from global economic trends exacerbated the tendency to backwardness. The root cause of Soviet backwardness was the imbalances that developed in the Soviet economy with the onset of Stalinist industrialization. These imbalances were principally the overproduction of industrial goods in preference to consumer goods, the development of industry and economic infrastructure over services and social infrastructure, and excess demands for investment and for labour from Soviet industry. The effect of imbalances only manifested themselves as promoters of backwardness after the initial basis of industrial economy had been built in the 1930s and during post-war reconstruction. Technological progress was considerable during these early periods because it was often basic – the extension of electrical supplies to the countryside for example – and was imitative of technologies and industrial organization already in widespread use in advanced capitalist states.[1] At first, therefore, the USSR experienced some of the classical benefits of backwardness – imitation and ability to miss out stages of development, use of the state to channel investment so as to achieve rapid growth from the basis of a low capital to output ratio – identified by Gerschenkron (1962). However, as Gerschenkron later noted, the growth spurt that lifted the USSR out of backwardness was also unique. The scale of the developmental burden that it imposed on its people and in the institutional arrangements that it put in place to force them to accept this burden during the Stalin period were found nowhere else in the world until the Chinese revolution and Mao's 'Great Leap Forward'.[2] Modernization under Stalin involved large coerced inflows of labour into industry from the countryside, the squeezing of the agricultural economy to provide investment resources, the coercion of labour so that the costs of production remained low for the state and planners had a large surplus to redistribute, and the rapid expansion of extractive industries and the construction of new forms of plant such as hydroelectric dams based on the exploitation of labour to provide cheap materials and energy to fuel more growth. This could only be achieved, Gerschenkron (1970, pp.116-19) noted, by the 'maintenance of a permanent condition of stress and strain', premised on 'the existence and creation of enemies' internal and external, the 'incessant exercise of dictatorial power', extreme proscription of dissent, and 'creation of an image of the dictator as incarnation of supreme wisdom and indomitable will power'.

Over time, however, the combination of despotism with the imbalances of the planned economy produced backwardness. Despotism locked in the imbalances and as the initial spurts of economic and technical progress died down, the ability of the Soviet economy to develop new sources of growth was impeded. Unlike other backward, late developers, the USSR was not able to shift from the production of industrial goods guided by the state to a balance of industrial and consumer goods production and a moderate overall rate of growth after its initial developmental spurt. International competition with the capitalist world and the high military expenditure that this involved combined with the bureaucratic power of industrial ministries to prioritize industrial goods production. Investment in these sectors remained high and crowded out the development of consumer goods and services. Moreover, the predilection of Soviet planners was to specialize so that vast industrial complexes with a small number of economic functions and requiring equally vast amounts of investment were created. At the start of the 1990s, Russian industry was on average five times more monopolized than West European industry, and in some sectors, such as machine-building, monopoly levels were up to fourteen times higher (Kuzin, 1993, pp.36-7). The inability to switch from industrial to consumer good production and the structure of economic power that favoured military and industrial good production meant declines in both labour productivity and investment returns. Having no access to consumer goods or services, workers had no incentive to produce and earn more; money could not be used to improve lifestyles. Excess demand for labour and ideologically-guaranteed full employment meant that there was no sanction of unemployment for unproductive labour. Excess demand for investment meant that although the rate of investment as a percentage of GDP was high in the USSR, there was a general shortage of investment as resources were spread thinly between competing interests, especially after military production and prestige projects such as aerospace had taken their large cut from the investment budget.[3] The effect of this was to delay the completion of investment projects for roughly twice as long as was the norm in capitalist economies (Hewitt, 1988, pp.89-90). To try to cope with this investment levels were raised, growing at a far greater rate than in the West and outstripping general economic growth (Kornai, 1992, pp.167-8). In short, the USSR got increasingly fewer returns on investment over the course of its history.

These problems were cumulative and exacerbated by the contradictory nature of change post-Stalin. The political structures that had overseen high initial levels of development became a drag on progress. The coercion that had helped force the rate of development to dizzy heights in the 1930s was eased as Khrushchev ended mass terror and dissent became less severely proscribed. However, at the same time, institutional structures, systems of management and lines of responsibility were tinkered with, rather than fundamentally amended. As a result, the arbitrary interference of political authority, the 'maintenance of a permanent condition of stress and strain', did not diminish. Without coercion, and in the absence of material incentives, the party had to rely on exhortation and moral appeal to try to maintain growth. When these failed, the party became more closely involved in trying to organize production and solve economic problems. However, as the economy became more complex, the party became less efficient and useful when interfering in the economy so that it too became an impediment to change (Rutland, 1993). Despotism, in other words, became less effective over time, especially as the tasks before the party-state grew more complex. Although over-bureaucratized the USSR never developed an efficient bureaucracy (Robinson, 2002; Suraska, 1998).

For the Soviet leadership, backwardness meant that control of foreign trade was more important, not less. Control over foreign trade and manipulating the system of subsidies between imports and exports helped Soviet planners to shore up the cracks in the Soviet economic system, compensate for problems in maintaining labour productivity and rates of natural resource extraction, and sustain modest increases in living standards. This practice developed at break-neck speed in the 1970s. Trade between the USSR and the outside world grew spectacularly. Between 1975 and 1985, foreign trade grew at eight times the rate of national income growth, and was worth 27 per cent of national income. However, this growth was largely based on the export of one product: oil. The USSR took advantage of high oil prices after 1973 to reap huge profits. By the mid-1980s, energy sales accounted for 80 per cent of Soviet foreign currency earnings (Gustafson, 1989 pp.263-4).

The revenue generated by Soviet energy sales went a considerable way to subsidising industrial production and increases in living standards at a time when the rest of industrialized world was closing down inefficient plants and seeking to rationalise industrial production through job cuts, efficiency drives and technological modernization (Kotkin, 2001). The USSR, in contrast, pursued technological innovation slowly and haphazardly, and sought to maintain social stability through broadening the social contract between regime and people based on incremental improvements in living standards (Cook, 1994). Energy sales thus perpetuated, rather than ameliorated Soviet tendencies to backwardness. Soviet industry did not, for example, have to take account of the rising costs of energy in the 1970s and their profligate use of energy imposed significant costs on the central state in terms of subsidies (Dienes, 1985; Gustafson, 1989). The fact that exporting industries did not accrue profit from their export activities meant that they were not able to use profits to modernize and become more efficient. Again, the energy sector is a good example of this. Although it accounted for the bulk of Soviet hard currency earnings, it was deprived of investment until crisis hit the sector in the late 1970s; the revenue generated by oil sales had, until this time, been spent elsewhere. Deficient investments in energy meant that the USSR did not develop new energy sources during the boom years of the early 1970s, or improve efficiency in the energy sector to keep energy costs low. By the time that crisis hit the energy sector at the end of the 1970s, the technological level and organization of the energy sector had deteriorated to such a level that the investment needed to head off crisis was enormous and threatened to deprive *all* other industrial sectors of new investment in the early 1980s (Gustafson,

1989, p.36). By 1990, maintaining oil production required resources equal in volume to the total investment budget of the USSR (Kriukov, 2001, p.172).

The end result of trifling political change, economic imbalances and oil dependency was that whilst its economy was 'modern', in that it was largely industrialized and supported a welfare state, the USSR would not have been able to increase its role in the global economy even if it had wanted to. The USSR combined an advanced industrial structure that was capital intensive (thanks to the expansion of investment referred to above), with low productivity and poor quality production (certain areas such as arms and aerospace excepted, but they were closed to international trade for security reasons). As a result, the USSR began to lose comparative advantage relative to other industrial economies, except in the energy sector (Collins and Rodrik, 1991, p.51). Although trade expanded as time passed, the USSR was still peripheral in the world economy. Trade with the non-socialist world also grew after Stalin's death, by 1990, it accounted for only 2.1 per cent of exports in the world economy and 2.3 per cent of imports – less than Belgium, the Netherlands and Italy, and a long way behind the USA and Japan (Goskomstat, 2000, p.630). As we have seen, the bulk of its exports were energy products. Consequently, and as energy sales came to dominate foreign trade, the USSR increasingly had the foreign trade structure of an industrially *un*developed state; it exported raw materials, rather than industrial goods to which value had been added in the process of their transformation from raw materials into manufactured objects. In 1950, the USSR exported more consumer goods (4.9 per cent of exports) and industrial goods (12.3 per cent of exports) than energy products (3.9 per cent of exports); by 1987, however, 46 per cent of Soviet exports were from the energy sector (Goskomstat SSSR, 1987, p.32). Poor quality meant that Soviet industrial and consumer good were unsaleable on world markets. Much Soviet production created 'negative value added goods', manufactured objects worth less on world markets than the raw materials used to produce them (McKinnon, 1993; Gaddy and Ickes, 1998). Only about 7 to 8 per cent of Soviet production was of 'world standard', that is exportable to non-CMEA countries by the late 1980s (Åslund, 1989, p.17). Technological developments in the rest of the world had simply left the USSR behind in the 1970s and 1980s; only 4 per cent of Soviet plant was of an equivalent technological par to world standards by 1991 (Kuzin, 1993, p.33). Few of the major technological innovations that transformed industry in capitalist states after World War Two were first discovered or utilized in the USSR (Kornai, 1992, pp.298-300; Amman and Cooper, 1982).

The energy crises of the late 1970s made Soviet leaders aware that their economy was in a potentially perilous state. They were also conscious that the security of the USSR was threatened because it lagged behind the West in what the Soviets called the 'scientific-technical revolution', the development of new technologies and administrative practices aimed at improving the efficiency of production (Hoffman and Laird, 1985). Calls under Brezhnev for the 'acceleration of scientific and technical progress' (*uskorenie nauchno-tekhnicheskogo progressa*), and later under Gorbachev for the 'acceleration of socio-economic progress' (*uskorenie sotsial'no-ekonomicheskogo progressa*), proved ineffective (Robinson, 1995, pp.91-3, 97-101). The isolation of the domestic economy from changes in prices internationally meant that the only stimuli to change economic practices came from within the Soviet party-state leadership; fear of economic loss due to lack of international competitiveness did not reach down to lower levels of the economic system and create a social constituency for change. This meant that efforts for change, whether they were the exhortations of Brezhnev, the anti-corruption and labour discipline campaigns of Andropov, or the increasingly frenetic economic and political reforms of Gorbachev, were defeated easily by the collective intransigence of the Soviet bureaucracy. The *apparatchiki* of the party-state found the certainties of neo-traditional Soviet political and economic practices more attractive than the uncertainties of taking the lead in reform, especially since they could only see the costs of reform to them personally; the costs of not reforming were hidden by the isolation of the Soviet economy from global trends and by propaganda that extolled the virtues and modernity of Soviet economy.[4] Consequently, reform was honoured in theory, but subverted in practice.

The problems of Soviet economy and institutional rigidities were finally joined by declining social cohesion and state fiscal crisis under Gorbachev to produce a fatal mixture. Gorbachev's attempt to build a social constituency for change that went beyond the party-state bureaucracy to draw in the Soviet population through political reform foundered due the fact that his reforms relied on old fashioned party-led campaigns for change that were easily subverted by bureaucrats, and because the Soviet state's ability to fund welfare payments to the population decreased after 1985. The global economy played a walk on part in this crisis as the economic strains on the central budget caused by the anti-alcohol campaign, the disruptions of reform, the Chernobyl' disaster and the Armenian earthquake were exacerbated by exogenous factors. As oil prices fell in the late 1980s and import prices remained stable, the central state's budget was heavily squeezed. The Soviet state was running a yearly budget deficit of about 9 per cent of GDP in the late 1980s (EIU, 1991, p.37). Foreign borrowing – 'chaotic and large-scale' during this period – covered some of the central state's revenue shortfall as the USSR's short-term foreign debt doubled between the end of 1987 and the end of 1989 alone (Lushin and Oppenheimer, 2001, p.288; IMF et al, 1991a, p.40). This borrowing could not cover all of the state's deficit since the collapse of economic activity under Gorbachev shrank the tax base and the appropriation of state property and resources by bureaucratic entrepreneurs denied it sources of traditional revenue (Solnick, 1997).

Gorbachev tried to alleviate some of these crisis phenomena by opening up the Soviet economy. But the increasing weakness of the central Soviet state meant that it could not overcome the economic distortions created by the Soviet system to make the USSR a more attractive investment destination. Gorbachev tried to open up the USSR's economy to Western investment in an effort to bring in new technologies and management practices, and to offload some of the state's investment responsibilities on to foreign business. Joint ventures (JVs) between Soviet and foreign firms were legalised and by the time of the USSR's demise, about 2,300 were registered. Their influence was small since they were unproductive and often set up to provide Western companies with a formal presence in the Soviet economy. Most were in services of one kind or another (computer and management consultancy, travel, trade and light industry), and were small and not well capitalized (Belyaev and Chichkanov, 1992, p.43; Hewett with Gaddy, 1992, pp.79-80). The geographic spread of JVs was also limited, with most in Moscow and St Petersburg (Faminskii, 1993, p.259). The experience of JVs showed that there were limits to how far foreign investment could help transform the Soviet economy without broader structural change. The USSR lacked both the public and the private infrastructure to support large inflows of foreign capital and enable it to make a profit. The Soviet planning system had no need for institutions such as commercial banks, insurers etc, which support market activity. Some such institutions began to develop in the late 1980s, but they largely took advantage of the arbitrage opportunities afforded them by the coexistence of market and plan to make large profits at the expense of the society as a whole. They were not, therefore, a platform that could support foreign capital in an effort to resuscitate the Soviet economy. The public infrastructure necessary for a market did not exist because the Soviet state had not developed such things as commercial law or arbitration services, and was anyway in a condition of financial collapse. The crisis of Soviet state finances meant that there were not the resources at the end of the Soviet period to restructure the administrative system and make it market supporting.

Ending isolation: the reformist imperative for reforging the weakest link

The global economy thus added to the burdens on the Soviet state in the late 1980s and early 1990s and did little to rectify it from its course towards collapse. External economic factors are not a smoking gun responsible for the bullet that killed the USSR; they were, at best, a contributory cause in Soviet collapse (Evangelista, 1996).[5] However, thinking on transition to market economy and democracy posited that exogenous economic factors and forces would play a significant role in securing the transformation of Eastern Europe and the former Soviet Union.

Liberalizing foreign economic relations and reattaching transitional economies to international economic trends was a central plank in mainstream economic thinking about the need for reform to destroy and rebuild (in the radical version), or transform (in the gradualist version), old economic structures.[6] In part, this was based on a realization that the collapse of state budgets in Soviet successor states meant that the only significant sources of investment for transitional economies were likely to be foreign funds and governments. You can neither rebuild nor transform without money, and state investment, the only kind possible under planning, would only slowly be replaced by indigenous private investment as and when transition began to have an effect. In the mean time, as Jeffrey Sachs – the main foreign advisor to the Russian government until January 1994 – insisted Western financial aid was an essential prerequisite for the successful economic transformation in states such as Russia, and 'economic integration with Western Europe' was likely to be 'the primary engine of economic growth' for transitional economies generally (Sachs, 1993; Lipton and Sachs, 1992, p.352). The IMF, in tandem with all the other main international financial institutions (IFIs) that had an interest in the area, declared that 'flows of foreign investment could be crucial in the transition to a market economy' (IMF et al, 1991b, p.75). There was some debate about the scale of investment needed and whether or not full-scale reconstruction to raise transitional economies to the same levels of productivity and wealth as advanced capitalist states was affordable (Collins and Rodrik, 1991, pp.76-83). But the need for investment from abroad was not a particularly contentious point. Post-Soviet economies were, as the figures cited above on the technical level of industry in comparison with the rest of the world attest, in dire need of modernization and it is generally assumed that foreign investment is the best conduit for the transfer of both 'hard' and 'soft' technologies (plant and business organization) (Dyker, 1999, 2001).

The effects of reintegration with the wider world economy were, however, supposed to be wider than this. Reformist thinking proposed that reintegration would help to break down traditional Soviet economic practices and structures, and thereby transform the nature of economic relations and the structures of power that rested upon them. It was to help achieve this as a part of the transformation of exchange relations that would occur in the movement from planned to market economy. And it was because of this role in transforming exchange relations that reintegration with the global economy would generate opposition and make officials of the state the crucial agents in the process of reintegration and reform. We therefore need to understand something of exchange relation under Soviet socialism and the implications of their reform.

Exchange relations, as they occur in capitalist economies, are radically different to those in a planned economy. The difference is created by the different functions of money and prices in the Soviet economy.[7] Capitalist markets largely set the value of goods impersonally; both buyers and sellers of goods have choices as to where they trade; the price of goods and services is determined by overall levels of supply and demand, and takes account of costs of production, of the labour, raw materials, that went in to their production. Finally, the value of a good or a service is expressed in a common, generally accepted unit of exchange, money. An act of economic exchange in a market thus has a *common* or *universal* character with all other exchanges in a national economy. Goods and services of a similar type can be purchased for roughly the same price across a national market (and in many cases beyond), and for the same, commonly accepted unit of exchange, money; one type of good can be compared to another because it is possible to judge their relative worth in monetary terms. Market exchange and the value of goods, services, and resources are thus reasonably transparent. The resources – land, raw materials, labour power, factories, shops – possessed by a person or group can be valued in terms of money, the income that they generate from them can be compared and evenly taxed by the state across the whole national economy. The ability to develop economic power depends on the possession of money since this is necessary to purchase more property, modernize a factory, invest etc. Economic activity that does not take account of costs (measured in money) and demand (the estimation of which creates an idea of what monetary return can be expected of producing and supplying a good) cannot break even or be profitable; any one engaging in such activity may expect to go bankrupt.

The Soviet system was very different to this in both its usual operation from the 1920s onwards and in its legacy.[8] Goods in the Soviet economy had a monetary value assigned by state planning agencies. These prices were arbitrarily determined by central planners without regard to the costs of supply, what a product might cost in terms of raw material, labour etc, and without regard to demand. Political priorities mattered more than economic costs. This gave exchanges in the planned economy a *particularistic*, rather than a universal, character. The price of a good was a reflection of its political importance, whether the Soviet plan priorities valued it as important for socialist construction, and if it was scarce, access to it was according to the political importance of their consumer. Since prices were set arbitrarily, no accurate profit and loss calculations could be made of economic activity. If a firm made a 'loss' and had a deficit of roubles due to overspending or poor efficiency, the result was not bankruptcy. Credit did not come from a commercial lending organization concerned to make a profit, but from the state, which only cared about fulfilment of the plan. For this reason, it was often claimed that Soviet enterprises only had 'soft budget constraints' (Kornai, 1986 and 1992, pp.140-44). If an enterprise spent more than its budget allowed, it did not face the 'hard' constraint of not having any more money to spend, a situation in a market economy that would mean an end to economic activity (bankruptcy). More soft credit would be made available to the 'bankrupt' firm from the state in the form of increased subsidy, investment would continue through the mechanism of the plan, tax obligations to the state could be waived, etc. Enterprises would thus continue to trade no matter what their financial status. Soft credits would generally not have to be returned to the state and did not incur interest payments. Naturally, the ease with which such soft credits could be accessed, and the amount made available, was a function of the particular political importance of an enterprise and its production.

Money did not, therefore, fully play an effective accounting function as it does in a market; success and failure were not measured in monetary terms. There were also strict political limits to what could be done with money. The state owned or controlled all significant property and resources; development priorities and investment were determined and controlled through the planning system. Money earned either by a firm or an individual could not be used to consolidate control over economic activity by the purchase of more land, machinery or business outlets, and shortages meant that money could not, by and large, be used to buy up consumer goods. The demonetization and particularistic character of exchanges in the planning system facilitated another form of particularistic exchange. The official allocation of goods and services and their pricing in the plan was paralleled by unofficial exchanges also took place outside of the planning system (such as black market deals), or to supplement it (the unofficial exchanges arranged by party-state officials and economic managers to compensate for breakdowns in the plan). These exchanges were also particularistic because value was assigned to goods and services by the actors involved in each individual exchange independently of any similar exchange that might have been going on somewhere else in the system; each exchange and the value of goods exchanged were, unlike exchanges in a market economy, unique to that exchange (Urban, 1985, pp.210-13). Again, and as in the official system, these transactions took place without reference to what goods had cost to make, what someone else might pay for them, or what price the state had formally attached to them. These particularistic exchanges were highly personal, based on acquaintance, mutual affinity and trust, rather than on a desire to make profit and avoid loss, as in monetized exchanges in capitalist economies. The value of goods was the value assigned to them through personal relations and such things as considerations of the political power of traders – bureaucrats, party officials and economic managers – the value of being connected to them and the favours that such connections might bring in the future. Particularistic exchange was thus the basis upon which patronage networks, corruption, and simple networks of mutual aid based on friendship and extended families, were based.[9]

As the Soviet system fell apart, particularistic exchange and soft budget constraints changed character and developed. From being an important, if unofficial, mechanism that helped to keep the Soviet system functioning when the plan failed, 'unofficial' particularistic exchange increasingly became a mechanism that allowed the maintenance of soft budget constraints. The flow of goods to enterprises did not become commercialized – based on monetary, market exchange – as planning collapsed, but took place in the form of barter. This barter was often conducted through the networks of particularistic exchange that had always supplemented the plan. In effect, then, as the ability of the state to set prices arbitrarily and subsidize them through soft credits decreased, unofficial, personal forms of particularistic exchange took over. The importance of this development was not only that it kept factories going in a time of crisis. It was also a means of safeguarding the semi-legal ownership of property acquired through 'spontaneous privatization' (Johnson and Kroll, 1991). Trading through barter and/or without regard to the monetary value of goods traded meant that production that was not commercially profitable was still possible. And since they were able to maintain production, enterprise directors were able to keep their positions and prestige, and continue to control the resources that a factory had.

Particularistic exchange was thus necessary for much of Soviet industry to keep up at least a semblance of economic activity and a means by which sections of the *nomenklatura* could protect the resources, and hence the power, that they controlled through spontaneous privatization. This meant that managers kept personal status and position, and also that they could derive personal economic gain even as the rest of the economy declined. Goods and resources could be transferred between elite members at low, fictitious prices, and the state could be deceived and not paid its due in the form of taxes. This form of economic activity and the wealth derived from it was not profit seeking, where returns on economic activity are produced through meeting demand and maximized by being efficient in the use of labour and resources. It was rent seeking, taking wealth from economic activity by extracting it from the public purse, or by manipulating distortions in the economy caused by policy. Even sectors of the economy that had a comparative competitive advantage in the world economy were not immune to favouring rent seeking over profit seeking; they were able to manipulate the differences between domestic and international prices to their advantage. An example of this would be Russian oil where fantastic revenues were earned both before, and after, the start of reform from the international resale of oil brought cheaply on domestic markets (Pleines, 1999). Such arbitrage opportunities depended on many of the same personal ties and interactions – such as bribery – that had characterized unofficial particularistic exchange under the plan. In sectors with a relative comparative advantage, as elsewhere, the personal ties that underpinned particularistic exchange could be used as a barrier to the acquisition of power by those outside of elite networks leftover from the communist system. Particularistic exchange devalues resources not held by members of networks since they cannot be converted into other goods or services. In the USSR and its successor states, this meant that the resources held by the mass of the population and the state, were devalued. The chief resource held by the population at large was cash money and the chief means that any state has of accumulating resources is through taxation and the gathering of money. However, money had no great power whilst particularistic exchange prevailed since access to economic resources did not flow from the possession of money, but from connections. Particularistic exchange and the networks that it created and sustained where thus social and political phenomena as much they were economic, so that economic action was thoroughly 'embedded' in social and political structures (Granovetter, 1985).

The centrality of particularistic exchanges to the organization and operation of late Soviet, and hence post-Soviet economy, meant that how to transform it in to a more universal, monetarized form of exchange was a key political question. Economic policy choices, radical or gradual, were obviously seen as the main means of dealing with particularistic exchange. However, the ability of government to implement policy of whatever type was far from certain given that there was likely to be much opposition to change from those with a vested interest in maintaining particularistic exchange practices. Moreover, although policies might be introduced to limit the availability of soft credit and restore the connection between money and value, establishing prices for all of the goods produced in the transitional economy would be very hard and costly in time. Economic agents would have to establish what levels of demand were and assess costs. It was far from certain they would have a motive to do this. Leaving aside the questions of skill, time and energy that would be required, breaking time-honoured particularistic exchange relations would require accurate information about future profits and losses. If economic agents did not have some expectation of gaining by switching from particularistic to universal exchange, where they knew their accomplices and could arrange matters to their mutual benefit, why should they bother? What would be their motive to dissolve what were in their terms 'profitable' associations? In other words, to make calculations about whether or not it was worth breaking with particularistic exchange relations was dependent on possessing the sort of knowledge that only breaking with particularistic exchange could provide.

Economic change away from the forms of exchange prevalent in the Soviet system thus faced an agency problem: who would do undertake it? Society as a whole, if we assume that it has an interest in economic reform and the prosperity that might flow from it, might be expected to be in favour of change. However, economic reform is a public good and as a result is subject to collective action problems.[10] The majority may have a latent interest in reform in that they might gain from it, but they have low incentives to organize and agitate for reform; they will incur personal costs if they do organize and agitate for reform, but will gain from the public good of economic reform if they free-ride. The uncertainty of economic reform's success reinforces free-rider problems. The immediate benefits of free-riding are clear: you avoid the personal costs of political and/or novel economic activity, evade the attention of those who have power from the old system and who might oppose change, and continue to derive benefit from traditional economic activity and relationships. The benefits of reform, however, are deferred until reform begins to be successful. In contrast, opposition to change was almost certain to come from those groups that benefited from particularistic exchange and gained rent. Such groups have incentives to oppose reform. Their losses (the ability to infringe the property rights of others, to make profit from unstable currencies, privileged access to goods and resources etc) are born directly by them and outweigh the gains that they would derive from the public good of reform.

Collective action problems associated with reform and opposition to it from those groups who would lose their privileged position meant that the key to launching reform was the attitude of politicians and state officials: reform needed policy entrepreneurs to get off the ground. It did not matter what reform option, radical or gradual, was chosen; the need for policy entrepreneurs was constant. Radical reform was more reliant on them since it proposed what amounted to a full-on assault on vested interests and planned to ignore and subvert any existing economic institutions and practices (Murrell, 1992). Gradual reform strategy was less reliant on them since it sought to minimize opposition by building up support for reform through an evolving mix of policies. It was assumed that such mixes would create shifting majorities in favour of change. However, gradual reform was in need of policy entrepreneurs too: someone, after all, had to construct a policy mix that would create an initial constituency for reform.

Any move to the market thus had to escape a vicious circle by breaking with the past under conditions of high uncertainty that deterred support for reform. The international economy's importance to the reform process was supposed to help in this escape by creating incentives to change. It would do this by introducing some notion of what the 'true' market price of goods, production, labour and property were from outside and highlighting the opportunity costs of not reforming and behaving as good capitalists. Trade was supposed to be of particular importance since through it engagement with the global economy would break particularistic exchange down by importing 'a ready-made price system', 'the set of relative prices ... that predominates for goods traded throughout the rest of the world' (Eatwell et al, 1995, p.146; Fieleke, 1992, p.275; Blanchard et al, 1993, p.23; Blanchard et al, 1991, p.30; Åslund, 2002, p.77). Liberalized foreign trade would also help satisfy consumer demand so that monopolies, which were more prevalent in the USSR than in capitalist states, could not raise prices – once they were freed – and take super profits (Karavayev, 1992: 10). Finally, it would stop sectors that had relative comparative advantage in the global economy from taking rent through arbitrage activities. Foreign direct investment (FDI) would also have an effect in creating universal exchange. Foreign investors would price assets and assess profitability as a prelude to expending any money. In doing this, they would expose the true costs of goods for the first time. This would change economic behaviour generally and not just where there was a receipt of FDI. Enterprises that did not get foreign investment would have to mimic those that did if they wanted to stay in business. Engagement with the global economy would thus, though one channel or another, directly or indirectly, fill the 'systemic vacuum' that exists in a transitional economy due to the 'discrepancy between the complex structure of an industrial society and as yet underdeveloped exchange communication' (Dietz, 1991, p.103; Astapovich and Grigor'ev, 1993; Faminskii, 1993; Macmillan, 1993).

The role imagined for the international economy in the transformation of post-Soviet economies was thus great. As a force coming from without and not marked by the particularism of Soviet economy it would cut through obstructions to reform and reduce the uncertainties of it, and provide the post-Soviet state with means to overcome obstacles to reform in its own right. This was supposed to help recommend reform, and in particular its radical variant, to politicians. Reintegration with the global economy would reduce the electoral uncertainties of reform and offset some of the risks in choosing a radical reform strategy. The electoral advantage of reintegrating with the global economy came from the way that it would help to break down particularistic exchange, weaken the power of groups engaged in it and empower broader social constituencies. As a result, opposition would be blunted and sources of political support for reformist politicians would be clearly delineated. We might expect this to be a significant consideration given the shapelessness of the democratic movement in the USSR, in which support for action against the Soviet system was broad and the political constituencies of individual politicians and political groups was poorly defined (Urban, 1994; Fish, 1995). This electoral incentive tended to favour the adoption of radical reform since radical reform would, it was promised, shake out positive social support more quickly and pacify the rest of society by rapidly restoring living standards. Gradual reform, on the other hand, was more complex an electoral strategy since it required coalition maintenance is effective in order to supply politicians with positive support. Although drops in living standards might not be as severe under gradualism, recovery would be delayed. It should not be surprising that radical reform strategies were more in favour of opening up to the global economy than gradualist strategies. The more open the economy became, the more rapidly particularistic exchange would be broken down. Gradualists, on the other hand, saw reintegration with the global economy as one policy tool amongst many. In the long-run, it would be necessary to achieve full reintegration with the global economy, but in the short-term openness could be finessed sector by sector according to the needs of coalition building and maintenance.

Radical reform was thus simpler and more direct in promising benefits from reintegration with the global economy. It brought another incentive with it too: it was the strategy most in favour with IFIs and their chief sponsors, the major industrialized powers. Adopting radical reform was consequently a way of unlocking access to foreign advice, foreign loans, and to securing membership of international bodies like the IFIs themselves and international trade regimes. The money that could come from abroad was a resource that reformist politicians could use as a source of patronage (Wedel, 1998). It was also a way of shoring up short-run legitimacy since support for reform, its leading proponent argued, demonstrated faith in the competence of transitional governments during a time when their people had only limited experience and capacity to judge the success of governments at running market economies (Sachs, 1993).

Finally, in helping to end particularistic exchange, reintegration with the global economy in support of reform would empower politicians and the state by changing the balance of power in their favour. The collapse of communism generated what was effectively an institutional *tabula rasa*: political institutions existed, but were without direction, unstable, and unwilling and/or incapable of transforming social practice. State power was weak in comparison to 'social power ... the empirical question of who ... is capable of employing whatever resources in order to protect himself and take advantage of others'. The source of this social power was the 'assets and resources acquired under the old regime ... [and] easily converted into individually useful resources, thus generating positions of power and advantage unregulated by legal rules' (Elster et al, 1998, p.25). The value of the resources accumulated by holders of social power was realized through particularistic exchange and protected by it. As has already been argued, the prevalence of particularistic exchange in some form acts as a barrier to the acquisition of power by those outside of networks leftover from the communist system and devalues resources held by actors other than social power holders. By helping destroy particularistic exchange, engagement with the global economy was supposed to help author a change in the structure of power, altering the balance of power between state and social power in the state's favour. The capacity of the state would increase and its ability to regulate the economy would grow as social power was controlled and particularistic exchange was replaced by market exchange that required the state to safeguard property rights, provide public goods such as protection from criminality and facilitate profit-maximization rather than rent-seeking by enforcing contracts. Of particular import was the fact that as particularistic exchange decreased and was replaced by monetized exchange, the state would be able to monitor and tax economic activity more effectively. Many of these benefits would flow from reform if it was successful no matter what, but the international dimension of reform increased the autonomy of the state since it would mediate between the global economy and domestic forces. Reintegration in the global economy would require the creation of institutions and policies that could open up the post-Soviet economy so that the state would have arguments for taking action independent of social power holders.

Conclusion: the problems of moving from reformist theory amidst post-Soviet realities and the rest of this book

Moves towards openness in foreign economic relations always require the action of the state, but it is this usually expected that this action occur in tandem with pressure from those economic sectors that enjoy a comparative advantage in the international economy, if not as a direct result of such pressure (Frieden and Rogowski, 1996). This was not the case in the former Soviet Union. The nature of Soviet economy meant that there were few economic interests that had an incentive to push for reintegration with the global economy as the USSR collapsed. If moves toward reintegration were to come, politicians and the state had to perceive the direct benefits of it for themselves, as well as the abstract, down-the-line benefits that reform might deliver for the population and economy as a whole.

Although we can outline what these benefits might be in theory, in practice the benefits of economic liberalization and policies to facilitate global markets breaking down particularistic exchange and the centres of power that it created were not always apparent to the elites that took control as the USSR collapsed. The legacies of Soviet isolation stood in the way. Post-Soviet elites were faced with the worst of all economic worlds. The relative backwardness that they faced on the early 1990s was very different to the backwardness that had existed at the time of Stalin's rapid industrialization. Then, there was a low capital to output ratio and the injection of new technology and plant into industry enabled a growth spurt. However, and as we have already discussed, the USSR had developed backwardness in a new way, combining high investment in plant and capital with low productivity. Investment would thus not bring great returns by unlocking the potential of labour to produce. The former USSR was over-industrialized, its industries too specialized, to enable quick returns from combining foreign capital and technology with cheap labour, or by reaping the benefits of liberalized foreign trade and exporting cheap goods.

The fact that backwardness would not bring advantage meant that post-Soviet leaders had to calculate the advantages of reintegration with the global economy with the disadvantages of alienating economic elites and the benefits of maintaining some state control of industrial production and revenue. In short, post-Soviet leaders had to compare the uncertain advantages of reintegrating inefficient and uncompetitive economies in the global economy, with potential downturns in output and shortfalls in tax revenues caused by the economic contraction that would follow reform and the absence of tax collection systems, with the certainties of revenue collection from industries under state control. This calculation was complicated by the fact that there were frequently close connections between political and economic elites in post-Soviet states. It is debateable whether the *nomenklatura* of the USSR was a class or an elite, whether it had any sense of a corporate interest or not, and the extent to which it survived and in what forms at different levels of the political and economic systems. What is not debateable, however, is that many members of the political elite that came to power as the USSR collapsed were unsure of their ability to act or exist independently of old elites and unwilling to test their ability or luck too far. They had little social base to fall back on except other successor elites. As we have already been mentioned, the political constituencies of individual politicians and political groups across the post-Soviet space were poorly defined at the time of collapse. Social mobilization in the collapse of Soviet power was sporadic and did not, as in great social revolutions such as that of France in 1798 and Russia in 1917, involve the wholesale destruction of the power base of the former ruling elites. They kept control of the bulk of economic resources and had a mechanism to deny the emergence of new power centres in particularistic exchange.

Not surprisingly, therefore, willingness and ability to gamble on the benefits of reform, radical or otherwise, and reap the theoretical benefits of reintegration with the global economy, were generally low. Across the USSR as a whole, and excluding the Baltic states, which were beneficiaries of special circumstances, decisions to reform were rare. Only Russia embarked on radical reform and it too soon succumbed to the problems of launching reform in the face of backwardness and stepped back from reform. Other states, most notably Belarus, Uzbekistan and

Tajikistan, barely moved at all. The norm was half-hearted reform, as reluctant elites were dragged along by a combination of Russian and international pressure.

The next three chapters in this book look at these processes in the three states of Belarus, Russia, and Ukraine. These three states have certain common characteristics that facilitate comparison. At independence in 1991, the three states had very similar social and economic structures. The bulk of their people reside in urban locations; on average just under 70 per cent of the population of Russia, Ukraine and Belarus were urban at the end of 1980s, compared to an average of 56 per cent in the USSR as a whole (excluding the Baltic states). All were essentially industrial economies at independence and possessed a wide spread of industries. On average, agriculture and industry contributed 19.3 and 41.1 per cent of GDP respectively in Belarus, Russia and Ukraine, whereas they contributed on average 31.1 and 26.7 per cent of GDP respectively in other post-Soviet states (excluding the Baltic states and Turkmenistan).[11] This meant that they faced post-Soviet development from what has been described here as the classic post-Soviet situation of over-industrialized backwardness. All were over endowed with defence industries and inefficient industrial sectors such as machine production (Popov, 2001, p.31). Finally, they share cultural traits. Although all are multi-ethnic thanks to their having been a part of the USSR, the bulk of their populations are Slavic and the main religious affiliation is Orthodoxy. But despite their common attributes, each of these states represents a case of one of the three responses to reintegration with the global economy: Russia tried to achieve integration and the benefits of reform; Ukraine was dragged towards reform and Belarus has tried to avoid it.

Russia, as Chapter 2 points out, tried to leap to the market to solve the political problems before its leaders, who believed that it was too big to fail. When it did fail because reform policies could not open it up to the global economy quickly enough for external economic factors to support reform, Russia entered a period of drift. Russia turned towards the global economy once more in the late 1990s as sources of domestic finance dried up, but it was again unable to push forward reforms necessary to support its increasing financial dependence on the outside world. As a result, and as confidence in other emerging markets declined, the Russian government found itself in a position where it could not service its debt or defend the rouble in 1998. Although the economy has since picked up thanks to high oil prices and import substitution caused by rouble devaluation, many of the structural problems of the economy remain and the state's ability to generate and sustain policy responses to them is still unclear.

Russia's problems show that reform policies and faith in the transformative power of the global economy are not enough to secure growth and marketization. Russia's failure to progress unambiguously to the market has been cushioned by its energy resources. Ukraine and Belarus have not had this advantage and have had to struggle to define their relationship to both the global economy and their Russian neighbour. Chapter 3 by Marko Bojcun on Ukraine highlights the problems of trying to find a new place for oneself in the world independent of Russia. With no history of economic independence, as old economic connections have collapsed, and as its leaders have sought to further its independence, Ukraine has found itself without a stable position in either regional or global markets. Whilst it has some of the advantages of Soviet modernization since it possesses some high tech sectors, and segments of its labour force are skilled, it has not been able to develop strategies that can foster its development in the global economy. Without the pull factors of energy and raw materials that Russia has, it has not been able to secure high levels of inward investment or reap great benefits from trade, and has seen its debt burden increase whilst its economy contracts. Bojcun concludes that what integration with the global economy has occurred in Ukraine has been haphazard, although it retains great potential as an energy corridor from Russia.

Belarus has many of the same structural problems as Ukraine, but unlike it did not seek to secure economic independence in any significant measure after 1991. In Chapter 4, Julia Korosteleva establishes what the specific nature of Belarus's developmental path is. Belarus has not engaged in any major structural reforms, but has tried to maintain output through promoting reintegration with Russia. This has been done to preserve the power of Belarusian political elites. Korosteleva describes how this has been achieved via financial repression, which has seen the state suppress or co-opt the financial sector, use inflation tax and seigniorage to direct resources to support industrial production and construction. This has produced economic stability in that industrial production has not suffered the same levels of transitional recession in Belarus as elsewhere, but the cost of such a strategy is too great for Belarus to endure over the longer-term. However, thus far, reform choices have been avoided in Belarus thanks in large measure to Russian support in the form of trade and energy subsidies. These subsidies have been provided under the guise of promoting Russian-Belarusian integration, but as Korosteleva notes, this project has been more rhetorical than real and is dependent on Russian interests. Belarus's choice of avoiding marketization and suppressing its financial system in the interests of continuity is thus a risky strategy that arguably surrenders more of Belarusian economic sovereignty than Russia and Ukraine's efforts at reintegrating with the global economy.

The next three chapters of the book turn to comparative issues, looking at trade, how far the failures to link to the global economy are path dependent, and the status of the area as a periphery to the new global capitalism. Nadia Lisovskaya's chapter looks at the problems of trade liberalization as a mechanism for reintegration. As we have seen, trade was supposed to play a special role in the transformation of post-communist economies through the importation of prices. However, trade development has been stifled by structural and institutional problems. The absence of stable currencies because of Soviet legacies and the failure – or avoidance – of stabilization policies has meant that much trade has taken place through barter or through unofficial channels in the form of shuttle trading. Problems with joining the WTO and unfair trade practices have compounded these problems, as have policies that have sought to tax exporters in order to fund domestic budgets. The result has been that trade has exacerbated legacies of the past rather than aided recuperation. The chief difference between Russia, Ukraine and Belarus in terms of trade, Lisovskaya argues, is their resource endowments. Russian, and to a lesser extent Ukrainian, possession of natural resources have given them positive trade balances despite the lack of change in the two states and the structural and institutional obstacles to developing trade that they display, whilst Belarus has become dependent on Russia.

Chapter 6 places the relative failure of Russia, Ukraine and Belarus to achieve reintegration with the global economy in comparative context. Robinson argues that the global economy's effect on post-communist transformation pre-dates the collapse of communism in 1989-1991. The communist state had already evolved by this time, particularly in Eastern Europe, with the development of foreign trade and debt build-ups compensating for the failures of central planning and the limited resources that it created for consumption and development. He argues that these changes created hybrid state forms in Eastern Europe that in some cases made them more amenable to post-communist economic transformation since they had domestic constituencies for reform. The evolution of the state and the creation of such constituencies were far less marked in the USSR, however, due to its reliance on energy sales. As a result, continuity was more prevalent across the former Soviet Union, with classic communist states being replaced in many states with equally unaccountable authoritarian regimes that have taken rent from energy sales, or from Russia in the form of subsidy – something that we have by this time already seen in Korosteleva 's chapter on Belarus. Ukraine, and in particular Russia, have not totally succumbed to this trend, but are not yet sufficiently reformed, or integrated in to the global economy in ways that would foreclose more rigid state controls over the economy in rentierist fashion.

Finally, although Russia, Belarus and Ukraine have not been as successful in terms of economic reform as Chapter 6 points out, it must be remembered that the whole post-communist space is operating as a new periphery to the developed capitalist world. This is analyzed in Chapter 7 by Anastasia Nesvetailova, who argues that Eastern Europe's success relative to the former Soviet Union is still marked by a patchy, geographically and sectorally concentrated pattern of re-integration with the global economy. Global capitalism has simply been unwilling to bear the cost of transforming the region as a whole and has doomed parts of it to a future of economic dependency, preferring to dominate through divide and rule strategies, co-opting parts of the post-communist elite, whilst suppressing the social whole within the international financial and trade system. Consequently, the 'market' as a pure economic institution has not had a transformative effect as the orthodox paradigm on transition from communism has argued and economic models cannot explain the patterns and forms of capitalism that have emerged. Instead, Nesvetailova argues, the absence of social institutions to support market exchange, something that is unique to each country, has produced a plethora of forms of capitalism across the region, many of which are distinguished by their lawlessness and deepening inequality.

The picture painted in all of the chapters of this book is then, a pretty depressing one. The weakest link in the chain of capitalism fractured by the revolutions of 1917 has been restored, but unevenly, tentatively, and with less than edifying results. This does not mean that a return to the past and relative economic isolation is likely; sections of some of the regions economies are more or less integrated in the global economy and will likely remain so as this generates wealth to the state. However, given the weakness of reintegration and the fragility of reform in the region, periodic crisis, slumps and shallow recoveries with political crises are likely to continue so that the future is uncertain and largely unpredictable.

Notes

1   Although it should be noted that in many ways the USSR was not a particularly effective copier of technologies even during the first spurt of growth under Stalin (see Berliner, 1976; Amman and Cooper, 1982).

2   Even then, the result was different. China remained a largely rural economy after the 'Great Leap Forward'. The number of workers and employees had outgrown the number of agricultural workers in the USSR by 1939. By the late 1980s only 12 per cent of the Soviet labour force worked in agriculture (Goskomstat SSSR, 1987, p.176). Even today, the amount of value added to China's GDP as a percentage by agriculture is double that of Belarus, Russia and Ukraine (World Bank, 2002, pp.236-7).

3   High demand for investment was caused by the absence of self-restraint on demands for investment such as exist in capitalist economies where investment, in the form of borrowed money, has to be repaid through the generation of profit. In the Soviet system, failure to make a return on investment would be covered by soft-budget constraints that would see debts and losses written off by the state (see Kornai, 1992, pp.162-3).

4   A belief still remains in certain quarters that post-Soviet international economic failure is due to unfair competition – which certainly exists – rather than because of the backwardness or faults of post-Soviet industry (see, for example, Sergeev, 2001, p.121).

5   The case for external economic forces – globalization – being responsible for Soviet collapse is made in Lockwood (2000). Lockwood argues that inefficiency and relative backwardness forced the USSR to change due to pressures of military competition, but it could not pull change off. Not many people would disagree with this. Lockwood's argument is distinguished by the terms that he uses, most notably globalization and Marxist categories, and the teleology of his argument. The chain of reasoning that he presents to make a case for exogenous factors being vital to Soviet collapse is a syllogism: globalization as a stage in capitalist development breaks down state power (autonomy) because it is a fetter on production; the USSR had the most powerful/autonomous state of all and it was the biggest fetter on production amongst all the political systems of the world; since globalization breaks down state power, the USSR's destruction must have been because of globalization. This argument, like so many orthodox Marxist arguments, cannot be gainsaid except that time proves it wrong (remember Lenin and imperialism as a fetter on development). It takes plausible reasons for Soviet collapse – economic backwardness in the world and institutional rigidity – and explains them by reference to an unfalsifiable variable, globalization as an outcome of world historical development. All we can do to disprove this argument is change the terms of debate and say that globalization is not what Lockwood thinks it is and therefore did not have the effect that he claims it had. There are more than enough studies of globalization that define it differently to Lockwood without adding to them here. Anyway, it would not take us beyond what we already know: the Soviet Union had a weak economy in comparison to that of the capitalist world by the 1980s and lots of economic, and attendant social, problems; this troubled its leadership and

led to reforms that did not work. We may as well, therefore, leave Lockwood's argument to be proved or not by history, by the fulfillment of the teleology that his argument invokes and upon which it ultimately rests: capitalism is doomed as it shifts to a global scale. If he turns out to be right (and if he turns out to be right for the right reasons) he has my apologies in advance for doubting him.

6   The differences between the radical and gradualist approaches to reform are primarily concerned with the arrangement of reform, the sequencing of policy, rather than with its ends, the creation of a market. The differences are described in Åslund (2002, pp.70-112;) Lavigne (1999, 118-20); Murrell (1992). A more technical discussion can be found in Roland (2000).

7   This next section draws on Robinson (2002, pp.104-07).

8   A longer discussion of these issues can be found in Woodward (1999).

9   Whether networks etc are the best terms to use here and whether it is correct to talk about exchange are moot points. Discussion of different terms that could be applied, as well as examples of the types of interaction referred to here, can be found in Ledeneva (1998 and 2001).

10   The basic aims of reform (low inflation, stable currencies facilitating equal exchange, greater availability of goods and services, secure property rights) are, if achieved, non-exclusive even if the higher aspirations of reform (growth and increased economic prosperity, more resources available for consumption) are not achieved or are attained unequally. For a longer analysis of economic reform as a public good see Hellman (1998). For a critique of this view of economic reform, see Woodruff (1999, pp.9-10). Woodruff's objection is that this characterization of reform creates a particular view of the state and its role. Whilst this is true, it is also true that the outcomes of reform are non-exclusive so that the definition of reform as a public good has to hold.

11   Calculated from figures in Statkomitet SNG (2000) for 1991 or 1992. The Baltic states are excluded because of their unique developmental path; Turkmenistan is excluded because its figures are unbelievable even by post-Soviet standards.

Chapter 2

A Fickle Benefactor:
Russia and the Global Economy
as a Resource for Change

Neil Robinson

Introduction

The collapse of communism in the Soviet Union created high hopes for the integration of Russia into the global economy. Integration would, as Yeltsin put it in his speech announcing radical economic reform, 'considerably ease our movement along th[e] road [to a market economy] and speed up reform' (*Sovetskaya Rossiya*, 29 October 1991). Engagement with the global economy was seen by Russian reformers as one way in which the end of communism could become 'an avenue to European civilization', whilst others claimed that 'the integration of Russia's domestic economy into the world economy is a fundamental aspect of Russia's national interest', and believed that Russia would achieve membership of all the major international economic agencies within a short-time and form links with Europe so as to take part in its 'single monetary system' (Bogomolov, 1992, pp.33-5; Shokhin, 1994, p.105; Belyaev and Chichkanov, 1992, p.12).[1]

Reality has fallen far short of these aspirations. This chapter looks at Russian reformers attempts in the 1990s to restructure the political economy of Russia. Russian reformers saw the global economy as a powerful resource that could be used to support the struggle to reform Russia. At first, it was hoped that changes in trade, foreign investment and aid would help the initial push for radical economic reform through 'shock therapy'; later, it was hoped that the opening of debt markets to foreigners would assist reform efforts. The aspirations of reformers were, however, the same no matter what the foreign economic strategy used: it was believed that foreign money would help consolidate the state's control over fiscal policy so that financial tools could be used to force marketization and structural changes on to the Russian economy. The chapter will explain why the different foreign economic strategies failed, explaining, *inter alia*, the collapse of 'shock therapy' in the early 1990s and the 1998 crisis. The chapter will conclude by explaining how unexpected effects of the 1998 crisis and high world oil prices have worked to alleviate financial pressures on the state under Putin and what this means.

Why radical reform?

The Baltic states excepted, Russia was unique amongst the former Soviet states in unambiguously making a choice for radical economic reform in the wake of the USSR's collapse. At one level, the decision for radical reform was inevitable. Radical reform was the best way of accessing international resources. Unlike the other newly independent states, there was no great regional power to which Russia could turn to for economic aid in the same way that all of the CIS states were to receive economic subsidies after independence from Russia. The only source of similar aid for Russia was the global economy. Access to resources that were held in private hands overseas meant economic liberalization and openness. Radical reform was also necessary to unlock the coffers of international financial institutions (IFIs) and foreign governments. The G-7 states effectively passed the task of co-ordinating the international response to Soviet economic collapse at their 1990 Houston summit to IFIs with the International Monetary Fund (IMF) as the lead institution. The immediate result of this was a multi-agency and multi-volume study of the Soviet economy that argued that the Gorbachev reforms were 'relatively gradual' in approach and asserted that only radical economic reform would actually work to transform the Soviet economy (IMF et al, 1990, pp.18-19, 47-8; see also IMF et al, 1991a, 1991b, 1991c). This more or less ended the effective – as opposed to the academic – policy debate before it had even begun since it in effect, established a series of policy hurdles that had to overcome before resources would be disbursed from IFIs and Western governments.

International factors could, however, have been ignored except for two other factors. First, it seemed to many that Russia was too large and too important to fail. The USSR under Gorbachev had made great efforts at achieving partnership with Western powers and had promoted the idea that international problems should be solved by co-operation. The Russian government believed that once freed from the last remnants and concerns of the Soviet state, it would be even more successful in developing partnership with the West and that as a partner it would draw economic benefits from participation in international financial institutions. On top of this, there was a belief that it would simply not be possible for Russia to be poor. Russia's natural resource potential is far greater than that of any other major industrial power: twice that of the USA, five to six times greater than Germany's and 18 to 20 times that of resource poor Japan (L'vov, 2001, p.26). It was thought that this great potential would act as a buffer for the economy and in tandem with the strategic partnership that would be forged with the West, would give Russia a reform safety net like no other post-communist state.

Second, and reinforced by the above, the calculations about reform made by Russian leaders were very different to those in the rest of the post-Soviet space. The leaders in most other states calculated that the risks of reform were too great and either embarked on half-hearted reforms, or avoided them altogether. Russia took a different course because the ongoing collapse of the USSR in the aftermath of the failed August 1991 coup created a crisis of government that Yeltsin, as the newly elected President of Russia had to resolve at the same time that he could no longer avoid taking direct responsibility for the economic fate of Russia. Adopting a radical reform package appeared to resolve both of these problems in a way that was politically advantageous to Yeltsin to a point where it appeared that the pay-off of action would far exceed any political losses caused through the pursuit of a radical policy. Moreover, it appeared that the benefits of action would be concentrated on Yeltsin, whilst the costs would be born amongst opponents real and potential.

The time horizons of radical economic reform were short and expectations of results were therefore less uncertain than might have been the case with a more gradualist programme. Radical economic reform promised that there would be economic stabilization based on price liberalization, currency stabilization and convertibility, and commercialization of economic activity by 1993. This would be followed by national economic recovery between 1993 and 1995 – at the same time that property rights were to be redistributed – when there would be a return to a pre-reform level of GDP (Russian Government, 1992, pp.47, 70). There would not be an improvement in popular economic fortunes before Yeltsin's second term electoral contest, but people would be no worse off and certain public goods associated with economic transformation such as property rights and a stable currency, would have been delivered. Yeltsin, of course, would have the credit of these successes because it would be the executive that had delivered them.

The 'lack of a long-term' in reformist discourse meant that rhetorically there was a seamless and endless pay-off to reform: the public goods of reform would segue from the immediate benefits of adopting reform policies. This might have been enough to prompt the adoption of reform, but radical reform was also attractive for shot-run political reasons. At the onset of reform, Yeltsin occupied a position at the apex of a state that barely existed. Although it had begun to appropriate the functions and resources of some parts of the old Soviet state, much of the Soviet state's resources had been transferred into private hands (Solnick, 1998). Reform was not so much concerned with getting such resources back as with creating alternative sources of power and altering the terms of power granted by resource possession. As was argued in Chapter 1, the transfer of resources from the Soviet state into private and semi-private hands took place through particularistic exchange where value was identified and created by the actors involved in exchange, rather than by impersonal market relations. Although the Yeltsin regime was far from free of connections with the old *nomenklatura*, it had a general interest in either destroying, or altering the terms on which resource possession created power. This would enable it to gather resources as a state through taxation, fix the value of any resources that it accumulated, and make it easier to perform other desirable state functions such as economic planning, the promotion of economic development etc. Market reform would destroy particularistic exchange and replace it with market exchange based on a state-licensed unit of exchange (a stable currency) and in the process author a change in the structure of power in the state's favour (Woodruff, 1999). The capacity of the state would increase and its ability to regulate the economy would grow as particularistic exchange was replaced by market exchange that required the state to safeguard property rights, provide public goods such as protection from criminality and stable money, and facilitate profit-maximization rather than rent-seeking. The costs of this were low because they would not be born by those forces or institutions that supported the president, but by those actors who possessed resources acquired due to position under the old regime. Benefits would be concentrated on the presidency at the apex of the state with its new fiscal powers. In short, the Yeltsin regime had little by way of state power at the start of the reform process and therefore had little to lose; any improvement in the position of state agents in relation to those who had power from past position was almost an absolute improvement.

Finally, the adoption of a radical reform variant was attractive because it solved some immediate and pressing institutional problems. The collapse of Soviet administration engendered by the August 1991 coup came before the Russian presidency and its attendant institutions had established their relationship with the government of the RSFSR – the Council of Ministers, under Prime Minister Ivan Silayev – or the parliament. Yeltsin resolved the struggles that were growing between the agencies of the Russian government at the end of October 1991 by asking parliament to grant him the power to issue mandatory decrees to begin the process of radical economic reform. The granting of decree powers and the subsequent reorganization of government resolved the power struggle and created the basis of a Yeltsin government made up of reformers in place of the remnants of the Silayev government (Yeltsin, 1994, pp.163-64; Gaidar, 1999, p.61). This was reinforced by Yeltsin's use of his decree powers to try to assert control over regional government. Elections for heads of regional administrations were cancelled so that the heads of regional administration and Presidential Representatives to the regions appointed by Yeltsin to insure compliance with Russian government laws and decrees as the August coup collapsed were kept in place to implement economic reform. In rapid order, therefore, Yeltsin had created what is often called the 'executive' or 'presidential' 'vertical', a hierarchy of administrative bodies responsible to the President and supposed to ensure the implementation of government policy throughout Russia (Kuvaldin, 1998, p.24).

How was radical reform supposed to fulfil its promises?

Calculations about power – personal, governmental and state – were central to the decision to undertake radical economic reform. Although considerations of foreign support were important, external factors could not on their own secure reform. This was because support from outside could only influence reform outcomes after the basic elements of market exchange had begun to be laid. It is difficult to attract investment to an economy, or trade from it, when there is little notion of value and costs and hence uncertainty about the potential to accrue profit. The solution to this problem for the reformers of the early 1990s was to design reforms that would enable external influences on economic transformation to be fully effective resources for change as quickly as possible. However, since the power of the state was weak, the success of reform depended on the policy mix and the ability of the government to convince its opponents that they would be successful and that resistance would be futile. The most important thing to put in place in order that external economic forces could come to the aid of the reformist government were prices that were a relatively accurate reflection of value.

The sequencing of reform – price liberalization and financial stabilization before the privatization of industry – was thus not only designed to alter power relations in the Russian economy, but also to highlight where investment might be made profitably from outside the country, and to increase demand for access to foreign markets and capital internally.[2] Successful price liberalization and financial stabilization policies would have led to a cut in government subsidies to industry and the creation of a market for resources. Central government would cease to offer subsidies by choice; local government would be financially squeezed with the cutting of the state budget so that it would not be able to replace the centre as a source of largesse and rent. Enterprises would be made dependent on private investment and credit, which would require transparency in corporate governance (Robinson, 1994 and 1998). Economic activity would become commercialized in the absence of subsidies and this would help establish the conditions for an inward flow of foreign investment capital and goods into Russia by creating some basic information about economic costs and profitability. Controlling inflation would help to facilitate the introduction of foreign capital by expediting the creation of a convertible and stable rouble.

Between them the creation of a market, the cutting of the state budget and a growing inward flow of foreign capital would expose the weaknesses and inability to compete of Russian industry and force further change in corporate governance. The power of foreign capital and of the new entrepreneurs from the nascent private sector would grow and balance the power of the old managerial stratum with a new economic class that would be a social constituency for the government. Essentially, the reformers were trying to create a virtuous circle. Commercialization of enterprise behaviour under the conditions of price liberalization, financial stabilization and foreign capital inflows/foreign trade would insure that the most efficient and productive owners would begin to emerge before large-scale privatization in the second stage of reforms. In light of this, the reformers were not so concerned about the policy design of privatization. Concessions could be made (and were) because change in the general economic environment would mean that privatization would soon lead to a transfer of 'property into the hands of the most effective owners' (Chubais and Vishnevskaya, 1993, p. 94).

The failure of 'shock therapy' and the limited influence of the global economy, 1992-1994

Reformist aspirations to achieve rapid reintegration with the global economy thus depended on the success of radical economic reform. Only when it had created some basic economic structures such as commercialized economic activity and a stable currency would foreign economic forces have any significant purchase on the Russian economy, and hence on the balance of political power. Radical reform was launched with the liberalization of prices in January 1992, but was heavily contested and compromised fairly quickly thereafter. Aid did come from IFIs, but this was never more than enough to stabilize politics for a short time by temporarily funding deficits. There is little point in recounting the blow-by-blow undermining of the reform process. Basically, political opposition was too great for Yeltsin to be able to maintain a credible commitment to reform and guarantee his own political survival. This failure was inevitable. The Gaidar-inspired government and key members of the Presidential Administration were divided from the onset about the merits of economic reform (Robinson, 2000). As political conflict developed in 1992 these divisions became ever more apparent and facilitated the introduction of economic pragmatists into the government to balance the neo-liberal reformers. This process reached its logical conclusion in December 1992 when Yeltsin compromised on the composition of the government and replaced Gaidar as Prime Minister with Viktor Chernomyrdin. This helped to split the opposition to Yeltsin. The industrialists, who had been most threatened by radical economic reform, broke away from radical political groupings, whose opposition was more ideological than self-interested, and the opposition bloc in the legislatures underwent realignment (Henderson and Robinson, 1997, pp.189-92). Chernomyrdin's appointment meant that neo-liberal economic reform measures could only be implemented haphazardly and were subject to countervailing pressures from pragmatic ministers brought in to government to shore Yeltsin up politically.

The compromising of reform by political conflict meant that serious effort to replace particularistic exchange with market exchange was derailed. Russian industry was able to ignore the government's injunctions and incentives to commercialize, and carry on as usual, trading on credit, building up inter-enterprise debt and seeking subsidies from local authorities to maintain soft-budget constraints. The slow transformation of the economy and political conflict delayed the creation of mechanisms and institutions that would have enabled the entry of foreign capital or permitted trade to support the commercialization of economic activity.

The failure of 'shock therapy' to create an opening for foreign capital meant that the nature of Russia's engagement with the global economy evolved from the late Soviet situation, rather than changed dramatically and fundamentally. Foreign direct investment made little impact on Russia in the early 1990s, and even subsequently has been comparatively small in scale.[3] As Table 2.1 shows, Russia has attracted less per capita FDI and FDI as a percentage of GDP than the average of all post-communist

Table 2.1 Foreign direct investments in Russia in comparative perspective

	Cumulative FDI, 1989-2001 (US$ mln)	Cumulative FDI per capita, 1989-2001 (US$)	FDI as a per cent of GDP, 2001
Russia	6,762	47	0.0
Central and eastern Europe and the Baltic states		1,401	4.9
South-eastern Europe		299	5.0
CIS		196	3.1
All post-communist states		603	4.1

Central and eastern Europe and the Baltic states: Croatia, Czech republic, Estonia, Hungary, Latvia, Lithuania, Poland, Slovakia, Slovenia
South-eastern Europe: Albania, Bosnia-Herzegovina, Bulgaria, Croatia, FYR Macedonia, FR Yugoslavia, Romania
CIS: Russia, Armenia, Azerbaijan, Belarus, Georgia, Kazakhstan, Kyrgyzstan, Moldova, Tajikistan, Turkmenistan, Ukraine, Uzbekistan

Sources: Calculated from EBRD (2002, p.67)

states, much worse than the Central and eastern European and Baltic states, and even worse than the South-eastern European states, many of which have been war ravaged and slow to reform. The failure of commercialization made much of Russian business activity too opaque to invest in. Moreover, legislation needed to improve chances of attracting foreign investment and the development of institutions and governance to regulate foreign economic activity were stalled. Neither foreign investors nor the state were able, nor at times willing, to enforce transparency in corporate governance and break the power of managers left over from the Soviet era (Blasi et al, 1997). Share registers and accounts remained closed so that an investment in a Russian enterprise did not lead to a say in its operation. Legal enforcement of property rights was weak and lack of clarity in ownership and corporate governance increased the risks of investing in Russia considerably. Where not tied to Russian investment, foreign capital investment has generally been small, only rising above 3 per cent of total investment once, in 1999 (Goskomstat, 2001, p.4571). We should also bear in mind that this is a share in a small, and for most of the period, declining investment figure. Domestic investment has plummeted in Russia since the fall of communism, only rising at the end of the 1990s after the 1998 crash. The fall was particularly marked in the first post-Soviet years. Overall, investment was at 35 per cent of the 1990 level by 1995, and fixed investments fell 18, 5, and 12 per cent in 1996, 1997 and 1998 respectively (Russian Government, 1997, p.39; EBRD, 1998, p.225).[4]

We also have to question whether capital inflows are actually *foreign*. Capital flight from Russia has been a persistent feature of post-Soviet economy. Estimates of the amounts of capital flight vary, but are uniformly high (Loungani and Mauro, 2001). It is difficult to estimate how much of this money returns to Russia from countries with consistent records of large-scale foreign investment activity in Russia such as the USA and Germany. However, what appear to be anomalies in figures on the source of FDI indicate that some exported capital comes back into Russia as 'foreign' money, or is reinvested as profit by Russian-owned, foreign-registered front companies, to claim tax and other incentives. In the first nine months of 1995, for example, the largest amount of foreign investment in roubles Russia came from Cyprus, a favoured destination for exported capital; in 1997 Switzerland, another nation favoured by Russian money-launderers, was the third largest investor in Russia (ahead of Germany) and Cyprus has consistently been in the top ten foreign investors, generally above France and Japan, in the late 1990s and 2000 (*Finansoviye izvestiya*, 22 February 1996; *Izvestiya*, 6 June 1996; Goskomstat, 1998, 337 and 2001, p.579). Since much of the exported capital will have been earned through particularistic exchange (for example, through manipulations of the foreign trade system, or the sale of primary goods at a rouble loss, but a dollar profit), the repatriation of capital through front companies can be expected to sustain vested interests and empower them with resources relative to those controlled by the state.

The low levels of FDI in Russia, and the fact that some of it is 'non-foreign' in nature, mean that the influence of foreign capital on the Russian economy in general has been low. The relatively small amounts of FDI entering the Russian economy throughout the period 1992-1997, but especially in 1992-1993, were essentially 'enclave' investment, limited to a few sectors and regions, and could not and did not produce a general change transformation in national economic fortunes (Kuznetsov, 1994, pp.112-14). Foreign money has only consistently gone into the energy sector, trade and financial services; for example, 49.2 per cent of all foreign investment (excluding financial instruments such as bonds and bank credits) in Russia was in these three sectors in 1997, the year in which Russia witnessed the largest inflows of foreign capital (calculated from Goskomstat, 1998, p.336). The only industrial sector that has been penetrated significantly by foreign capital is the energy industry, but as in the rest of the economy foreign capital was not necessarily productive: in 1996, for example, 11 per cent of energy enterprises had foreign involvement, but they accounted for only 5.2 per cent of energy production (Goskomstat, 1997, pp.335-36).[5] The influence of foreign investment has also been geographically uneven. Money has, fairly predictably, followed money. The regions that are consistently at the top of the investment table are also nearly always regions from which JVs export most and which are generally the wealthiest (Moscow, Tyumen, St. Petersburg). Most of the capital inflow has gone to Moscow and the 'central raion' (Moscow and its surrounding districts), and to one or two other regions like Tyumen, the oil producing centre in Western Siberia. The distribution within regions is also very uneven. In 1994, for example, Arkhangelsk *oblast'* displaced Moscow at the top of the national investment chart on the basis of investment in just two energy projects; in the first half of the same year 10 firms in Moscow received 60 per cent of foreign investment in the city (Goskomstat, 1997, p.657, *Finansoviye izvestiya*, 1 September and 9 June 1994).

Table 2.2 Russian foreign trade by commodity group, selected years (current prices, % of total, excluding CIS)

	1992		1996		2000	
	Export	Import	Export	Import	Export	Import
Value (US$ bln)	42.4	36.9	71.8	31.7	89.2	22.3
Food and agricultural products	2.5	25.3	3.7	25.4	1.0	23.9
Minerals, including oil	51.2	2.7	46.9	3.7	54.5	1.7
Chemicals	6.0	9.3	7.0	12.2	6.7	20.7
Leather, animal skins	0.2	1.6	0.5	0.4	0.3	4.5
Wood, pulp and paper products	3.4		4.2	4.2	4.5	3.9
Textiles	0.6	10.7	0.8	4.4	0.6	4.9
Metals, metal products	10.5	3.2	21.2	4.9	23.5	36.3
Machinery, electrical equipment, means of transport	8.4	35.0	7.5	32.0	7.5	0.3
Other	17.1	11.2	7.0	10.3	1.4	3.8

Source: Adapted from WIIW (1995, pp.269, 275, and 1996, pp.340, 347, 1997, p.360, 367); Goskomstat (2001, pp.609-10)

Foreign trade's influence on the Russian economy also followed Soviet patterns. The profits that could be generated through foreign trade made it an attractive source of patronage for Yeltsin. He granted large exemptions to import and export duties that undercut international markets and created vast profits for clients and lobbies (Aven, 1994, p.92; Åslund, 1995, p.147). This was a useful means of securing his continued tenure in office, but meant that the chances of international markets providing Russia with a 'ready-made price system' through trade were slim. Table 2.2 shows the structure of Russian imports and exports with non-CIS economies. Changes since the Soviet era are marginal even up to 2000, let alone in the early years of transition. Russia imports more food than the USSR did, more textiles and means of transport, but its main import is still machinery. Its main exports of fuel (mineral products in Table 2.2), raw materials (metals, timber) and semi-manufactures (chemical and metal products) form roughly the same proportion of goods traded abroad as they did in the Soviet period (see the data in Lavigne, 1995, p.85). The CIS remained a market for poor quality Russian goods, at least in the early years of transition, as trade followed paths established in Soviet times and under the division of labour created by planning within the USSR. In 1997, for example, machinery and means of transport made up only 8.1 per cent of Russia's exports to non-CIS countries, but 19.5 per cent of exports to CIS states (Goskomstat, 1998, p.374). This perpetuated Russia's isolation from international markets. The only real difference to the Soviet period in foreign trade has been the drop in the value of imports from non-CIS countries and Russia's trade surplus. The drop in the value of imports reflects the declining purchasing power of the Russian domestic market; and Russia's trade, and hence current account surplus, whilst of value to the economy, has at times been based on an increased volume of exports fetching lower prices on world markets, and is generally unstable because of fluctuating energy prices and production levels (UN ECE, 1994, p.68).

After shock therapy: setting the scene for foreign deficit financing

The failure of shock therapy combined with the relative smallness of FDI inflows into Russian enterprises and the basically unchanged nature of foreign trade relations after 1991 meant that engagement with the global economy could not aid the help the cause of radical economic reform. It did not bring about a fundamental change in the management of the enterprises, or wipe out particularistic exchange. Managers who had taken advantage of *perestroika* to transfer control over enterprises into their own hands were not removed from post and engaged in survival strategies – most notably trading on credit[6] – that weakened efforts to commercialize economic activity, stabilize the currency and control inflation. The failure of commercialization, reformers' sanguine view that ownership mattered less than the economic environment in which ownership was operative, and privatization legislation that enabled managers to maintain their control over enterprises, meant continuity before change. Privatization introduced massive changes in that the state's stake in many enterprises fell dramatically, but there was not necessarily a correspondingly dramatic change in management, and hence in the networks of trade and mutual support that economic actors engaged in (Robinson, 1998).

The limited gains from economic reform in 1992-1993 meant that the will to reform the economy died down after 1993, even though Yeltsin won his political battle against the legislatures in October 1993 and gained considerable powers under the December 1993 Constitution. The result was a hiatus in developing relations with the global economy between 1993 and 1996. The Russian government remained keen to attract foreign capital, at least rhetorically, and continued to press for things such as membership of the WTO and the G-7, and reacted to pressure from IFIs (for example, by ending many foreign trade concessions and cutting export tariffs in 1996). However, there was no great reformist push of the type needed to attract foreign capital in large quantities. For example, no money was allocated by the Ministry of Finance in 1995 to co-fund investment projects involving foreign partners and approved by the Ministry of the Economy (Grigor'yan, 1997, p.14).

The hiatus in developing relations with the global economy evolved as economic policy drifted to a crisis in 1994. The poor performance of pro-government, reformist parties in the December 1993 elections to the new State Duma and the subsequent resignation from government of Gaidar and Boris Fedorov (the Minister of Finance) lead to a gradual dissolution of financial discipline during 1994. Chernomyrdin declared that the era of 'market romanticism' was ended and the government became a 'coalition of lobbyists' (*Segodnya*, 21 January 1994). These lobbies gradually had an affect on the budget as expenditure on agriculture and other subsidies was increased (*Izvestiya*, 18 May 1994, *Segodnya*, 15 October 1994). The state lacked the ability to finance these subsidies because of its inability to collect taxes. The shortfall in tax collection in 1993 had been 30 per cent (*Rossiiskie vesti*, 5 March 1994). Matters did not improve over the course of 1994, and by the autumn, just before the rouble crisis, projected tax returns for the year were just above 50 per cent (*Segodnya*, 27 September 1994). Outflows of credit from the Central Bank of Russia (CBR) grew at a faster pace than provided for in the budget (9 per cent of GDP in the first 9 months of the year instead of hoped for 5-7 per cent, *Segodnya*, 17 December 1994). Finally, the government did not keep control of interest rate policy. The CBR's discount rate was reduced over the course of 1994 until it reached a negative rate of return against inflation.

The growth of the budget deficit and the different pressures on the rouble produced a crisis in October 1994 when the rouble collapsed against the US dollar. The crash was in part caused by commercial banks speculating on leaked information about government plans to realign the rouble against the US dollar in the hope that this would enable it finance some of the budget deficit, and in part by the build-up of inflationary pressures in the Russian economy caused by the growth of that deficit. The immediate economic affect of the crash was a jump in the monthly inflation rate and a fall in living standards. The political affect was a realignment of the government (Anatolii Chubais was promoted to first Deputy Prime Minister), and some tough talk and calls for more fiscal prudence. In the summer of 1995, a fixed rate corridor was introduced for the rouble to control speculation. However, the state possessed no more effective policy tools or powers available to enforce tax collection or fiscal austerity than before the crisis. Deficit financing thus remained a problem. In the absence of any larger political change, or help from external forces, the shortfall in state finances was to be filled by the one set of actors in Russia with some liquidity, the commercial banks.

Whether the turn to the banks by state actors was a deliberate move towards the creation of a patronage contract between state and commercial interests is open to debate. There were already close links between state actors and banks. Many commercial banks had their roots in old social power networks and practices and were tied to political structures from the first. Indeed, the Russian government classified the largest banks as 'authorized' banks and used them to manage state money in the absence of its own financial apparatus. But deliberate or not, any contract that did emerge was inherently unstable because the banks came to the aid of the government in two contradictory ways after the 1994 rouble crisis. On the one hand, the banks began to fund the budget deficit as the market in government stock (GKOs, short-term government discount bills, and OFZs, government fixed coupon bonds) set up in 1994 began to take off. This was helped by the rise in the CBR discount rate after the rouble crisis and soon reached a point where treasury bills could be used to replace

CBR credits as a source of deficit financing. This method of deficit financing was justifiable in reformist eyes in that it was not inflationary. Like 'shock therapy' before it, therefore, it might serve to stabilize the rouble and this could encourage inward investment and change the configuration of economic power. The boom in treasury bills, as Treisman (1998, p.255) has noted, not only funded the budget deficit, it also allowed the banks to secure an alternative source of profit to the inflationary speculation that had fuelled the growth of the banking sector in 1992-1994. Commercial bank investments in government securities rose eightfold between the rouble crisis and mid-1996 and were equal to 7.1 per cent of GDP in 1996, rising to 12 per cent by May 1997 (EBRD, 1997, p.197).

On the other hand, the commercial banks came to the aid of the government by proposing a 'shares for loans' programme in the spring of 1995. Under this scheme the banks gained control of major and strategic industries not privatized in 1993 and that promised a profit through the production of goods for export or in near monopoly conditions (oil, telecommunications, certain metals etc). Again, this had attractions for reformists in that it appeared to link industries to sources of finance, could be justified as a means of changing corporate governance in major strategic industries, and was supposed to create new revenue sources for the state budget. Income from the first round of privatization had been very low since privatization had been voucher, rather than monetary, privatization. The 'shares for loans' scheme consolidated bank power as they expanded their fields of activity and influence. The auctions of blocks of shares were organized by banks themselves to their financial advantage, were less than transparent and comprehensively denounced (especially by the losers) as corrupt and insider-dominated. The terms of the initial 'shares for loans' scheme called for banks to manage a block of shares won at auction until September 1996 on provision of a loan to the government and investment in the company whose stock the bank held. Thereafter, if the government did not redeem the loan, the shares could be sold on with the bank taking back its original loan plus 30 per cent of any capital gain, the rest going to the government. In all cases where the 'shares for loans' scheme was completed until the end of 1998, auction winners subsequently brought the firms they had managed and often did so at bargain prices. In the first of the 'shares for loans' sales, for example, Menatep won control of one-third of Yukos (Russia's second largest oil holding company) for a loan of US$159 million. When Menatep sold its share of Yukos on, it went to one of its subsidiaries for US$160.1 million so that the state's share of the capital gain was only US$770,000. In another sale, Oneksimbank sold another oil firm to one of its subsidiaries for below the original loan price so that the state got nothing. The consolidation of ownership over strategic industries through shares for loans transformed them from finance houses in to 'financial industrial groups' (FIGs) (Johnson, 1998).

The contradiction between these two means of assistance to the state from the banks was their different sources of high profit. High profits from 'shares for loans' were based, first, on making sure that the government did not get a true market price for the assets that it was disposing of, and, second, on avoiding paying large sums in tax on either the limited amounts of money that could be squeezed out of domestic customers, or on foreign currency earnings. Profits from GKOs on the other hand, required that the government's revenues were maintained so that there was confidence in its ability to meet debt repayments. Amongst other things, this meant that taxes had to be paid. In the short-run, this tension was managed because the government maintained the profitability of securities and hence commercial banks' commitment to investment. It achieved this by securing a low inflation rate and providing the banks with concessions. The concessions to banks were that they were allowed to have the GKO market to themselves because foreign purchase of government stock was at first banned, and that certain 'authorized' banks were licensed to trade in GKOs as agents of the state to their financial advantage (Johnson, 1998, p.353). The government kept inflation low by not paying some of its bills (such as wages) and provided industry and local authorities with non-monetary subsidies in the form of fuel supplies. By mid-1996, Gazprom (the gas monopolist) had 'practically replaced the CBR as the source of centralized credit' and was owed 57 trillion roubles by its customers (US$10 billion) (*Nezavisimaya gazeta*, 4 June 1996). In return for making these fuel deliveries, oil companies and Gazprom received tax and exporting concessions (Treisman, 1998, pp.260-4). Tax concessions were equivalent to 7.2 per cent of GDP by the end of 1996 (EBRD, 1997 p.121). Cumulatively, these actions helped bring yearly inflation down from 837 per cent in 1993 to about 14 per cent by the end of 1997 (EBRD, 1997, p.118).

Hitting rock bottom: global financing of the Russian state and the August 1998 crash

The problems of the state's relationship with the banks built up gradually after 1994. Between 1994 and the start of 1997, the relationship between state and the banks became increasingly close. The large banks and FIGS were major contributors to the Yeltsin re-election campaign in 1996. Their leaders' involvement in politics was formalized after Yeltsin's successful defence of his presidency. Vladimir Potanin (from Oneksimbank) and Boris Berezovsky entered the government as, respectively, first Deputy Prime Minister with responsibility for economic policy and a Deputy Secretary of the Security Council. But no matter how close the government and the banks became, deficit financing through the sale of short-term debt could only be a temporary solution to Russia's problems. The government's failure to failure to pay some of its bills, the replacement of monetary with non-monetary subsidies and the granting of tax concessions, all further weakened the state's ability to raise taxes and contributed to the demonetization of much of Russia's economy in the form of barter and the non-payment of wages by companies.[7] This in turn hit the government's ability to raise money to finance its budget through the securities market. The demonetization of the economy had to be reversed at some point if the state was to have a solid revenue base and be able to roll its debt over. There also had to be some control on the growth of the deficit, which had been pushed up by the expansion of the GKO market and the high interest rates the government paid on its short-term debt. By the end of 1996, government debt was roughly 50 per cent of GDP (Korhonen, 1998, p.5). This need became particularly pressing as the demonetization of the economy also meant that the banks could not sustain their funding of the budget deficit. By autumn 1996, the stock of GKOs and OFZs had risen above the total stock of rouble deposits in the banking system (EBRD, 1998, p.13). International pressure also grew to change the relationship of the government to the economy in the wake of the presidential elections of 1996. The elections were seen as having led to financial indiscipline because of the spending promises made by Yeltsin during his campaign and the drop in state revenues whilst the outcome of the election was uncertain. In October 1996, the IMF delayed a US$10.2 billion transfer of budgetary aid because of the shortfalls in state revenue. An alternative source of funding had to be secured that could tide the state over whilst it resolved some of the structural problems of the economy. This alternative source was global finance, which it was hoped, would achieve what trade, aid and FDI had not been able to do.

Accessing global financial flows meant that state revenues had to be secured to insure investor confidence. The domestic bond market was opened up to foreigners in late 1996. There was a promise of profit in this for the banks since they would be the agents through which trading was to take place; the state would gain because its budget deficit would be funded despite the lack of liquidity in the Russian economy. At the same time, the state moved to improve its budgetary position by increasing its revenue flows. The first signs of change came in the autumn of 1996 with reform of the administration of tax collection to squeeze defaulters. This was bound to bring the government and the banks into conflict since many of the biggest tax defaulters were the energy companies that the banks had a stake in thanks to the 'shares for loans' sales.[8] In the spring of 1997, this aspect of strategy became more focused. Potanin was removed in a government reshuffle, and Chubais and Boris Nemtsov (the ex-governor of Nizhny Novgorod *oblast'*, a favourite of the World Bank and Western financiers), were brought into government as first Deputy Prime Ministers with, respectively, responsibility for economic reform and the Ministry of Finance, and for energy monopolies. This was quickly followed by an order from Chernomyrdin requiring companies in debt to the state to hand over 50 per cent plus 1 share of their equity to the government (*Financial Times*, 17 March 1997). Nemtsov applied pressure to Gazprom in particular, and it paid its back taxes in the summer (*Izvestiya*, 30 December 1997). Nemtsov further tried to break up the power of the energy lobby by pressing for improved corporate governance and government oversight, and for conditions in which foreign capital could balance the power of the large commercial banks in the sector (*Segodnya*, 10 July 1997, *Financial Times,* 9 and 19 September 1997).

The policies of building solid state finances through tax reform, the personnel mix (Chubais and younger reformers like Nemtsov), and an anti-inflationary policy all sat well with foreign investors and the financial press. Russia even made some headway in negotiations with IFIs in 1997, joining the Paris Club and announcing that it would balance out its debt repayments (favourably renegotiated with the London Club a few weeks after the Paris Club deal), with new income from debtors.

Foreign money began to flow into Russia in a variety of ways. The assault on the energy industries and the drive to push up tax revenue made some energy concerns open up to the West. The demand that Gazprom pay its back taxes, for example, led it to take out a US$1 billion loan from Credit Lyonnaise and Dresdner Kleinwort Benson (*Financial Times*, 30 June and 11 July 1997). The GKO market exploded in 1997 after Russia received its first credit ratings from international ratings agencies and issued its first Eurobonds in September and October 1996. The major influx of foreign money into GKOs came in the first six months of 1997 and financed 56 per cent of the budget deficit when taxation revenue was still very low (BOFIT, 1997a and 1997b). By the end of 1997, foreigners owned 33.9 per cent of the market in GKOs and OFZs; in the space of a year, the value of foreign holdings of short-term government debt had risen threefold and doubled in percentage terms (*Russian Economic Trends*, 1998, 7 (1), p.58). Eurobonds issued by the Russian government and some cities and firms were well received in Western markets after Moscow issued the first non-federal government Eurobond for US$500 million (*Finansoviye izvestiya*, 26 June 1997). Foreign money also began to enter the Russian stock exchange in large quantities for the first time on the back of the boom in treasury bills. The value of stock traded on the Moscow exchange rose by 155 per cent in the first half of 1997 to a value of about US$100 billion (*Financial Times*, 14 July 1997). In total, an estimated US$44 billion of foreign capital was invested in the Russian economy over the year (*Nezavisimaya gazeta*, 12 August 1998).

The inflow of foreign capital into the market for treasury bills and the increase in tax collection had the desired effect of controlling the government's debt problem. Interest rates on government stock fell to 9-10 per cent in the summer of 1997 from a high of over 100 per cent in 1996 and the rate of increase of state domestic debt fell to less than 2 per cent month by the autumn of 1997 (it had tripled in 1996) (*Izvestiya*, 15 October 1997). But whilst government policy made Russia look more attractive as an investment proposition, there was no real objective change on in the state's financial position, or transformation of the economy outside of the stock exchange and bond markets. The government's revenue situation was still precarious. It could force up collection of tax payments in cash for a short time, but it could not increase its revenues in general. Tax collection at the end of 1997 was about 15 per cent higher in cash terms than at the same time in 1996, but the overall level of enterprise tax indebtedness rose over the course of 1997 by 50 per cent and including tax penalties was worth US$93 billion (BOFIT, 1997c and 1998a, p.2).

The drive to increase tax collection was not, therefore, an unqualified success. Politically, it was even less successful since it exposed the tension between the government and the banks and FIGs. Pressure to pay taxes grew at the same time that profits from GKOs fell due to declining yields and as profits from access to government and profit from political influence declined.[9] The exposed tension displayed itself in competition for the blocks of shares to be allocated by the next round of the 'shares for loans' scheme and in the 1997-1998 privatization round. Control of these shares would have spread the risk of government strategy leading to losses for banks/FIGs since they were in firms where there was potential for income generation through export earnings (Norilsk Nickel, the Rosneft oil group), or linkage with foreign investors (the Svyazinvest telecom network). Tax losses could thus have been offset against new income streams.

Competition to control these enterprises intensified over the summer of 1997 and soon became political as access to politicians was seen as a key ingredient to a successful bid. The result was that at the same time that there was some move to increase state power by isolating it from economic interests, competition between these interests began to erode the organizational integrity of the government. A rolling governmental crisis developed from the summer of 1997 as the perception that Oneksimbank was doing better than everyone else in the 'shares for loans' auctions took hold. Oneksimbank won the Norilsk Nickel and Svyazinvest auctions and its rivals accused Chubais of favouring it unfairly. Yeltsin attempted to mediate between the rivals, but to no avail. The banks were determined to compete for Rosneft and bureaucratic conflict and criticism of the government from bank/FIG owned media mirrored their struggle. In November 1997, Chubais and three officials close to him were accused of corruption for taking a very large book advance from an Oneksimbank subsidiary (*Nezavisimaya gazeta*, 13 November 1997). The three officials lost their posts and Chubais lost control of the Ministry of Finance (*Kommersant*, 20 November 1997).

The Chubais scandal accelerated the development of a government crisis. In January 1998, Yeltsin tried to solve the government's problems by a redistribution of functions, from which Prime Minister Chernomyrdin appeared to emerge victorious. But then Yeltsin removed the whole government on 23 March 1998 on the pretext that pension and wage arrears had not been dealt with, and a new Prime Minister, Sergei Kiriyenko, was proposed. This turmoil came at precisely the wrong time, just as the crisis in Asian markets began to affect other emerging markets and as Russia began to suffer from balance of payments problems. The latter were the result of Russia's trade patterns. As we have seen, Russia ran a large trade surplus after 1991 by exporting fuels and metals. In 1997, the prices of these goods fell on world markets, whilst imports rose by 7 per cent. Income from fuel and metals sales fell, according to Kiriyenko, by 20 to 40 per cent and state revenue dropped off by Rb28 to 30 billion (*Rossiiskaya gazeta*, 11 April 1998). Further losses of 'several hundred million dollars' were projected as taxes on oil exports were cut to increase competitiveness (BOFIT, 1998b, p.1).

On its own, the decline in Russia's trade performance would not have been a problem. The Russian current account was still positive. However, combined with governmental crisis and pressure on government finances, it magnified the effect of declining investor confidence caused by the crisis in Asian markets in late 1997. Most of the foreign money that had entered the government debt market in late 1996 and

1997 was in short-term debt that matured in under a year. Maintaining investor confidence was therefore very important because as debt matured the government sought to roll it over in new GKO issues. When this confidence began to decline as a result of the Asian crisis and in response to government troubles (international credit rating agencies reduced Russia's credit rating several times after October 1997), money began to leave the government debt market. Foreign investors withdrew US$5 billion from the government debt market in November 1997 alone (BOFIT, 1997a). To counteract falling confidence, the government raised interest rates. The yield on GKOs rose from an average of 26 per cent in 1997 to 65.1 per cent by June 1998 (BOFIT, 1998c). The cost of government borrowing thus rose whilst worries remained about revenue generation because of continued tax collection problems and the falling current account surplus. Doubts about the overall financial health of Russia were compounded by failure to sell a stake in Rosneft, the oil group whose sale stirred up the 'bank wars' in the first place. Rosneft was overvalued and no bids were received; the government lost another Rb12 billion (*Kommersant*, 27 May 1998).

By August 1998, there was no confidence either in Russia or abroad in the ability of the government to service its debt or to implement reform measures that would enable it to regain confidence. The new look of the government after March 1998, the intervention of the IMF, swapping short-term debt for longer term bonds, the adoption of a reform package, promises of major cuts in the 1998 budget by presidential decree, and the appointment of 'foreigner-friendly' personnel like Boris Fedorov, the former Minister of Finance, to head the State Tax Service and Chubais, one of the casualties of the March purge, as Russia's representative to IFIs, produced only momentary relief. Russia did not have solid enough financial institutions to win back investor confidence. The banks in particular were exposed by the forward options on the rouble they had taken out with foreign banks, the size of their GKO holdings and lack of reserves. The government did not have the reserves to prop up the rouble over a long time, or broad political support for measures that would restore confidence. The Duma moved slowly in support of the government's anti-crisis package during July 1998. By the time it dissolved for the summer, it had voted through new laws creating only about one-third of the extra tax revenue wanted by the government. As a result, the IMF held back US$800 million of the extra aid that it had granted Russia to support the rouble (*Izvestiya*, 21 and 28 July 1998). In early August 1998, the price of Russian debt plummeted once more and the stock market began to sink to new lows (between October 1997 and devaluation the market lost 84.9 per cent of its value). On 17 August, Kiriyenko announced that the rouble would be allowed to float in a wider band so that it could be devalued by over a third by the end of the year (it soon broke this barrier). A moratorium on payment of foreign commercial debts and a freeze on domestic debt repayment were also announced.

Table 2.3 Selected economic indicators, 1998-2003

	1998	1999	2000	2001	2002	2003
GDP increase (%)	-5.3	6.4	10.0	5.0	4.3	6.8[a]
Industrial production (%)	-5.2	8.1	11.9	4.9	3.7	6.7[b]
Fixed investments (%)	-12.0	5.3	17.4	8.7	2.6	11.8[b]
Inflation (consumer prices, year end % change)	84.4	36.5	20.2	18.6	15.1	13.6[b]
Exports (US$ bln)	74.4	75.6	105.0	101.9	107.2	
Imports (US$ bln)	58.0	41.1	44.9	53.8	61.0	
Current account (US$ billions)	0.2	24.6	46.8	35.0	32.8	
Budget balance (% of GDP)	-5.9	-1.4	1.2	2.9	1.4	3.3[c]
Foreign currency debt (% of GDP)	50.1	87.7	55.3	44.4	36.2	34.1[a]
Foreign currency debt (US$ bln)	158.2	143.4	133.1	123.5	124.8	

[a] As of first quarter, 2003
[b] As of 1 May 2003
[c] As of April 2003

Source: BOFIT (2003, pp.1-3)

Unexpected revival: economic recovery, 1999-2003

The outlook for the Russian economy in the wake of the August crisis was bleak. The financial system appeared all but destroyed as banks could not meet their foreign debt obligations, and the state could meet neither its international or domestic obligations. Russia defaulted on its Soviet-era debt in September and December 1998, one major bank (Oneksimbank) defaulted on a Eurobond in February 1999 and several of Russia's regions defaulted on loans. Although the IMF has disbursed some money, it is not enough to cover Russia's debt repayment commitments to the IMF, let alone other creditors. The World Bank changed its policy toward Russia and would no longer provide loans to cover budget shortfalls (*Izvestiya*, 22 December 1998). The Russian budget for 1999 made provision for only US$9.5 billion for debt servicing, but debt servicing obligations in 1999 were US$17.5 billion. To cover this full amount would have required 80 per cent of budgeted expenditures in 1999, an impossible commitment for the government to make (BOFIT, 1999, p.2). It thus appeared inevitable that Russia would be unable to meet debt repayments and would be forced to be a supplicant to international economic agencies for some time to come. Moreover, given Russia's straightened circumstances it looked like any resources generated from these agencies would be earmarked for debt servicing, rather than reconstruction. Access to such funds also looked uncertain since the collapse of the rouble weakened the influence of market ideology in government. The new government under Yevgenii Primakov government, which included Yurii Maslyukov, a former chair of Gosplan, was ideologically more committed to state action than its predecessor was. Primakov himself argued that 'the market is not capable of putting all things in their correct place and so the government has to take on the function of supporting and regulating domestic producers' (*Nezavisimaya gazeta*, 21 October 1998).

Against this background, the recovery of the Russian economy was unexpected. The bases for recovery were the very weakness of the economy and changes in international oil prices, rather than economic policy in the first instance. As Table 2.3 shows, industrial output and GDP both rose after 1998. The weakness of the rouble meant that consumers turned back to Russian producers because they could no longer afford foreign made goods: the value of imports fell by US$17 billion in 1999 and continued to be relatively low in 2000-2002. Inflation fell as domestic demand was dampened by the rouble crash and as the government avoided pumping money into the economy. It did not reach the lows of 1996-1997, but at least this time round the fall in inflation was not based on the demonetization of the economy as the amount of barter in industrial sales fell from 46 per cent to 33 per cent between January 1999 and January 2000 (BOFIT, 2000, p.1) Investment picked up only slowly in 1999 in comparison to the growth in GDP and industrial production, but grew in 2000. At the same time, the value of exports grew as world oil prices rose to levels not seen since the Gulf War of 1991. In these circumstances, tax payments on foreign economic activity rose due to the weakness of the rouble and improved world oil prices. Tax payments may also have improved as barter has declined in industrial sales. The crash made paying taxes in cash cheaper than before: the rouble was so weak that there was little point in converting earnings into dollars and paying taxes in kind rather than in cash; the collapse of the GKO market meant that it was no longer possible or attractive to divert money that should have been earmarked for tax payments into the government securities market. The strength of Russian trade helped to stabilize Russia's current account surplus, taking some pressure of the rouble and allowing it to stabilize in relation to other currencies. In 2000, the Russian government managed to post a budget surplus for the first time, and the growth of the economy meant that the size of Russia's foreign debt relative to GDP became more manageable – even if it did not shrink particularly in dollar terms.

Both the Russian government and the economy and population in general seem, therefore, to have gained from the coincidence of the 1998 crash with oil price rises. As a result, the global economy looks to have had some positive influence on Russia's economic transformation at last. However, the way in which global economic factors have influenced Russia positively in aggregate terms illustrates the continued weakness of the Russian economy and of the Russian state to transform it. Recovery is still minimal and very much both oil dependent and oil focused, and although some policies have been put in place by Vladimir Putin to try to take advantage of the relative economic up-turn since 1998, the outcome of these policies and their political viability are open to question.

The oil-dependent nature of Russia's recovery is such that 80 per cent of the variation, and increase, in industrial production since 1998 can be explained by the strengthened price of oil (Gaddy, 2002, p.130). Similarly, the state's positive budget performance since 1998 is oil dependent. Andrei Illarionov, President Putin's economic adviser, has estimated that a fall of US$1in oil prices would lead to losses of to the state budget of US$1.4 billion (cited in Hanson, 2003, p.372). To this must be added the effects of exchange rate changes, where appreciation of the rouble, and a corresponding decline in Russian economic competitiveness, can also have dramatic effects on economic fortunes and state finances: Ruatava (2002, p.18) estimates that a 10 per cent rise or fall in oil prices leads to a 2.2 per cent rise or fall in GDP as does a 10 per cent rise or fall in the rouble exchange rate. Changes in oil prices can therefore have a dramatic and negative effect on Russian economic fortunes. Moreover, the benefits of recent economic recovery are not evenly spread. Over the years of post-communist economic transformation, investment in industry has made up just over a third of total capital investment in Russia. The share of the oil and gas industries in this investment has risen during the post-1998 boom from 10.9 per cent of total capital investment in 1998 to 17.7 per cent in 2000, a rate of increase that accounts for all of the percentage rise in industrial investment (Goskomstat, 2001, p.570). The increased competitiveness of the Russian economy under devaluation and the rise in industrial production have not, therefore, given rise to significant levels of increased investment across the economy, although the riches of the oil industry have helped to stimulate a revival of the Russian stock and bond markets (see also, Gaddy, 2002, p.137). Russia consequently is still waiting for the right conditions for long-term recovery despite its short-run successes. Moreover, it should be remembered that the short-run recovery is still relatively small. For recovery to 1989 GDP levels from 1998 onwards will require 15 years of growth at 5 per cent a year (Popov, 2000). Russia has achieved this level of growth since 1999, but it still obviously has a long way to go.

The oil-dependent nature of the post-1998 boom and its partiality show that the Russian economy is in remission, rather than cured. A cure requires policy and the imbalances in economic recovery are indicative of the continued weakness of the Russian state. It still cannot both draw up policies and implement them to help insure change and growth. The Russian state is stronger post-1998 than it was before it thanks to its budget surplus and the personal authority of President Putin after the drift of the later Yeltsin years. Putin has also taken action to further strengthen the state and invest its institutions with more authority by weakening regional authorities and curtailing the power of some business interests. These have been backed up by an impressive legislative and administrative record, with new tax codes, reductions in tax rates to encourage payment, moves towards restructuring the electricity sector, enforcing better corporate governance, new land codes, pension reform, money laundering and bureaucratic interference in the economy. There are, as Tompson (2002) has pointed out still significant problems of forcing compliance with legislation and policy, although as he goes on to argue Putin seems to have a strategy of gradually building up support for structural change that might alleviate some of the opposition to change and free-riding on it that have beset previous efforts at reform.

However, whilst there are some positive features to policy and Putin's style of rule, they are not always consistent, nor are they necessarily policies that will lead to a deepening of structural economic change. Inconsistency in style of rule is, perhaps, unavoidable. Consensus may be necessary to build support for polices and reduce the risk of their being undermined. However, at the same time, Putin is faced with an economy in which property ownership is broadly regarded as illegitimate because of the manner in which privatization, in particular the 'shares for loans' scheme, took place. There are inherent contradictions between consensus building with powerful economic elites over policy, maintaining popular trust and putting in place mechanisms necessary for the operation of a market economy. For example, improving the legal basis of economic activity and respect for the state and the rule of law requires either continued action against groups who benefited illegally or unfairly from the redistribution of property under Yeltsin, or their amnesty. Amnesty is however, a political risky strategy. However, action against vested interests leads to political confrontation and creates uncertainty about the economic future. The actions taken from the summer of 2003 against the Yukos oil group are a good example of this. The campaign had a political dimension since it served to warn that support for political parties that would campaign against the government in the December 203 Duma elections would not be tolerated, and at the same time proving President Putin's continued commitment to dealing with past abuses of privatization (*Vremya novostei*, 3 July 2003). However, at the same time, the case undermined business confidence by highlighting the fragility of property rights – never mind how the property was acquired – in Russia and the uncertain relationship between business and state that still exists despite the recent period of growth. As a result, the Yukos affair undid some of the benefits of growth. Growth should lead to confidence and a longer-term perspective on economic activity by Russian businessmen. Political uncertainty, on the other hand, shortens the time horizons of businessmen and can encourage such things as capital flight and warn off foreign investors. Even the Russian government recognized this, with Illarionov, Putin's economic adviser, accusing the procuracy of taking action harmful to national economic interests, and the Prime Minister, Mikhail Kasyanov and Minister of Economic Development and Trade, German Gref, calling for a privatization amnesty to reassure foreign investors of the stability of the economic system (*Nezavisimaya gazeta*, 15 July 2003; *Kommersant*, July 18, 2003).

Finally, it is not as yet certain that all the economic actions that the Putin administration has taken are actually in support of economic reform. As Gaddy (2002, p.141) has noted, Putin has been far more successful at implementing policies that are consistent with moving towards the market than policies such as major land reform that are essential for structural change. This means that the actual ends of policy are somewhat ambiguous. Tax reform is a case in point. The system of taxation in Russia has been in dire need of overhaul to simplify them, reduce tax evasion and avoidance and to create incentives for people to stop operating in informal economies and join the national market. Low, flat rate taxes on income and corporation tax under Putin have simplified the tax system, made it more effective, and reduced the overall tax burden. Potentially these measures support market transformation in that they create investment funds, pull people out of the informal economy and in to a monetized, and more extensive market economy, and weaken the discretionary revenue raising and expenditure powers of regional authorities so that their ability to run their own economic policies to the detriment of the nation as a whole is diminished. However, low, flat rate taxes such as those introduced in Russia are also a common feature of economic systems that are reliant on energy sales for revenue generation and in which states increasingly slough off responsibility for general economic development in favour of consolidating control over energy revenues and using these as a source of patronage. Such states generally have underdeveloped state administrative capacity as a result, even where they have bloated bureaucracies because of patronage. Without large-scale renationalization, Russia's ability to develop in such a direction may be limited by the structure of ownership in the energy sector. However, without compensating growth in the non-energy sector and with incomplete reform of administration, it stands on the cusp of rentierism, a point we shall return to in Chapter 6.

Conclusion

Russia shows that arguments about the transformative powers of global markets can be dangerously seductive, but are meaningless where there is nothing domestically to support them. In the 1990s, when the prices of commodities were low, the global economy could not serve as a significant resource for change even though it held out the prospect of transformation. The Russian state could not create structures that would enable the global economy to have some purchase on Russia and help effect its transformation. The result was continued relative isolation from the global economy and perpetuated state weakness as the government turned to deficit financing by commercial banks that was based on exploiting demonetization. When this strategy proved unsustainable, the government turned to global finance to help stabilize it and kick start change. Stabilization proved elusive again, however, since the state did not manage to resolve its revenue collection problems quickly enough and the turn to global finance coincided with a crisis of government. Ironically, the collapse that this failure produced has led to some stabilization of the Russian economy and some growth, but on a very limited basis – the sale of oil and its taxation. The one-sided nature of this stabilization and the limited revival of the rest of the Russian economy shows another side of the fickleness of the global economy as a resource for change; where there are no structures, either social or institutional for it to work with and through, only the most basic forms of economic development such as resource extraction seem to be possible. Great wealth can, of course, be generated from this but without a state that can use its share of this wealth to stimulate the rest of the economy, this benefit of the global economy is no more effective a force for change than trade or direct investment or bonds were before it.

Notes

1   At the time they were writing Bogomolov was a member of Yeltsin's Presidential Consultative Council, Shokhin was a Deputy Prime Minister, and Belyaev and Chichkanov were Deputy Ministers of Foreign Economic Relations.
2   The basic reform strategy was laid out in speeches made by Yeltsin in October 1991 and January 1992 (*Sovetskaya Rossiya*, 29 October 1991, *Rossiiskaya gazeta*, 17 January 1992), in the memorandum on economic reform written by Gaidar and Matyukhin (the head of the Central Bank) (*Nezavisimaya gazeta*, 3 March 1992), and in the government's 'medium-term programme' of economic reform (Russian Government, 1992).
3   There are no commonly agreed FDI figures for Russia, especially for the early years of transformation. This reflects the confusion in Russian statistical sources on foreign economic activity caused by the multiplicity of agencies gathering data on it, the different techniques used by them and, until recently, the lack of a single authority with which foreign economic actors in Russia registered. For descriptions of the problems of data on foreign economic activity in Russia (see Fel'zenbaum, 1994, p.12; Urinson, 1994; *Finansovie izvestiya*, 3 May 1994).
4   Some estimates of the extent of the fall in capital investment since independence estimate the decrease to be even higher (see Volkov, 1996, p.6. A full review of the investment crisis in Russia can be found in Loginov et al, 1997, pp.64-97).
5   Excludes electricity (where 0.5 per cent of enterprises had some foreign involvement), includes oil, gas and coal. No other sector had more than 5 per cent foreign involvement. Even in those parts of the energy industry with a significant foreign presence (oil production and processing), share of production was small (24.5 per cent and 14.7 per cent foreign involvement and 9 per cent and 3.2 per cent production share respectively)
6   This built up massive levels of inter-enterprise debt. The immediate effect of this in 1992-1993 was to prompt the Central Bank to issue credits to enterprises to clear debt; these credits had inflationary effects and weakened efforts at financial stabilization. This strategy was continually used between 1992 and 1998 and the crisis of that year. Total company arrears at the end of 1993 were the equivalent of 5.2 per cent of GDP; by the end of the third quarter of 1998 they were 48.4 per cent of GDP. The bulk of this debt was to suppliers as firms continued to trade with one another to keep afloat

or engaged in non-monetary exchange (barter). But tax debts, wage arrears and outstanding loans to banks also grew over time (*Russian Economic Trends*, 1998, 7 (4), p. 87).

7 Estimations of the extent of barter in the Russian economy by the end of 1997 vary from 40 per cent to 70 per cent (EBRD, 1997, p.26).

8 Many of the most significant defaulters on tax payments were industries in the energy and petrochemical sectors controlled by FIGs. These enterprises ran up tax debts that were often much higher than the average for the industrial sector (*Russian Economic Trends*, 7 (3), 1998, p.36).

9 The classification of the largest banks as 'authorized' banks and their use as managers of state money was brought to an end, for example, as Yeltsin ordered that all federal accounts be lodged with the Federal Treasury by the start of 1998 (*Rossiiskie vesti*, 25 September 1997).

Chapter 3

Trade, Investment and Debt: Ukraine's Integration into World Markets

Marko Bojcun

Introduction

The past ten years have seen the renewed development of capitalism in the countries of Central and Eastern Europe, Central Asia and the Transcaucasus, and their steady integration into world markets. It still remains unclear where all the individual states that emerged in the wake of the collapse of the Soviet bloc will eventually settle in the hierarchy of the world capitalist order and how they will become grouped into regional markets and security regimes on the continent of Europe and Asia. The countries of Central Europe are now moving rapidly towards integration with the single market of the European Union and the NATO security regime. Countries east of Central Europe face greater uncertainty. The Russian Federation attempted unsuccessfully in the 1990s to regroup the ex-Soviet area into a new supranational economic and security order on the basis of the Commonwealth of Independent States (CIS). More recently, attempts to promote the regional economic integration of the ex-Soviet area have focused on the transcontinental fuel and energy trade through the Caspian Black Sea Corridor. Both Russia and the United States of America have long-term interests in controlling this trade. The Western states view the oil and gas reserves of Central Asia as a promising supplement to, and even a replacement of, the Middle East's supply. However, important questions remain unanswered with respect to the exploitation of Central Asian gas and oil: will long-standing Russian interests in Central Asia clash with those of the Euroatlantic states? And will the USA and the West European states co-operate or compete with one another in furthering the integration of this region with the Western centred order?

This chapter examines the recent entry and insertion (the 'push and pull') of the second largest Eastern European state into world markets and explores the competing alternatives for its regional economic integration. One side of the renewed development of capitalism in Ukraine concerns the domestic process, which I have examined in a separate article (Bojcun, 1999). The complementary side of this process is the direct impact of external markets and capitals upon the national economy and the nation state, which is the focus of this chapter.

The state and capitalist development in Ukraine

Until the last decade of the twentieth century, a Ukrainian state had made only two brief appearances on the world map – once in the latter half of the seventeenth century and once again in fits and starts during the years of war and revolution from 1917-1920. So it hardly played much of a role in the development of capitalism in Ukraine or influenced the country's place in the international division of labour. It is significant that the year 1648 marked both the birth of the contemporary interstate system and the beginning of the first failed attempt in the modern era to establish an independent state centred in Kyiv. The Ukrainian Hetman state, created in 1648 in the midst of an anti-feudal peasant war against the Polish nobility, sought lasting protection against Poland from the Russian autocracy in 1654. Russia, however, eclipsed the Polish-Lithuanian Commonwealth and absorbed the Hetman state completely by the end of the seventeenth century, reducing it in status to a set of provinces. The erosion and loss of its national political autonomy coincided with the ending of the first major phase in Ukraine of wage labour, commodity production and long distance trade with Western Europe. These shoots of capitalist development had appeared in the early seventeenth century on the periphery of the Polish feudal order and had contributed to the social and national conflicts provoking the 1648 war. But they were destroyed as the greater part of Ukraine was absorbed into the Russian Empire, which had codified serfdom in 1648 and would retain it until 1861.

The second major phase of capitalist development took place in the late nineteenth and early twentieth centuries when Western finance and the Russian state jointly undertook industrialization and the commercialization of agriculture in the Ukrainian provinces of the Russian Empire. The absence in this period of a Ukrainian state, and indeed the relative weakness of the Russian state among the Great Powers, marked this phase of capitalism with features of dependency: the expatriation of surpluses, underdeveloped end product and consumer goods industries, land hunger and weak domestic demand. Nevertheless, the joint effort of Western finance capital and the Russian state in these four odd decades before the First World War to invest in and build an industrial sector and commercial agricultural sector meant that Ukraine became one of the six, and arguably the most dynamic, centres of capitalist development in the Russian Empire. This placed it firmly into the semi-periphery of the evolving world capitalist economy at the beginning of the twentieth century, albeit as part of a multinational and imperial Russian state (Bojcun, 1985).

The present, third phase of capitalist development in Ukraine is occurring in the presence of a nation state. However, the Ukrainian state, beginning as a territorial administrative division of the Soviet state, is at a fairly nascent state of institutional development, and the economic crisis of the 1990s has retarded that development. Moreover, throughout much of the 1990s the state leadership progressively withdrew both from state ownership and from state regulation of the economy. In effect, the Ukrainian elite has divided functionally into political, state-administrative and economic branches since the Soviet system started to collapse in the late 1980s; economic activity acquired autonomy from state regulation that was unprecedented since the 1920s.

At the same time the Ukrainian state has already made a number of important contributions to the redevelopment of capitalism in its territory. It has established the infrastructure of a national market (securing borders, creating a national currency, regulating imports and exports, licensing) and increasingly it has elaborated a national economic strategy of recovery and competitiveness in the global economy. The most ambitious national strategy was elaborated in the programme of the President's Administration (entitled 'Ukraine: Progress in the 21st Century') in February 2000 (Kuchma, 2000).

Despite all its institutional weaknesses and lack of resources in dealing with the social costs of moving to a market economy, the state nevertheless played an influential role in fostering the private accumulation of capital by the five or six oligarchic formations that today dominate Ukrainian industry, trade and politics. These formations, typically built on the super profits accruing from trade in Russian and Central Asian oil and gas in the mid-1990s. They invested these profits into domestic production, mass media outlets and political parties. They depended on various state institutions at each stage of this process of acquiring economic wealth and political influence: to gain access to state-procured energy carriers and state transit facilities, to secure licences and contracts to trade aboard, to guarantee their loans and pay their debts, to privatize nationalized assets and to expatriate capital for safe-keeping abroad. Indeed, by the end of the 1990s, the swaying of Ukrainian foreign policy between Russia and the Euroatlantic states could be attributed largely to the tensions between a section of the state elite that still hoped for Western/European integration and that section which was now a captive of Ukrainian businesses tied to the operations of much bigger Russian businesses.

Finally, the new Ukrainian state appeared on the map in 1991, precisely at a time when the room for manoeuvre of all but the most powerful states in the world was being hemmed in by the might of globally mobile finance and the international financial institutions. In addition to the traditional function of the state to project its national interests abroad, the state is obliged to mediate between the interests of foreign capital entering its territory and its own population. The obligations assumed by the state in return for loans, foreign investment, economic assistance have had a direct bearing on the domestic economy and state social policies, as well as on the development of democratic institutions and practices. For Ukraine, such external pressures have had at least two important consequences. They have required the state to shift the burden of its foreign debts, state and corporate (because corporate debts were guaranteed by the state) onto the population at large, thus driving down their living standards. And they have fuelled the bitter infighting within the state – notably between President Kuchma and various anti-Kuchma coalitions since his re-election in 1999 – which is a phenomenal form of the struggle between different oligarchic formations tied to competing external economic interests. Such fighting has spilled out from the inner sanctum of the state, resulting in the legal prosecution, physical intimidation and murder of political opponents and investigative journalists, and the mutation of the political process as a whole in an anti-democratic, authoritarian direction.[1]

The former Soviet bloc enters the world market

The Soviet bloc broke up at a historical point in time when then steadily growing volume of world economic output was outstripping the capacity of the world's population to pay for and consume this output. This disparity was caused by the unequal global redistribution of accumulating wealth, which left the poorer countries' people unable to meet their consumption needs while the banks and corporations of the rich countries found it increasingly difficult to find new opportunities for productive investment. The objective limitations on productive investment influenced how the core capitalist states, their banks and corporations would exploit the newly opening markets of the ex-Soviet area after the break-up of 1991. Essentially, these territories were to be exploited as new consumer markets to absorb existing production, as additional, possibly alternative, sources of fossil fuels and raw materials and as debt markets. With one significant exception Western investors have not considered them as a terrain of significant productive investment. That exception is the oil and gas fields of Central Asia and the pipelines – existing and yet to be built – delivering fuel to Western markets.

The economic division of labour and trading regime of the Soviet bloc in the form of CMEA did not survive the break-up of 1989-1991. Each state, new and old, now bore liabilities in terms of incomplete production cycles and skewed economies from the perspective of their national-territorial coherence that could be overcome only by forging ties anew with other national and regional economies. Each state faced entry into the world capitalist economy on its own. The whole region experienced significant economic disruption and decline in the course of transition from the largely autarchic CMEA to the open seas of the world market.

The nature and extent of international assistance to the post-Soviet bloc countries have been quite different to the American assistance offered to Western Europe under the Marshall Plan after World War Two. The Marshall Plan extended a sum equivalent in current value to $75 bn, the bulk of which was spent in the first four years of the Plan. Total committed aid to the former Soviet Union under the EU's TACIS programme amounted to $3.7 bn for the whole of the 1990s. Total EU commitments under the PHARE programme to East Central Europe for the same period were $10 bn, but not all of it was actually disbursed. The Marshall Plan was driven by long term objectives of economic recovery of Western Europe, requiring its European participant states to rebuild a regionally integrated economy that was open to international trade (Triulzi, 1999, p 26). With respect to the Central and Eastern Europe in the past decade, the alliance of Western states has not sought their regional re-integration, but rather their rapid insertion individually into world commodity, capital and debt markets. The European Union has embraced the goal of integrating the Central European and Baltic Sea flank of post-communist states into its single market and political institutions. However, it has no agreed perspective on the long-term integration of the bulk of the ex-Soviet area, other than to create free trade areas with its individual states. Foreign direct investment into the former CMEA countries of East Central Europe and the Soviet Union has been small, relative to the region's investment needs (see Chapters 2 and 7).

Reforging the Weakest Link

Table 3.1 Regional GDP per capita as a percentage of the 'leading nation' (Great Britain in 1870 and 1900; USA in 1913 and thereafter)

	1870	1900	1913	1950	1973	2000
World Average	27.4	27.5	29.0	22.3	24.8	21.9
Western Europe	64.7	67.3	69.8	53.5	74.0	74.0
Areas of recent European Settlement: USA, Australia, Canada, New Zealand	74.8	87.6	98.7	96.7	96.8	96.5
Eastern Europe, excluding USSR	35.9	35.1	38.2	23.9	30.8	13.3
Territory of USSR	31.4	26.5	28.0	29.6	36.5	16.6

Source: adapted from International Monetary Fund, *World Economic Outlook 2000*, Table 5.2.

The 26 states in question have a population of 400 million people and a combined GDP of some US$1,000 billion. This amounts to around 3 per cent of world economic output. Foreign direct investment into the region by 1997 had grown to $18 bn per annum, amounting to less than 2 per cent of the region's GDP. The Central European states which were preparing to join the European Union were at the time drawing foreign investment equivalent to 3 per cent of their GDPs, whereas the states of the former Soviet Union were drawing investment equivalent to 1 per cent of their GDPs (Lankes and Stern, 1998).

The region of the former CMEA countries accounted for 10 per cent of the value of world trade in 1970, declining to 2 per cent by 1994. Although their share of world trade in fact peaked in the 1970s, the fall was most precipitous after the break-up of the Soviet bloc in 1989-91 when intraregional trade was severely disrupted, each country's foreign trade objectives were redefined and the proportion of manufactured goods in exports progressively diminished (Rohach and Shnyrkov, 1999, pp.81, 134).

A study of the International Monetary Fund provides other evidence of this region's downward movement through the world economic hierarchy. Table 3.1 shows that living standards on the territory of the USSR rose in comparison to those of the economically most powerful nations throughout the twentieth century until 1973, but then fell back dramatically by year 2000. The factors leading to this comparative fall include both the economic crisis that enveloped the Soviet nationalised economy by the 1980s and the acceleration of that crisis in the period of denationalization and transition to the market. East Central Europe exhibits a different pattern over the twentieth century, falling back further than the USSR as a result of the Depression and World War Two, recovering, but then showing the same tendency of decline by the end of the century.

United Nations' statistics show that the economic output of the Soviet bloc slowed and then stagnated in the 1980s, but contracted dramatically in the first half of the 1990s. At this point, the former member states of CMEA parted ways: the CIS region's output continued to contract, albeit more slowly, in the latter half of the 1990s, whereas the Central East European region's output returned to positive growth rates. By contrast, total world output and trade, and the aggregate output both of developed and developing countries maintained overall positive annual growth rates throughout the 1980s and 1990s (UN, 1999, Tables 1.1 and A.3).

Ukraine enters the world economy

Broadly speaking, Central Europe started to recover from the shock of the break-up and the economic slump of the early nineties more quickly than the former republics of the Soviet Union. Ukraine's economy went into precipitous decline in the early 1990s and continued to fall until the end of the decade, returning to positive growth rates only in 2000. A convincing explanation for the contrast in fortunes holds that 'Association Agreements with the EU (by the Central European states, leading to their accession to the EU) have brought early benefits of market access and massive technical assistance' (Lankes and Stern, 1998, p.6). Indeed, the IMF has predicted that the divergence in economic performance between those countries accepted for EU accession and those so far denied 'appears likely to widen in the period ahead' (IMF, 2000a, p.26). Insofar as the EU represents those European states with the greatest investment capital and most advanced technologies, entry onto the world market by way of close engagement with the EU is an attractive prospect for all the postcommunist states of the region.

In 1991, the research division of Deutsche Bank released a study concluding that Ukraine had the best economic potential of all republics of the Soviet Union to make a successful transition to a market economy. It compared favourably to the West European states in terms of its agricultural and heavy industrial per capita production as well as the level of education and training of its workforce. It possessed transit capacity for oil, gas, electricity and telecommunications; power generation equipment plants, aeronautical and aerospace industries, a powerful arms industry, shipbuilding, precision instrumentation and an impressive network of research institutes. The country's productive capacity well exceeded domestic demand, which accounted for the high proportion of industries geared to export (Halchynsky, 1999, pp.38-45).

However, these assets represented merely a significant potential to enter the world market on favourable terms, not its guarantee. In addition to coping with the unfavourable international economic conditions the realization of this potential depended also upon the pursuit of appropriate strategies by the country's leadership. On this front, Ukraine possessed some obvious deficits. Historically, it had lost its best intellectual assets to Moscow and the central Russian or Soviet governments. The brain drain continued in the 1990s, but now in all directions and especially to the West. As mentioned above, a state-building experience was largely absent and the state institutional capacity of the ex-Soviet republic was lacking. So although the new Ukrainian state under President Kravchuk was able to walk away from the USSR with a good portion of its armed forces (because they were held on Ukrainian territory), it did not manage to negotiate a division with Russia and other successor states of other important joint assets. For example, all USSR property abroad and the savings of all

Ukrainian citizens in Oshchadbank USSR - totaling 84.3bn rubles, or $150bn at the prevailing rate of exchange - were lost to the Russian Federation (Halchynsky, 1999, p.45).

The lack of cohesion or discipline within the new Ukrainian elite was evident in the way its members used the institutions under their control to accumulate personal wealth. By 1995 around one half of the country's GDP passed through the shadow economy, where the mechanisms exist to conceal, divert and expatriate wealth. According to the World Bank in 1999 the Ukrainian unofficial or shadow economy was proportionally larger than that of Lithuania, Russia, Poland or Romania (IMF, 1999, p.15).

The brain drain, the weakness of elite cohesion and discipline and the lack of state and institution building experience all contribute in some way to explaining why it took the state leadership so long to elaborate a national strategy of domestic economic recovery and competitiveness on the world market. Ukraine was the last country in the entire region to introduce its own currency, the *sina qua non* of any national economic strategy, the *hryvnia* in September 1996. After following a monetarist programme of austerity and tight money supply in order to bring down inflation and achieve a measure of macroeconomic stability, the President's Administration under Leonid Kuchma began only in the late 1990s to depart from IMF neo-liberal orthodoxy and to develop an economic recovery programme of its own.

Trade

An important component of this strategy concerns trade: repositioning Ukraine's technologically advanced sectors for more effective competition on the world market, and prioritizing the country's involvement in key regional markets and market regimes (World Trade Organization, EU, Russia, the Central European Free Trade Area, the Asia-Pacific region). Simultaneously, the Verkhovna Rada (parliament) has adopted policies concerning discriminatory trade practices of other states vis-à-vis Ukraine, addressed issues of insurance and credit risk of exporters, adopted its own anti-dumping code and began to align the country's national product standards and norms with international ones (*Zerkalo nedeli*, 30 June 2000). However, the question must surely arise in the wake of ten years of economic decline and degradation of the country's productive assets as to whether the doors to a strategically advantageous export structure have already closed?

The trading pattern of the decade 1988-1998 consisted of the following trends: a steady decline in the country's trade with countries of the former Soviet Union from 80 to 56 per cent; a decline vis-à-vis Central Europe from 20 to 10 per cent; a growth in trade with the EU member states from 6 to 20 per cent, and with both China and Turkey, each with more than 5 per cent of total trade turnover by 1998. Overall, Russia remained Ukraine's dominant trading partner, and its markets played a critical role in Ukraine's recovery from 2000 (see below). And while trade with the EU increased, it was increasing at a faster rate with Turkey, China and other Asian countries (Burakovsky and Biletsky 1999, p.6; Filipenko, 1997, p.15).

With Russia, Ukraine exchanged its metals and food products for fossil fuels, timber and other primary goods. With the EU, Ukraine traded its metals, chemicals and minerals for West European machinery, electrical equipment, transport vehicles, processed food and light industrial goods. It ran up significant trade deficits with both Russia and the EU, which were offset, but not equalled, by its trading surpluses with other countries. In the prevailing conditions of domestic economic contraction, trade relations with both the EU and Russia served to promote 'conservatism of the existing production structure and technological backwardness' (Burakovsky and Biletsky, 1999, p.15). In other words, foreign trade stimulated an expansion of the proportion of raw materials and semi-finished goods within the country's GDP even more with its major partners.

The proportion of GDP exported by Ukraine has traditionally been high, but it did not always indicate a healthy economic state of affairs. For while exports may serve to stimulate an already expanding domestic economy, their maintenance at high levels in a period of domestic contraction means that domestic consumption has been suppressed. This was the case between 1993 and 1998 when the proportion of exported GDP doubled to over 40 per cent. The proportion rose to 53 per cent in 1999, when falling world prices of raw materials and semi-finished products put great pressure on export earnings and required an increase in the volume of exports. By contrast, Russia's exports constitute around 15-20 per cent of its GDP. Ukraine's per capita earnings from exports were $233 in 1999, compared to $500 for Russia, $690 for Poland, $2371 for Hungary and $2612 for the Czech Republic (Halchynsky, 1999, p.155; *Zerkalo nedeli*, 30 June 2000).

The Ukrainian state has tried to promote the export of its technologically advanced sectors, but here it faces stiff competition from transnational corporations of the core states in the aeronautical, aerospace and nuclear power sectors, and from the fast developing economies of Asia in the machinery and equipment sectors. In the arms trade, however, Ukraine now ranks among the top ten producers in the world and has cultivated markets in Pakistan, China and India. It wants to co-operate in military hardware production with western core states, but here it faces three countervailing pressures: Russian arms producers that want to maintain joint production with their Ukrainian counterparts; the direct competition of Western corporations; and the rivalry of Central European countries like the Czech Republic and Poland for joint production and conversion contracts from NATO. One might assume that the export earnings of the arms industry, which formally remains under close state supervision, should provide investment capital to regenerate other, civilian sectors of the economy. But as in these other sectors, unofficial trade remains significant and the expected revenues do not always make their way back to the state treasury (Burakovsky and Biletsky, 1999; *Zerkalo nedeli*, 22-28 June 2002).

There have been serious obstacles to the expansion of trade with the EU. The main one is the long-standing protectionist EU regime that places limits on the import of metals, chemicals, textiles and foodstuffs into the member states. Such limits prevented Ukraine from mounting an export drive westward of the kind of goods it could sell in volume and at competitive prices. Throughout the 1990s, Ukraine remained in the category of countries defined by the EU as having a nationalized economy, which freed the EU from GATT/WTO rules and let it use protectionist measures against Ukrainian exports. The proportion of Ukrainian exports to the EU that were subjected to anti-dumping investigations rose in the 1990s from a quarter to one third (Pashkov, 2000, p.61). In October 2000 the European Union's Council of Ministers removed Ukraine from this category, recognizing it as a market economy in anti-dumping investigations. The EU's decision was greeted in Kyiv, but the fact that it co-incided with moves on Russia's part to draw Ukraine into the newly formed Eurasian Economic Community led some to question the EU's motives (UCIPR, 2000).

The Ukrainian government has been involved in negotiations since 1993 to join the World Trade Organization. WTO membership would considerably reduce the ease with which anti-dumping measures are applied; in 2001 there were over 100 such cases pursued by 13 countries (mostly steel and chemicals). However, the government still faces a list of unfulfilled membership conditions. And it recognizes that in the process of acceding to the WTO it will be required to lower the existing barriers to imports, which will inevitably destroy certain lines of domestic production. Therefore, the Ukrainian government faces both external pressures to conform to WTO standards and admit foreign participation in its domestic market, while at the same time trying to address the interests of its domestic producers (*Zerkalo nedeli*, 22-28 June 2002).

Investment

Ukraine had the lowest rate of foreign direct investment (FDI) on a per capita basis for all the transitional economies in the 1990s. Cumulative FDI for the period 1991-2000 was $4 bn, compared with $20 bn for Hungary and $30 bn for Poland. Around a third was put into foreign and domestic trade, followed by food processing and light industry, machine building and metallurgy. On a state-by-state basis the USA was the largest contributor of FDI in the 1990s, providing around 18 per cent. The Netherlands, Germany and the UK together contributed 25 per cent, Russia 7 per cent and Cyprus 5 per cent (EU, 2001, p.7; Berengaut et al., 2002, p.11).

The official statistics do not reflect the true size of Russian FDI (Bednazh, 2000, p.12). If one also takes into account Russian offshore funds coming from Cyprus and other locations, as well as the unregistered investment being made into cross-border trade and privatized state assets through Ukrainian intermediaries, it rivals the American investment. The pace of Russian cross border investment into Ukrainian productive assets quickened in 2000 and 2001, especially in the fuel and energy sector and metals refining. The investment drive was supported by President Putin as part of a wider effort to regain Russian influence over the post-Soviet space. By exploiting Ukraine's state debt for Russian natural gas supplies (variously estimated at between $1.4 bn and $3 bn in 2000) Putin succeeded in getting his counterpart Leonid Kuchma to initial a debt for equity deal in November 2000. This deal was aimed prospectively at securing control by Russian firms of Ukrainian gas transit pipelines to Central and Western Europe. Meanwhile, other Russian companies were taking large shares or a controlling interest in major Ukrainian enterprises: Avtozaz, buying the Zaporizhzhia

Aluminium Plant; Lukoil buying the Odessa oil refinery, creating a joint venture with the Kalush refinery and planning to purchase 100 Ukraine petrol stations; the Tyumen Oil Company buying the Lisichansk oil refinery and a local television station; the metals conglomerate Russian Aluminium taking the Mykolayiv Alumininium Industrial Complex; Metalls Russia investing in the Donetsk Metallurgical Industrial Complex; the companies Alliance Group, Alfa Nafta and Tat Nafta taking part in the privatization of the Kherson, Nadvirna and Kremenchuk oil refineries respectively. (*Ukrayina moloda*, 21 February 2001; *Baltimore Sun*, 29 April 2001; Moscow *Interfax*, 12 February 2001).

A number of reasons can be cited to account for the relatively low level of Western originating FDI in Ukraine and for its application mainly to trade, services and other non-productive activities. The North American and West European regions are interested in securing new markets for their own products. The Central European states are more attractive than Ukraine because they have greater consumer purchasing power and their institutional and legal conditions are now better developed, more stable and secure for Western companies. As for Ukraine, not only does it lag behind in the harmonization of its legal and regulatory frameworks, but the widespread corruption of government at all levels has also made foreign investment difficult and the repatriation of profits hazardous.

The outlook of the Russian investor upon the Ukrainian economy is different from that of his Western counterpart. President Kuchma remarked in 2001 that 'a Russian businessman is not a foreigner. Conditions are precisely those in Russia, and the laws are more or less similar' (*Financial Times*, 1 June 2001). Moreover, the Russian and Ukrainian economies are still linked through numerous production and consumption cycles, providing opportunities for the expansion of Russian capital into allied Ukrainian industries and plants. Nowhere is the opportunity for expansion more promising, and indeed more necessary from the point of its long-term Russian interests, than the fuel and energy sector. The Russian Federation satisfies 40 per cent of the Central and Western European demand for natural gas. In ten years time it will be meeting 60 per cent of this demand. Ukraine is on the one hand a major consumer of Russian gas (satisfying more than 85 per cent of its needs), and on the other hand the major transit country in Europe for Russian gas, pumping 94 per cent of the supplies destined for Central and Western Europe through the trunk lines crossing its territory. Purchasing major shares of the Ukrainian gas transit system would guarantee transit security for the Russian exporters. But is it also the logical path for them to transnational status and competition with other major players in the European and Asian energy markets (*Gas Matters*, December 2000; *Oil and Gas Journal*, 19 February 2001, 19 March 2001).

There are long-term implications of Russian firms gaining control of Ukraine's gas transit system (and its electricity grid) that concern the latter country's economic sovereignty. Such implications have not been lost on the Ukrainian leadership. Throughout the period from 2000 to 2002, when the Russian government stepped up its efforts to exploit Ukraine's gas debts to secure equity in its gas transit system, Ukrainian leaders have been looking to establish a consortium of foreign investors working under the aegis of a state transit authority. Such a consortium would invest in the maintenance and expansion of the system's trunk lines, pumping stations and storage reservoirs. Interested Western parties have included Shell and Ruhrgas. The European Union, the World Bank and the International Monetary Fund have all addressed the issue of Ukraine's role in the European gas market and linked it to the need, in their view, to privatize the country's strategic industries and utilities, lobbying no doubt on behalf of the big Western players (*Financial Times*, 1 June 2001; *Ukrayinska Pravda* [www.pravda.com.ua], 1 June 2001; *Nashe Slovo* [Warsaw], 15 January, 25 February and 4 March 2001). By inviting foreign investment from both the main gas producing and gas consuming regions of Europe, President Kuchma and his Foreign Minister Anatoli Zlenko have tried to balance off the external interests bearing down on the Ukrainian economy and the state. In an interview given to *Rossiyskaia gazeta* on 18 April 2001 Kuchma acknowledged that 'we will be seeking compromises ... we are ... ready to examine the question of whether the pipeline should not be solely Ukrainian and whether both Russian and even European partners should be allowed to participate'. Zlenko said in Brussels on 24 April 2001 that Ukraine sought to develop closer co-operation with the EU, including 'the implementation of the European Union's energy strategy as an equal partner ... [and] the creation of an international mechanism for managing Ukraine's gas transportation system and invited strategic investors to participate' (CPCFPU, 2001). However, the government has not been united on this issue, with prominent ministers known to be backers of the Russian or the Western interest. Until his dismissal in April 2001 Prime Minister Yushchenko's cabinet was riven by conflicts between such rival entrepreneur politicians.[2]

Debt

Debt represents the third important path of Ukraine's integration into the world economy. The country's official foreign debt climbed throughout the 1990s, reaching a peak of £12.4 bn in 1999. The debt was not large in comparison with that of some Central European states, like Hungary. However, the contraction of Ukraine's GDP, the growing proportion of primary and semi-finished goods within the GDP and exports, and the chronic difficulties of raising domestic revenues through taxation together exerted enormous pressure on the country's capacity to repay the debt.

The debt burden was responsible for drawing the country into the international financial crisis of 1997-1998. From 1996 the government resorted to offering treasury bills on the domestic, and then foreign, markets in order to cover the state budget deficit. In the first seven months of 1997, when interest rates on treasury bills were high and confidence in the stability of the Ukrainian currency was still firm, foreign investors flooded the treasury bill market. By the end of 1997, 45 per cent of all treasury bills were held by foreign investors, 28 per cent by Ukrainian commercial banks (which had put 85 per cent of their investment portfolios into bills) and 24 per cent by the National Bank of Ukraine (NBU) (IMF, 1999, pp.30-40; Halchynsky, 1999, p.154).

The first signs of the financial crisis in East Asia undermined investor confidence in the transitional economies in Europe, in the first place in Russia and Ukraine. Foreign investors began to withdraw their money from treasury bills. In August 1997 the Ukrainian government switched over to international capital markets and floated a succession of high interest yielding bonds denominated in Euros and Deutschmarks, the total value of which exceeded \$2 bn by June 1998. But at the end of August when the financial crisis enveloped Russia and decimated its currency, investor confidence in Ukraine evaporated and capital inflow ceased altogether. In fact the National Bank, like its Russian counterpart, had been fighting a rearguard action for some months, selling its foreign reserves in an effort to hold up the *hryvnia*'s exchange rate. If in September 1997 the NBU had \$2.7 bn of reserves, by August 1998 they had fallen to below \$1 bn (IMF, 1999, p.47).

Debt accumulation is in some respects like an investor pyramid scheme, where the second round of investors is used to pay obligations to the first round, the third round to the second and so on. Faced with mounting wage and pension arrears, as well as a general crisis of social expenditure (from an inability to collect sufficient taxes) the state had first resorted to borrowing more money from residents in order to cover its annual budget deficit. When that proved insufficient, foreign investors were invited to buy bills whose proceeds were meant to cover repayment of bills that were already coming due. Bonds on international markets followed. In the end the loss of investors' confidence in the government's ability to pay back these loans with the promised interest drove holders of the Ukrainian debt to sell before their due date, taking a loss and undermining further the value of these loans in the eyes of other would-be purchasers. In the closing months of 1998 the Ukrainian government all but defaulted on its foreign debt when it negotiated a 'voluntary' programme with domestic and external creditors to change short-term debt into longer-term government bonds.

The international financial crisis impacted in several ways upon the Ukrainian economy: capital flight, devaluation of the national currency by some 80 per cent, an increase in the trade deficit and the loss of important export markets for metallurgical goods and foodstuffs. One positive by-product of the crisis was the decline of imports of consumer goods, which the Ukrainian public could no longer afford, leading to a certain revival of demand for domestically produced goods. On the whole, however, this crisis demonstrated how international capital and price movements could damage the domestic economy and the state's regulatory instruments.

The rapid fall in world commodity prices in 1997-1988 was largely responsible for Russia's default on its foreign debts in August 1998. Ukraine's economy is closely tied to Russia's, so Russia's crisis was bound to spread into Ukraine. Between September and December 1998 Ukrainian exports to Russia fell by one third, in January and February 1999 by 40 per cent. The flow of metallurgical exports between the two countries began to change direction (now from Russia to Ukraine). In 1998 as a whole the value of Ukrainian exports fell by \$2.8 bn, or by 13 per cent compared to the previous year (Halchynsky, 1999, pp.165-66). And while Russia's financial crisis was in most respects deeper than Ukraine's, the subsequent recovery of its foreign trade and its currency reserves was more rapid. This had to do with the fact that Russia has oil and gas, the world prices of which recovered in 1999 and allowed the country to return to a trade surplus. The world prices of other primary commodities did not recover in 1999, leaving countries trading in such goods and dependent on imported fuel – like Ukraine – with trade deficits. Central European states, by and large, withstood the international financial crisis, saw their economies grow in 1998 (with the exception of the Czech Republic and Romania) and even attracted investments that were fleeing out of the CIS region.

External factors and the economic recovery

The long economic decline which had begun under the Soviet system in the 1980s and which deepened in the 1990s came to an end in 2000. In that year Ukrainian GDP grew by 5.8 per cent and there was a trade surplus valued at $1 bn. The recovery continued in 2001 with a rise in GDP of 9 per cent (industrial output up 14 per cent, agriculture 10 per cent). Trade overall grew by 9 per cent, with exports up by 26 per cent, yielding an annual trade surplus in excess of $2 bn. The government was therefore able to reduce the foreign debt to $10.2 in 2001. Foreign investment started returning, including Ukrainian capital that had flown abroad in the 1990s (EU, 2001, p.6; Berengaut et al, 2001, pp.4-5, 9; *Ukrainian Economic Trends*, May 2001, p.5). Analysts of the European Commission and the IMF concur on the major causes of the Ukrainian recovery: the Russian economic recovery provided the export stimulus; the devaluation of the hryvnia in 1998 and a 40 per cent fall in real wages in 1998-2000 made Ukrainian commodities more competitive internationally; fixed capital that stood idle for much of the 1990s was reactivated because it could now return a profit (Berengaut et al, 2001, p.32; EU, 2001, p.6).

Conclusion

It is not easy to define where Ukraine finds itself in the hierarchy of the world economy. One analytical difficulty arises from the fact that it is a relatively new state and national economy. Such quantitative indices of national economic growth as GDP need to be compared with the indices of other countries of the world. The comparison, moreover, needs to be made several times over an extended period of time in order to have a sense of the direction of change of the global economy, its groups of countries and regions, and its individual states. There is little doubt that the region of the former Soviet Union suffered considerable economic damage and lost ground to other regions and groups of countries during the 1990s. However, the recoveries of individual countries of the FSU from its break-up and their transition to the market differ so much that these countries can hardly be treated as a group any more.

In the work of analysts dealing with global trends, the Ukrainian economy was disaggregated statistically from the economy of the Soviet Union and the CIS region only in the early 1990s. So while it has been possible on the basis of Ukrainian government statistics alone to track the country's economic evolution by comparing it with its own previous performance, including its performance in the Soviet period, it is more difficult to compare its performance over an extended period with other countries. For example, the United Nations Human Development Index (HDI), which combines measures of per capita GDP, education and life expectancy, placed the country in 1999 in 91st place among 174 countries in the world (UNDP, 1999, pp.134-137). We can only assume, albeit with confidence, that Ukraine would have been in a better position on the Index in 1990 had it figured there as a separate state. Most likely it would even have been higher than the 74th position it occupied in the 2001 HDI (UNDP, 2001, p.142).

The general impression left by the experience of the 1990s is that Ukraine has been moving downward from the upper quartile of the world's semi-peripheral states, where it stood at the end of the 1980s, to its lower quartile. Upon becoming an independent state it still had quite favourable prerequisites to cleave towards the group of core states of the world economy, most likely by way of integration with the EU. Now one faces a far more contradictory scenario: a country that on the one hand still possesses advanced technological sectors and a highly educated workforce, while on the other half its population lives below the official poverty line; its corporations launching Zenith rockets carrying communications satellites from the Pacific Ocean, selling world-class tanks to Pakistan, offering heavy lift Antonov aircraft to West European states while at the same time fighting to retain its primary goods markets in Russia and Turkey.

Ukraine still has no secure place in a stable regional market. It remains uneasily balanced between several regional markets. Membership in the European Union remains the principal long-term goal of its foreign policy. But the EU has ruled that out for the foreseeable future. Ukraine's leaders once saw the Central European Free Trade Area as a possible back door route into the EU, but CEFTA's construction as a regional market was put back when the Central European states' began accession negotiations in earnest with the EU. A long-term economic engagement with Russia is taken for granted, but it is constrained by Ukraine's fear of political and military domination by Russia. So strong was this fear in the 1990s that Ukrainian leaders refused to relinquish even a small part of their state sovereignty to the Commonwealth of Independent States even though there were obvious economic benefits from doing so. At the beginning of this century, new prospects have arisen for Ukraine's integration into a transcontinental fuel and energy corridor. But these are nascent prospects, and the respective involvement of Russian and Western states and finances in Ukraine's sector of this corridor remain unresolved. However, it is more than likely that Ukraine will take part in future supranational arrangements if they involve both Western states and Russia because that would reduce the risk of old dependencies reasserting themselves or new dependencies taking root. Nevertheless, the penetration of the Ukrainian economy by foreign, especially Russian, capital has been occurring quite autonomously from the designs of state leaders. And now the interests and strategies of such capital influence more powerfully than ever before the state policies of both Ukraine and Russia, and further attenuate their sovereign powers.

Notes

1   Christopher Chase Dunn (1989, pp.123-24) suggests that peripheral and semi-peripheral states are more likely than core states to become authoritarian because they are dependent on foreign capital, which in times of tension leads to the political exclusion, and possibly repression as well, of groups that oppose the priorities of foreign capital operating inside their country.

2   For a blow-by-blow account of these struggles the best source is the archive of the Internet newspaper *Ukrayinska pravda* (www.pravda.com.ua) from its inception in April 2000.

Chapter 4

Continuity over Change: Belarus, Financial Repression and Reintegration with Russia

Julia Korosteleva

Introduction

From the late 1980s transition economies began to transform into market economies and reintegrate with global markets. This chapter examines the case of Belarus, focusing primarily on developments in its financial sector and its strategy of integration into the global economy. The nature of transition in Belarus is the same as elsewhere in the post-communist world, but its policy-making and chosen path of integration into the global economy are very different. While most Central and Eastern European (CEE) countries embarked upon the transformation of their economies from early on in the post-communist era and were strongly committed to moving towards a market economy along an 'orthodox transition path', Belarus has often been retroactive. It has ducked the challenges of transition and introduced elements of a 'repressed' economy in which the financial sector serves the government's own ends due to controls over monetary and credit flows. Belarus differs from other transition economies not only in its divergent policy-making during the years of transition, but also in its chosen strategy for integration into the global economy. After the USSR collapsed, it made its 'radical' choice in favour of unification with Russia, rather than pursuing a strategy of EU accession as a majority of CEE countries did. However, since 1993 when the issue of Belarus-Russian integration first emerged on the agenda of the two countries, actual, substantive moves to reunification have amounted to little more than the signing of agreements. There has been little real action to promote union especially on the Belarusian side. However, with Putin's accession to power in Russia, new constraints have challenged the Belarusian mode of economic and political development, forcing some change.

In order to explain how Belarus is a divergent case, we need to have some idea of what it is that it is diverging from. To this end, the first section of this chapter reviews the initial shocks that all transition economies face at the beginning of transformation and discusses patterns of transition. In order to isolate the difference between Belarus and most other cases of post-communist transition, the discussion concentrates on the issue of financial reform and stabilization. One pattern of reform is the strategy of financial repression. Countries like Belarus and some other Soviet successor states have used this strategy to maintain industrial output. One of the main reasons for adopting this strategy is political; it avoids some of the more direct negative social costs of transition and gives an impression of continuity that is useful to dominant elites. The second section of the chapter discusses the political reasons for introducing financial repression in Belarus and the subsequent politicization of economic-policy making in Belarus. This is followed by reviews of developments in the financial sector over 1990s and its impact on the economic development of Belarus. Finally, we look at the divergent post-communist pathway of Belarus by investigating its strategy of integration into the global economy, and outlining further perspectives on the development of the country.

Distinguishing the basic pathways of transition economies

The initial shock for all transition economies was the collapse of the administrative planned system itself. This predetermined the transformational recession in transitional countries, which was marked by falls in output. The collapse of the CMEA, which resulted in the breakdown of trade agreements, the elimination of subsidies and increasing prices of imported energy and gas, and decreases in aggregate demand due to the priority given to stabilization in policy-making, all aggravated the downward trend of output in post-communist countries. At the same time, price liberalization caused a strong upward inflationary pressure. It is reasonable to assume that the best policy mix in these circumstances would address both the decline of output and the sharp surge in inflation. However, the orthodox approach to this issue favoured a policy of curbing inflation by all means. This meant reducing central bank credit since excessive money supply was regarded as the primary cause of inflation. Price liberalization, stabilization, privatization, and cuts in government expenditures were regarded as a common remedy for all transition economies to achieve success in transformation. This pattern of transition was characterized by a sharp initial fall in output at the expense of social costs, but was followed by recovery and growth.

Countries that were strongly committed to driving towards the free market – most of the CEE countries and the Baltic countries – followed this orthodox approach and introduced deflationary policies with high positive interest rates and the tightening of money emission as the major anchors of stabilization policies.[1] These policies of credit restriction induced domestic enterprises to turn to non-bank money via the use of barter and increase of inter-enterprise arrears. In turn, this policy of credit crunch triggered further sharp drops in output in emerging economies. It also had a negative effect on enterprises that performed well and which deserved to get credit by all standard criteria. Owing to an adverse selection effect, they had to pay higher rates of interest on credit. Banks raised their provisions because of bad loans and sought higher profits through higher spreads between their lending rates and the cost of their borrowing from the Central Bank (Lavigne, 1999, p.187). Later, when capital account liberalization was introduced in these economies, it made enterprises turn to borrowing from foreign markets.

Differences between transition economies are noticeable because of variation in the pacing and the sequencing of reform implementation. Since the pace and the extent of removing capital controls vary, the effects are of orthodox policies vary too. However, most of these countries underwent banking or currency crises after initiating capital liberalization, a fact that strengthens the argument that liberalization should be gradual and undertaken after institutional and structural reforms have been implemented.

Other countries, notably the majority of states of the former Soviet Union (FSU), were slower in responding to the challenges of transition. Their patterns of transition also vary from country to country. States such as Russia and Ukraine made more progress towards reforms. Belarus, Uzbekistan, Turkmenistan have lagged behind, but have performed better in terms of output decline. They chose a policy of maintaining output and employment accompanied by repressed inflation. The liberalization of prices and of foreign trade occurred at a slow pace and subsidies to enterprises still prevailed. Indiscriminate financing of favoured industrial and agricultural enterprises by the banking system continued unabated. This policy of credit emission created inflationary tendencies. The dominant policy of negative interest rates aimed at supporting state-owned enterprises in these countries had a devastating effect on domestic savings. Under these conditions, legal tender began rapidly to lose its credibility. No amount of legislation on legal tender, or the administrative measures introduced in some countries, could make people accept the official currency. Its rate of depreciation in conditions of high inflation reached the point where money lost its attractiveness both as a store of value and as a means of exchange. Dollarization became a common feature of these countries. However, we should note that the problem of substitution of national currency was not only a concern of FSU countries. It was typical, to a greater or lesser extent, across the whole region, particularly during the early stages of transition. The introduction of a foreign currency component into the money supply makes the policy of monetary targeting more complicated.

Maintaining output and employment with repressed inflation required excessive government intervention in the economy and resulted in introduction of policies – price controls, multiple exchange rates, exchange rate restrictions, and subsidies to state enterprises – that are typical of repressed economy. Repression of the financial system was central to these developments. Restrictions on the financial sector as the intermediary between savers and investors enabled the continuation of soft-budget constraints. As a result, financial repression became the pillar of economic policy-making in those FSU countries that sought maintain output instead of securing orthodox stabilization.

Financial repression (FR) can be defined as a set of policies and controls, primarily in a form of interest rates ceilings, high reserve requirements and directed credit programmes, imposed by governments on the financial sector that restrain financial intermediaries' activities.[2] Interest rates ceilings can lead to credit rationing by the government due to the excess demand over supply in the loan market. The policies of FR are accompanied by the introduction of capital control restrictions to prevent access by potential borrowers to foreign markets, as well as preventing domestic money holders from switching from savings in banks to purchases of foreign assets.

Although several reasons for the use of FR have been identified, FR is generally regarded as a form of taxation and is generally associated with fluctuations in government revenue due to loss of direct taxes. This loss can be offset by FR, which is often associated with the concepts of seigniorage and inflation tax (IT) in the literature on financial development. All three are forms of discriminatory taxation on the financial system and transfer resources from private to public borrowers. IT is a tax on nominal assets. Since most government debt takes the form of non-indexed nominal assets, the value of that debt is eroded when prices rise. In turn, debt-holders suffer a capital loss. Not only householders (currency holders) lose in this case. Banks holding fraction of their assets in central bank as required reserves also suffer. The higher reserve requirements are the larger are banks' losses from IT due to increases in the inflation tax base. While the inflation tax base is money, FR affects the portfolio of non-monetary assets held by domestic residents.[3] De Melo and Giovannini (1993) argue it is to be expected that inflation tax is used together with financial repression. In turn, Fry (1995) argues that in classic cases of FR, the proliferation of financial instruments from which governments can extract seigniorage is encouraged. For example, this can be done through imposing taxes on private securities markets, because seigniorage cannot be easily extracted from these markets. Thus, the absence of private securities markets as such or the lack of their development in some transition economies with financially repressed systems is not surprising. FR together with inflation tax has an overall effect of transferring funds from the financial system to public borrowers and 'semi-public borrowers'. In transition economies, at least at the early stages of transformation, and in some countries even today, the distinction between public and private is blurred. As a result, it is common to have quasi-budget deficit alongside the budget deficit. This, for example, explains the phenomenon of low budget deficit in some transition economies when one would assume it to be much higher. In countries with a high share of the state-ownership, with slow pace of reforms and a high degree of state interference into economic activity, quasi-budget activities in the form of supplying 'planned funds', or in other words directed credits, to state-owned enterprises (SOE) become very common practice and was possible because of FR.

As we have already mentioned, political stance is correlated with levels of FR. Denizer et al (1998) have shown through a systematic analysis of the political economy of financial repression in the post-communist region that repressive financial controls are adopted not to finance deficits more cheaply than would be the case if there was financial liberalization, but to maintain authority and ensure the survival of those in power. Where inter-party competition is low, elites have been able to carry on a system of implicit subsidies by 'softening up' the financial sector to assure the continued flow of 'easy money' to large state-owned enterprises linked to the largest 'commercial' banks. Claims on public resources have been converted into preferential financing from the banks performing the role of state agents.

Belarus is a classic example of a financially repressed economy. Some moves were made towards financial liberalization in 1994-1995 through the introduction of positive interest rates, switching to market auctions as a way of reallocation of credit resources and introducing a policy of monetary tightening. However, these policies were reversed in 1996, and the elements of the repressed economy were reintroduced. The development of the financial sector of Belarus in the 1990s and the applicability of concept of FR to it are detailed below. First, we will look at how the choice of introducing FR was determined politically to assure the political longevity of elites and politicians that came to power as the USSR collapsed.

The politicization of economic policy-making in Belarus, 1991-1995

Under the Soviet system Belarus was the country's 'industrial assembly plant' specializing in the production of assembled goods, rather than the production of raw materials or services. The share of industry in GDP in 1990 was 49 per cent versus 22 per cent for agriculture and a 29 per cent for services. The military-industrial complex accounted for more than a half of Belarusian industrial production. The existence of price distortions in the Soviet system, which overpriced finished goods and underpriced raw materials and agricultural products underpriced, gave Belarus a positive balance in the system of inter-republican trade. As a result, and despite its lack of natural resources Belarus' economically favourable position within the Soviet Union enabled to have standard of living well above most other Soviet republics.

After the dissolution of the Soviet Union, the Belarusian authorities, dominated by the remnants of communist elite, were neither ready nor willing to undertake radical reform. Instead, they preferred to preserve the status quo (Silitski, 2002, p.226). Their main method of achieving this was to maintain trade links with Russia, to ensure the supply of Russian oil and gas at the prices that existed on the Russian internal market, and to preserve the fiscal arrangements of the single rouble zone that enabled them to generate credit through printing money whilst spreading the burden of inflation across the borders of Belarus to Russia. These policies helped the Belarusian economy avoid the sharp decline in production that was typical of the region, and guaranteed temporary political survival for the Belarusian leadership. Vyacheslau Kebich (Prime Minister from 1990 to 1994 and a presidential candidate in 1994) also raised the question of re-integration with Russia in 1993. This was a populist strategy aimed at winning the favour of a population that felt nostalgic for the Soviet Union. Moreover, lobbying on this issue together with trade-offs between Russia and Belarus in other areas of cooperation, allowed the Belarusian nomenklatura to avoid reforming the economy thanks to the economic concessions gained from Russia (see below and Lisovskaya and Korosteleva, 2002).[4]

However, despite taking the measures described above to prevent a sharp decline in output, Belarus nonetheless went in transition recession due to the collapse of the CMEA, which resulted in the breakdown of trade agreements, the elimination of subsidies and increasing prices for imported energy and gas. Kebich's government responded to this recession with policies that aimed to minimize social costs by preventing declines in real wages and employment. Subsidies to enterprises paid from the budget and through directed credit programmes were introduced to maintain industrial output. Social guarantees and control of consumer prices acted to prevent decline in income. However, these expansionary policies put pressure on inflation, which averaged 2,000 per cent a year in 1993-1994. The situation in the real, industrial sector of economy continued to deteriorate, with further falls in output. In the run up to the 1994 presidential elections support for Kebich's government and its political credibility began to ebb rapidly due to the worsening of macroeconomic situation and declining living standards of the population. The economic situation was one of the reasons that Kebich failed in his bid for the presidency, victory going to Alexander Lukashenko, a relative political outsider.

Some changes were made to economic policy-making immediately after Lukashenko's accession to power in 1994. The period just after his election was characterized by the introduction of steps towards market-oriented reforms. With Stanislau Bogdankevich, a neo-liberal economist, at the head of the National Bank of Belarus (NBB), the years 1994-1995 were marked by a tight monetary policy and a policy of positive real interest rates. These efforts resulted in a relative stabilization of the economy (see below). However, all these positive changes in the economic policy-making in 1994-1995 were not due to the Lukashenko's government's adhering to market-oriented reforms. Rather, the start of reform was forced on the government because of the worsening macroeconomic situation and the frozen relations between Belarus and Russia. A cooling off of Russian-Belarusian relations was observable from the beginning of Lukashenko's leadership. Lukashenko dramatic rise to the presidency from a position of virtual anonymity – he had previously been a collective farm chairman and parliamentary deputy – made Moscow suspicious of him. The future prospects of monetary union and subsidized energy supplies became a matter of debate. Russian officials openly declared that promises of both monetary union and continued energy subsidies had been made in anticipation of Kebich's election to the presidency, and were dependent on eventual political unification, which Lukashenko was as yet unready to pursue (Silitski, 2000, pp.229-30). As a result, in 1994-1995, and just after his election, Lukashenko seem to renege on almost all of his election promises regarding maintaining price controls and reintegration with Russia, and switched to a more radical course of economic transformation through tightening credit and monetary policy, cutting subsidies to some state enterprises and partly liberalizing prices. However, as the prospect of further economic deterioration and a loss of popularity loomed, Lukashenko changed course again. He turned to Russia for political, economic, and symbolic support. Consequently, although 1994-1995 was a sort of watershed between the uneven and chaotic policies pursued by Kebich and more defined system's building policies of Lukashenko, the period can only be regarded as a poor attempt to stabilize the economy since the economy did not undergo any sustained, in-depth transformation as such.

The 'Belarusian miracle', 1996-2000

Lukashenko's u-turn meant that the years 1996-2000 were marked by reversal of the political and economic course of Belarus and the fuller introduction of elements of repressed economy. From 1997 onwards, the strategy pursued by Lukashenko appeared to bring some economic success since it lead to economic growth and the 'Belarusian miracle'. However, the longer-run sustainability of this success is highly questionable. The Belarusian miracle is particularly intriguing because despite undertaking no transformation per se, and achieving no macroeconomic stability, Belarus nevertheless demonstrated macroeconomic growth comparable to that in the Central European transition countries regarded as successful in transition from 1997 onwards. The roots of this 'success' lay in inflationary creation and state stimulation of demand through policies of unprecedented credit expansion, negative interest rates, and administrative price control.

The government emphasised a strategy of state stimulation of demand through credit expansion and negative interest rates because it saw decreases in aggregate demand as a key factor that had led to output decline. However, it was difficult to implement these policies unless the government had a high control over the economy. The easiest way to establish state control was through preserving and increasing the state ownership. This took place through the reversal of the Belarusian privatization programme. After 1995, privatization became artificial in character as it involved turning the state enterprises into joint-stock companies in which the state retained either a majority share, or at least a share larger than 25 per cent of the stock, so that government preserved control over the managerial decisions. In 1997, state control over industry was increased by the introduction of 'golden shares' that gave government control over managerial decisions no matter what the actual size of its share holdings. State control also had to be introduced in the financial system. This was achieved through the renationalization of the banking system in 1995-1996 and the subordination of the National Bank to the government, issues that we will return to below.

With the reversal of any financial liberalization and neutering of privatization, Lukashenko had all the necessary economic instruments to manage his 'puppet-show' economy. He declared that the aim of economic policy was a socially-oriented market economy, but in practice the Belarusian economy resembled the old Soviet planned economy, with state ownership, 'planned funds', price subsidies, and repressed inflation as the dominant features of the economic system. The growth figures certainly resembled the high returns on investment that Soviet leasers liked to boast about. The Belarusian economy achieved an astounding 10.7 per cent rate of economic growth. However, while the mechanism of resource allocation was based on channelling funds from those enterprises that enjoyed a surplus to those with a deficit and was typical of Soviet economy, in Belarus this was achieved not only through credits directed to preferential sectors of the economy, but also through such indirect instruments as relief from paying some taxes and customs duties for 'strategic' sectors of the economy at the expense of increasing the tax burden on the private sector, licensing of certain economic activities that aimed to crowd out the potential competitors from the market, rationing access to cheap natural resources, multiple interest rates, multiple exchange rates, restrictions in foreign exchange markets and price distortions. It should be noted that multiple exchange rates, restrictions in foreign exchange markets and price distortions were also common in the old Soviet planned economy. However, under the Soviet economy, all enterprises were relatively equal in terms of their eligibility to subsidies when they ran a deficit; in Belarus, preference is given to strategic state-owned enterprises that in the end are supported at the expense of the private sector, households and the financial system.

Lukashenko's 'puppet-show' succeeded. The measures introduced facilitated an increase in short-term living standards that raised Lukashenko's popularity among the people. Pursuing a strategy of maintaining full employment, Lukashenko banned layoffs in the industrial sector. Moreover, he increased real wages through periodic credit injections into public enterprises, provided subsidies to poor people, banned price increases and so forth. The policy of money-led stimulation of aggregate demand triggered a surge in household consumption and investment in 1997. The surge in investment activity was mainly due to the strong growth of housing construction, which was in turn financed primarily by directed credits at highly preferential rates (see the next section). Industrial output expansion and housing construction, with trade slightly lagging behind, were the main branches of the economy contributed to the economic growth in late 1990s. The role of Russia was also a significant factor in sustaining economic growth in Belarus, a fact that we will expand upon below. Finally, GDP growth can be partly explained by some statistical tricks and the practice of multiple exchange rates; GDP was always overestimated due to the use of the official exchange rate – 60 per cent lower than the market rate – in the national statistics.

The longer the 'show' lasted the more obvious the cracks in the economic facade became; Lukashenko's strategy was not sustainable in a long run. The viability of the strategy for economic growth was based on re-establishing practices typical of the Soviet command-administrative system that inhibited the operation of economy at its full potential. Some elements of market economy continued to exist alongside the dominant practices of planned economy despite the significant restraints upon them. However, the Belarusian authorities have not acknowledged this. They prefer to portray the Belarusian model of economic development as a socially-oriented market economy with a high degree of state regulation. Literally, the role of the state in economic regulation in Belarus has created a type of state capitalism that makes any transformation towards market economy harder since it restrains economic activity and significantly aggravates the economic situation in the country. We can see this in more detail by looking at the example of financial system.

Financial repression as a 'lifebuoy' for the Belarusian economic model

In this section, we provide an overview of developments in the financial sector in Belarus during the 1990s to distinguish the key features of its evolution over the years of transition and to unveil the extent to which the introduction of financial repression contributed to economic recovery in Belarus and what impact it has had on the future prospects of Belarusian economic development. The working assumption is that financial repression had a positive impact on the economic growth only in the short run; in the long run, it caused a decrease in real cash balances, and a lack of financial sources and funds that had an adverse impact on the economic growth. First, we will deal with the developments in the banking sector and capital markets before discussing monetary policy in Belarus.

The banking sector

A two-tier banking system was established at the end of 1990 with the enacting of both the 'Act on the National Bank of Belarus' and the 'Act on Banks and Banking Activity in the Republic of Belarus'. At the start of 2001, these acts were replaced with the *Banking Code*. The National Bank of Belarus (NBB) was established from the Belarussian branch of the former Soviet Gosbank. The second tier of banks consisted of two types of banks: specialist banks (which took the place of Soviet specialist banks on the territory of the republic), and newly founded commercial banks. The first type of bank included Belagroprombank (which supplies credits to agriculture), Belpromstoribank (credits to industry), Sberbank of Belarus (specializing in household deposits, financing budgetary programs and extending housing loans), Belbusinessbank (light industry and trade) and Belvnesheconombank (foreign trade) (Oesterreichische Nationalbank, 2000, p.85).

The number of newly founded commercial banks mushroomed in 1992-1994. Their development as market institutions was limited at the beginning of transition by a number of problems inherited from the past, such as a problem of bad debts, sectoral segmentation of specialised banks, and the absence of capital markets, and macroeconomic instability that undermined the credibility in the banking system. Sectoral segmentation of banks immediately brought to the surface the problem of creditor dependence and limited portfolio diversification, which made these banks exposed to the failure of their clients, who were mostly the largest state-owned enterprises. Another problem typical of the post-communist region was the appearance of 'pocket banks' that were established by enterprises to finance their own activities.

A positive feature of the banking system was the relative independence of the National Bank, which was subordinate to parliament according to the 1990 Law. Its monetary emission function was limited by a 5 per cent of GDP ceiling on NBB credit to government. However, in practice and under highly negative rates, monetary and credit emission to support state-owned enterprises remained pervasive in this period. Restraints imposed on the banking sector – such as high reserve requirements (20 per cent in 1992, then reduced to 8-15 per cent in 1993 differentiating by banks) – were at least in part prudential and were common around the region. However, negative interest rates had a significant detrimental impact on banks' operation. Liquidity problems were solved by permanent credit injections from the National Bank of Belarus at a very low, and also negative, refinancing rate. The problem of bad debts seemed endless. Inflation continually wiped out the stock of bad debts, but the problem remained unresolved structurally.

Positive changes in the banking sector development can be observed in 1995-96, when Bogdankevich introduced a policy of positive interest rates, tightened monetary expansion, and reduced reserve requirements. Moreover, a fixed exchange rate introduced at the end of 1994 appeared to be an anchor for stabilization policies. These measures were very effective in curbing inflation, which was brought down from a 4-digit rate in 1994 to a 2-digit rate in 1996. The credibility of the Belarusian rouble was partly restored and individuals' share of deposits increased. Finally, some 80 per cent of credits were reallocated through market mechanisms.

However, this policy was reversed in 1996 for the reasons stated above; to re-establish soft-budget constraints Lukashenko needed to gain a control over a banking system that by that time was partly liberalized. To do this it was necessary to have power over the NBB and to nationalize the banking system.

Lukashenko's attack on banks started with his criticizing them for reaping profits at a time 'when the government has debts to teachers, doctors, workers, pensioners'. Lukashenko further accused banks of diverting profits from the real, productive sector of the economy into 'speculative transactions' such as interbank loans (which according to Lukashenko's estimates earned 600 per cent profits), and from the sale and purchase of foreign currencies. He even accused bank clerks of having very high salaries (Silitski, 2002, p.46). The nationalization of the banking sector started with the merger of the state-owned National Savings Bank with the commercial Belarusbank in August 1995. Belarusbank had a bad loan portfolio that could be cleared by merging with healthier bank. At first glance, this consolidation with the National Savings Bank appeared to be a bailout for Belarusbank. However, at the same time it turned Belarusbank into a state agent channelling 'planned funds' to the industrial sector.

Further nationalization proceeded with Presidential decree no. 209 of May 24 1996 'On measures on Regulation of Banking Sector of the Republic of Belarus'. This approved a list of banks servicing state programmes and measures to be undertaken by the government to increase its share, and the share of state-owned enterprises, in the statutory funds of banks. Finally, it required the wages of bank clerks to be paid according to a tariff system for the public sector. This brought to an end reforms in the banking sector. Since then direct government interference in the commercial activity of banks has been wide and pervasive. In 1998, a presidential edict was issued to formalize and enhance the powers of the head of state over the NBB. Accordingly, the President of the Republic – Lukashenko – effectively has the authority to remove the chairperson of the NBB and to suspend and revoke any decisions of the bank (Oesterreichische Nationalbank, 2000, p.85). With the enactment of the *Banking Code* in 2001, it seemed that everything had changed once again, because the Code stated that the NBB only reported to the President of Belarus. However, this was just a declaration and *de jure* the monetary authorities were left with little room for manoeuvre in formulating and implementing their policies. For example, in 2001, while declaring that priority in macroeconomic stabilization should be given to tightening credit-monetary policy, the National Bank was forced by the authorities to finance the budget deficit created as a result of Lukashenko's pre-election policy of increasing the average salary to US$100. Moreover, the government dictated the way that this deficit was funded. Rather than an emission of money, the NBB followed the state's suggestion, brought government bonds and then forcibly sold them on to the 'system-forming banks'. The banks are the six banks that dominate banking services, service the major Belarusian economic sectors, act as state agents by servicing state socio-economic projects, and give the banking system its peculiar character. The state-controlled commercial banking sector has thus executed quasi-fiscal duties while government budget deficits have been kept at relatively low levels.

As a result of these measures, the banking sector in Belarus remains dominated by state-owned banks, in which both the state and large state-owned enterprises have majority shares. Foreign ownership in banking sector reaches just 12 per cent. The ownership of large state-owned enterprises in banks creates a problem of intertwining owner-creditor roles, which hampers financial prudence. There are currently around 28 commercial banks, the six largest of which are the 'system forming' banks that serve a clientele inherited from the previous system and have continued to assist government programmes by supporting certain economic sectors. In return for acting as state agents in servicing the government social-oriented projects and financing budget deficit, the system-forming banks have been supported by the authorities setting relatively soft individual indicators of banking performance for them (for example, they have less loan-loss provisioning than required by regulation). These banks control over 90 per cent of total assets, 90 per cent of enterprise lending, almost 100 per cent of lending to households and their capital accounts for 77 per cent of total banking capital. The banking sector in Belarus is thus highly monopolized and concentrated. This concentration of banking power has been cemented in place by the NBB's requirement that banks have a net worth of €10 million by 1 January 2002 in order to be able to service individual customers and their savings. There was some economic rationale for this, since the authorities wanted to increase the capitalization of the banking sector. The present level of capitalization is too low and accounts only for 4.7 per cent of GDP and the ratio of total bank assets to GDP accounts only for 38 per cent versus, for example, 70 per cent in Hungary, a figure that is regarded as relatively low. However, not all the Belarusian banks managed this level of capitalization, or even tried. Small and medium-sized commercial banks were forced to look for niches within the financial system, often turning to interbank loans, or the sale of foreign currency.

The sustained policy of soft budget constraints and directed credits has aggravated the problem of bad debts and undermined the solvency of the Belarusian banking sector. Overall, bad debts account for 13 and 17 per cent of total bank credits whereas according to the international standards their amount should not exceed 5 per cent. Since the Belarusian banks frequently reschedule debts the real amount of bad debts this is even higher than reported. Under such circumstances, it is not surprising that capital markets have not developed to any extent. Negative or low positive interest rates have made any financial instruments completely unattractive for potential investors. Since privatization was subverted by government actions, any possibility of a private securities market developing was effectively foreclosed. The weakness of capital markets gives the government more room for manoeuvre and more chances of increasing its gains from seigniorage. The securities market is mostly represented by the government securities such as short-term liabilities (GKOs), which along with credit emission remain one of main sources of financing the government deficit. Consequently, the capital market in Belarus is insignificant and barely plays any role at all in enterprises' financing. In comparison with most of the other transition economies, Belarus has achieved little progress in reforming its banking sector and developing capital markets. Its pattern of financial development is solely bank-based, while in other transition economies the role of capital markets in financing enterprise activities has been increasing over the years of transition. Moreover, banking activity itself is ineffective and highly restrained by the government, which has turned the banking sector into a 'tool' for maintaining the Belarusian economic model.

Monetary policy

The key issue for the Belarusian authorities at the beginning of transition was to preserve the rouble zone that replaced the Soviet system and was supposed to help in creating a common economic space throughout the CIS. The Central Bank of Russia had a monopoly on currency emission within the rouble zone, but the central banks of other CIS countries were allowed to issue credits to enterprises or to cover budget deficits. This created massive opportunities for free-riding on Russia's efforts at economic reform, and was a system of transfers from Russia to other states. The governments and national banks of smaller Soviet republics could afford an uncontrolled emission of money as inflation effects were spread widely throughout the post-Soviet space. Its free rider status allowed the Belarusian government to print enough money to pay wages, and credit state companies and collective farms, while suffering only a small inflationary impact. At the same time, as Russia attempted to restrict the supply of money, the deficit between cash and non-cash money in Belarus began to increase. The shortage of cash money triggered the introduction of Belarus' own currency, the Belarusian rouble (known as 'zaichik', or hare). Non-cash *zaichik* were converted at a rate 1:5 against non-cash Russian roubles, whereas the banknotes were exchanged at a rate 1:10. These variations in rates created favourable conditions for highly profitable speculative activity. The effect of these policies was a large transfer of wealth from Russia to Belarus, equivalent to 13 per cent of its GDP in 1992 and 8 per cent of its GDP in seven months of 1993 prior to the final break up of the rouble zone.

The economic impact of the rouble zone on Russia meant that it could not be maintained forever. Russian monetary reform in July 1993 and inflationary pressures on the exchange rate parity between *zaichik* and the Russian rouble put the end to the rouble zone and forced Belarus to announce the Belarusian rouble as the only legitimate means of payments in 1994.[5] As a consequence of the policy of money emission, levels of hyperinflation rocketed from 1,560 per cent in 1992 to 2,221 per cent in 1994.

As we have seen, some efforts were made from 1995 to control inflation and stiffen monetary policy. However, these measures did not last. The deterioration of the real sector of the economy led the Belarusian authorities to loosen monetary policy once more. The inability of the government to maintain its exchange rate commitments, because of insufficient foreign exchange reserves, led to devaluation. From 1996, the country has turned back to implementing measures typical of a planned economy. Alongside negative interest rates, margins controls, directed credits and high reserve requirements policies of multiple exchange rate and multiple interest rates were introduced. The official interest rate has only been used in a small portion of the credit market, mainly as a rate of return on GKO (short-term government liabilities). Otherwise, the interest rates charged by the NBB have varied widely (Rusakevich, 2002, pp.19-20). There has been a highly privileged rate on directed credits granted for housing construction programme, usually one tenth of the announced refinancing interest rate. With inflation between 63.9 per cent and 293.7 per cent per annum in 1997-1999, this rate was only 5 per cent per annum and credit was granted under the condition that it was to be repaid within 40 years. These credits amounted to between 6 per cent and 15 per cent of the total bank credits to the economy in 1996-1999. A privileged rate was also set for the majority of directed credits to agriculture. In 1997-1999, this rate was half of the announced rate. Meanwhile, rates for short-term financing (Lombard and overnight credits) are one and a half times higher than the announced refinancing rate, and compensated privileged interest rates. The fact that the real refinancing rate was more favourable for banks than the real deposit rate encouraged banks to seek cheap NBB credit resources rather than to attract the resources held by individuals and enterprises into deposits.

Market allocation of credit resources by the lender of the last resort were thus replaced by the administrative reallocation of credit in favour of the branches of economy – housing construction and agriculture – that were regarded by the Belarusian authorities as priority areas (Rusakevich, 2002, p.20). The National Bank has channelled these cheap credits through the banks, which are government agents in servicing social-economic programmes. Belarusbank is mainly used in financing housing construction, and Agroprombank services the agricultural sector. The National Bank has also granted directed credits to the Ministry of Finance, which in turn has reallocated them to the aforementioned banks. Basically, these credits are potentially bad debts. When such debts occur, the National Bank or the Ministry of Finance apply debts-for-equity swaps schemes to these banks, and increase state ownership in them. This action has another implication: it makes these banks' performance look better statistically because the percentage of bad debts decreases whilst capital increases. In reality, however, this is an artificial growth of capital.

Directed and emission credits as a way of the state reallocating financial flows can be regarded as quasi-budget expenses. The fact that these mechanisms are so

Table 4.1 Seigniorage and inflation tax in Belarus in 1995-2000 (as a % of GDP)

Year	Seigniorage	Inflation tax
1995	4.17	36.5
1996	2.78	3.42
1997	3.56	4.95
1998	5.85	7.27
199	3.91	19.35
2000	2.52	8.4

Source: author's calculations

extensive has meant that the actual budgetary situation in Belarus is not captured by official statistics, that the status of money has been eroded and that the tax base of the state is based on seigniorage and inflation taxes. Belarus has been among the limited number of post-communist countries that have managed to keep a budget deficit at less than 3 per cent of GDP thanks to controls over banking and credit. With increasing inflation and the Belarusian Rouble losing its credibility, a dollarization of the economy has occurred.[6] Since the ratio of foreign currency deposits to broad money exceeds 30 per cent, Belarus can be classified as a highly dollarized economy. The majority of other transition economies, realizing the inflationary nature of money creation, have switched to using more market instruments to carry out monetary policy. Consequently, by reducing money emission, these countries have cut themselves off from gains coming in the form of seigniorage and inflation tax. Belarus, on the other hand has tried to benefit from these as much as possible. Table 4.1 shows annually dynamics of the level of seigniorage and inflation tax as a percentage of GDP in Belarus.[7] In 1995, the level of inflation tax was very high, amounting to 33.24 per cent of GDP. Monetary policy tightening in 1995 had a positive effect, reducing both the levels of inflation tax and seigniorage in 1996 to 3.48 per cent and 2.78 per cent respectively. In 1998-1999, both seigniorage and inflation tax increased significantly due to the aftermath of the Russian crisis, before falling again in 2000.

Inflation tax, which falls on individuals and enterprises for the most part, is the primary means of financing housing construction and agriculture, the main sectors of the economy that absorb emission credits. Rusakevich (2000, p.22) has calculated that during 1997-1999 privileged credits amounting to 72 billions Belarusian roubles were granted by the NBB for housing construction purposes. During this time, the Belarusian rouble was devalued by BRB75 billion so that the state built around ten thousand apartments using an inflation tax on Belarusian citizens. He also estimates that total emission financing of 120 billion Belarusian roubles in 1997-1999 led to depreciation of money of individuals and enterprises by 245 billion Belarusian roubles.

Revenue generation through seigniorage is a trade-off between a higher rate of money growth increasing seigniorage and associated inflation decreasing it by lowering demand for money. As money grows, so to do prices; as inflation accelerates, a limit is imposed on government revenue from seigniorage.[8] This is exactly what happened in Belarus in the late 1990s. When the government reintroduced the practice of inflationary financing in late 1996 together with the policy of negative interest rates, it boosted aggregate demand resulting in economic growth in 1997. However, demand has declined since then and the ineffectiveness of monetary policy-making has been shown up. The coefficient of monetization decreased from 69 per cent of GDP in 1990 to 6.4 per cent in 1994.[9] In 1995-1996, it slightly increased from 6.9 to 8.8 per cent due to the tightening of monetary policy, but it fell further from 1997 onwards, reaching its lowest value of 5 per cent in 2000.[10] Although the authorities have recognized that demonetization is a problem, the policy responses to it have been vague and contradictory. Government guidelines seek to lower inflation, aiming to restrict it in the first instance to 20-27 per cent in 2002, but do not state how this is to be done: will it be at the expense of freezing prices or through controlling maximum profitability rates, or due to monetary tightening? Moreover, inflationary policies are not to be curbed since the government plans to follow the same policies of directing credits to housing and other sectors of the economy through monetary expansion: 'growth of money supply is envisaged to be between within 39-117 per cent as it is necessary for the National Bank to participate in financing budget deficits to the amount of 152 billion Belarusian roubles (including 132 billion Belarusian roubles for housing construction), refinancing of the banks at the amount of 55 billion Belarusian roubles'.[11] Not surprisingly, inflation remained high at about 40 per cent (EBRD, 2002, p.60).

Belarus's pattern of financial development has thus differed from the CEE countries and the majority of the FSU countries significantly. Financial repression after 1996 was introduced to sustain the Belarusian model of economic development, but the collapse of demand for money and the shrinking tax base of seigniorage show that although financial repression might have short-term positive effects on economic development, in the long run it disrupts the economy.

Avoiding the global economy: Belarus, Russia and the prospects of integration

From very early on in transition, most of the CEE transition economies pursued a strategy aimed at securing membership of the EU. This required progress both in transformation towards market economy and building democracy, and compliance with EU accession requirements. As much as anything else, the choice of CEE countries to move towards European structures was a strategic choice about how to reintegrate in to the global economy. This may not have been immediately apparent to all policy-makers, or at the heart of their decision-making, or clear to their peoples, but Europe was the prism through which they approached the wider world. Belarus has pursued a very different path. Instead of following the CEE countries in their strategic choice for Europe, historical and cultural background, initial conditions, political stance, reluctance to reform the economy, a desire to find an easy way to preserve the 'status quo' and maintain the status of those in power determined that Belarus would favour a strategy of Russia-Belarus integration. In common with the CEE countries choice for Europe, Belarus's strategy is a way of integrating into the global economy, albeit it in a more indirect way. It is also a much more uncertain way. The decision to move to the world economy via Moscow rather than via Brussels was based on internal populist motives rather than any strategic reading of Russian interests. Consequently, there is much ground for doubt about the future of Belarus's chosen course; it is dependent on Russian calculation of their best interest and has meant that Belarus is not well positioned to pursue an alternative strategy in the event that Russian politicians decide to change their policies towards Belarus.

Most of what passes for Russian-Belarusian integration consists of a set of agreements between the two states that date back to the mid-1990s. There is little point in setting out the content of these agreements, which have generally been greater acts of rhetoric than they have been declarations of intent, or statements of specific policies. Belarus has, however, gained economic advantages as a result of developing the integration issue. We have already seen that links to Russia were important in the aftermath of the USSR's collapse. After 1996, economic integration with Russia contributed to the revitalization of the Belarusian economy and provided it with a valuable alternative in the aftermath of international isolation into which the country fell after its condemnation by the EU and the November 1996 referendum that was used by Lukashenko to extend his powers. Belarus has made some moves towards economic openness, but these are much more limited than elsewhere in the former Soviet Union. Uniquely in the CIS, Belarus directs most of its trade to other CIS states. In 2001, 60 per cent of its export trade and 70 per cent of its import trade was with the CIS; on average, other CIS states conducted only 21 and 40 per cent of their export and import trade with other CIS states. Moreover, most of this trade is with Russia. In 2001, 88.1 per cent of Belarus's export trade and 93.6 per cent of its import trade were with Russia (Statkomitet SNG, 2002, pp.74, 78-9, 80-1). Likewise, Belarus's political stance and economic policies have meant that it has been less influenced than other states in the region by inward flows of capital. The weakness of capital and securities markets means that it has not attracted large amounts of money to portfolio investment, and the bastardization of privatisation and failure to secure monetary stabilization have deterred direct investment. On average, the CIS have attracted FDI of US$196 per capita by 2000; Belarus had a per capita FDI receipt of US$132 (EBRD, 2002, p.67).

The advantages of Belarus's links to Russia cannot be underestimated. In March 1996, after Yeltsin and Lukashenko signed the first formal agreement on joining the two states in a new 'Community of Sovereign Republics', Belarus's US$1 billion debt to Russia was written-off. Subsequently, Belarus received unlimited access to the Russian market and the opportunity to purchase oil and gas at low prices: 50 per cent of the world price for oil and 16 per cent for gas. The Custom Union between the two states established in 1995 gave Belarus control of almost all Russian exports and imports to and from the West as they crossed the Belarusian border. The Union did not last, however, as the Russian budget suffered large losses in customs payments. The experience of the Union showed the difficulties both states had in properly drawing up such types of economic agreement and the fact that neither was actually ready for this kind of unification. Despite this, Russia has colluded in establishing trade relations with Belarus that mostly take the form of barter. Only about 8 per cent of trade has been carried out on a cash basis. These barter transactions have usually taken the form of exchanges of the goods in which each side is obliged to supply the other with an amount of a product at a price fixed in the US$ dollars according to official exchange rates. This practice meant that the appreciation of the real exchange rate did not immediately harm Belarus's industrial exports to Russia. As a result, Belarus has been able to exchange its overpriced industrial products for under-priced oil and gas from Russia. The years that followed the formation of the 'Community of Sovereign Republics' witnessed a rapid growth of trade between the two states. This was achieved mostly due to the proliferation of barter schemes, which Lukashenko actively lobbied for in the course of his visit to Russian regions. Altogether, the annual amount of hidden Russian subsidy to the Belarusian economy was estimated to reach US$1.5-2 billion in 1997-1998 or 10 per cent of Russia's consolidated budget (US$25 billion). In 2002, thanks to an agreed 5 per cent decrease in the price of gas, these 'subsidies' increased by US$63.5 million a year.[12] Belarus is also by far the largest recipient of Russian investment in the CIS. In 2000, it received 82.2 per cent of all Russian investment and 58.9 per cent of all direct investment by Russia in the CIS (Goskomstat, 2001, p.579).

Without these subsidies in the form of low energy prices and favourable barter deals with Russia, Lukashenko would not have been able to sustain his 'transformation' model whilst the economy has constantly deteriorated. Trade with Russia has in large measure enabled the economy to continue to produce whilst by all normal criteria it has collapsed. The amount of loss-making enterprises in industry reached 44 per cent and in agriculture 61.9 per cent as of June 2002 (Zaiko, 2002); depreciation of equipment in industry increased from 50 to 76 per cent during 1992-1997 and reached 80 per cent by the end of the decade (Godin, 2001, p.156; Bogdankevich, 2002, p.4). The ability of Belarus to maintain this level of integration with the Russian economy in the absence of structural reform is, however, far from certain. Lukashenko's efforts at isolating Belarus from the West have become increasingly problematic with the accession of Vladimir Putin to the Russian presidency. The revitalization of the Russian economy and the renewal of its strength as a world power have meant that Russia is less prepared and willing to pay for its 'integration' with Belarus. Although policy has not been uniform or totally successful in the short-term, Putin has stressed the need for Russia to look increasingly to Europe in order to foster its own development. Developments elsewhere have supported this geopolitical course. As a result, the future prospects of Russian-Belarusian integration are doubtful. To keep the issue alive will require some movement toward reform on the part of Belarus since reform will lower the costs of integration to Russia. Some steps towards liberalization have been made starting in 2000. These included removing the system of multiple exchange rates, ending restrictions in the exchange market and achieving convertibility of current account, introducing a policy of positive interest rates, some relative monetary tightening.

Conclusion

In comparison with the CEE countries and the Baltic countries, and perhaps also in comparison to a majority of the CIS countries, Belarus has hardly begun to embark on the transformation of its economy. What reforms have been undertaken have been fragmented and controversial. Indeed, at present, Belarusian economic development has been a step backward in an attempt to break away from transitional challenges and to switch to elements of a planned economy. Whilst this Belarusian-style 'transformation' model has been widely regarded by the Belarusian authorities as leading towards a socially-oriented market economy with a high degree of state participation in national economy regulation, in reality the economic course was highly politicized and served the interests of the ruling nomenklatura. With time, the role of the state in national socio-economic development has taken a state capitalist form that has hindered any transformation towards market economy and significantly aggravated the economic situation in Belarus. Yet, despite undertaking no transformation *per se*, and achieving no macroeconomic stability, Belarus nevertheless demonstrated recovery from 1997 onwards. This has been achieved through inflation and state stimulation of demand through policies of unprecedented credit expansion, negative interest rates, and administrative price control that cumulatively take the form of financial repression. Although this financial repression has had positive short-term effects on economic development, in the longer run it appears to be disrupting the economy. These policies have kept Belarus relatively isolated from the global economy, which it has chosen to approach through integration and monetary unification with Russia. This chosen route to the global economy can itself be explained by the passiveness and unwillingness of the Belarussian authorities to reform the national economy. It has been easier for them sustain production through their relations with Russia and at the same time preserve the political viability of the Belarusian leadership, than to bear the costs of reform and face the uncertainties that economic openness might bring. The chosen strategy is not without its own difficulties, however. Instead of being dependent on the global economy, Belarus and its economic future have become dependent on the political climate in Russia. The cost of preserving sovereignty in the face of the global market has thus been a relative, and perhaps greater, surrender of sovereignty to another power.

Notes

1   Some transition economies, particularly Poland, Czech Republic, Estonia, adopted stabilization programmes based on exchange rate regimes. So basically there have been two main forms of stabilization programmes: one money-based, the other exchange rate based.

2   The phenomenon of FR has been widely studied in financial development economics. The idea of financial repression can be traced to the financial development frameworks of McKinnon (1973) and Shaw (1973) which support the idea that money and capital

complement each other, rather than substitute for one another as neo-classical theory argued. Currently, there is a large literature on FR and its effects on economic development including Fry (1995), Giovannini and De Melo (1993), Demetriades and Luintel (2001). The majority of researchers conclude that FR has a negative impact on maximizing welfare. However, the financial repression literature has been criticized recently, due to the experience of some unsuccessful liberalization episodes in Latin America, Asia and Russia (Denizer, et al, 2000).

3   Distortions in real interest rates (under condition of nominal interest-ceilings) due to inflation should therefore be included in the definition of financial repression rather than of inflation tax (De Melo and Giovannini, 1993).

4   For example, in September 1992 an agreement was signed on military co-operation of Belarus with Russia, which extended the stay of Russian troops in Belarus until 2000.

5   For more details on the rouble zone and the arrangements made by Belarus and Russia within it, (see Silitski 2002 and Conway 1995).

6   The term 'dollarization' serves as shorthand for the use of any foreign currency.

7   Seigniorage is calculated as the annual increase in the monetary base, divided by nominal GDP. Inflation tax is calculated as the inflation rate times the real stock of money base. Inflation rate, used to measure Inflation tax is measured on GDP deflator, because it is the government who benefits from inflation tax. It buys a much wider range of goods that the CPI covers. Another reason for using GDP deflator in these calculations is that inflation tax is expressed as a percentage of GDP.

8   The inflationary nature of monetary expansion is well known. Since seigniorage is a tax, it can graphically be represented as a Laffer curve with respect to the rate of money growth. Imagine the bell-shaped form of an inflation-tax Laffer curve. There is a maximum point at which seigniorage is optimized under a certain rate of money growth that can be called the revenue-maximizing rate of money growth. Under a moderate rate of money growth, less than the revenue-maximizing point, seigniorage exhibits an upward trend. When the money growth rate exceeds the revenue-maximizing one, the inflation rate increases at greater pace than the money growth rate. This leads to the decline in real cash balances, or in other words to a proportionally greater reduction in the tax base for seigniorage compared to the increase in the tax rate itself. As a result, revenue declines; graphically, seigniorage is on the downward sloping side of the Laffer curve. Thus, there is a kind of trade-off between a higher rate of money growth increasing seigniorage and the associated inflation decreasing it by lowering demand for money. When seigniorage is first imposed, that is at the beginning of inflation, there is no revenue-maximizing growth rate as such. The higher the growth is, the higher the revenue due to the lag in expectations. However, after households start correctly estimating expected inflation an adjustment in real cash balances tends to be instantaneous. Higher money growth leads to the higher inflation and correspondingly to a decrease in demand for real money and fall in the revenue from seigniorage. The productivity of this tax is thus made ineffective. For more details, see Cagan (1956), Romer (1996), Boichanka (2001). Another important implication is that despite nominal money supply continuing to rise, real cash balances decline and resulting in shortages of finance. This then negatively influences economic growth.

9   Calculated as a ratio of rouble broad money (M3) to nominal GDP.

10   The source of this data is the draft 'Concept of Development of Banking System of the Republic of Belarus, 2001-2010'.

11   Resolution of the Council of Ministers of Belarus and the National Bank of Belarus of December 28, 2001 'About the programme of measures to increase demand for money in 2002'.
12   Silitski (2002); interview with S. Stankevich, a specialist of the Division of Foreign Currency Transactions, JSSB 'Belarusbank', Minsk, March 2002.

Chapter 5

Merchandise Foreign Trade in Russia, Ukraine and Belarus

Nadia Lisovskaya

Introduction

The chapter aims to identify commonalities and differences in merchandise foreign trade of Russia, Belarus and Ukraine. Foreign trade is analysed from structural and institutional perspectives. Structural parameters of foreign trade refer to the volume and composition of imports and exports, their relation to domestic growth and development. The institutional aspect of foreign trade refers to the regulatory mechanism of foreign trade: tariffs, qualitative restrictions, export subsidies and other measures. The analysis covers the first ten years of transition, but this first needs to be contextualized.

The historical context of foreign trade in Russia, Ukraine and Belarus

The role of foreign trade in economic growth was generally insignificant for the USSR's centrally planned economy (CPE). Indeed, the Soviet economic system was characterized by export aversion. Tariffs, quantitative restrictions, export subsidies were non-existent as economic categories. These highly specific features of the CPE system are a long-term background factor, shaping the peculiarity of foreign trade development of Russia, Belarus and Ukraine after the collapse of the USSR.

The institutional-economic difference between central planning and market systems is reducible to a single notion: the institution of ownership. Ownership can be seen as a type of ultimate economic institution that causes or significantly modifies the rest of the institutional layout of a country's economy. One of the immediate institutional derivatives of state ownership is planned exchange. The appearance of planned, non-competitive exchange had two important structural consequences for the CPE, and consequently for its foreign trade.

First, the CPE was extremely inefficient, with inefficiency realized in high costs of production or value creation. Competition creates pressure that minimizes the costs of production in market economies; this pressure could not take place under central planning endogenously, that is, as a virtue of the system itself, since competition was non-existent. Costs grew in the course of producing new value until they exceeded the magnitude of the new value. This manifested itself in the low competitiveness of the Soviet products and negative economic growth for the whole economy. Structural change, in the sense of the transformation to a more efficient input structure and new output quality, could not take place under central planning. The factor, however, which did ensure some development in the USSR, was natural resource endowment. This created value 'from nothing', but this development originated not from a more effective use of known and already employed resources, but from the addition of new ones. This was therefore an extensive type of development; most of it was provided by Russia since it has extensive mineral resources, which went for export.[1]

Second, money almost ceased to exist as an economic category under central planning. Since prices were fixed in the CPE, money served as a means of fixed values. The fixed values did not remain unchanged in an actual sense since industrial products underwent physical aging, and consumer goods did not meet demand and were wasted. Money, therefore, expressed fixed values, whose actual magnitude was been inexorably decreasing as a result of the lack of development. Money's function as a means of payment, exchange and a store of value was limited as well.

The act of development implies extracting resources from current production for the sake of future production. In market economies, since all material resources are already employed in current production and they are counter-balanced by a corresponding amount of money, this resource extraction can be purchased by 'ad hoc money' – credit (Schumpeter, 1961). Credit is given to an entrepreneur on account for his or her future value creation. Credit implies that the money function as a means of payment is spread in time: money is given for goods yet to be produced. When an entrepreneur uses this ad hoc money for the purchase of material resources from current production, money performs the function of exchange in time: future goods are exchanged for present ones. This did not happen in CPEs. All the values of goods and the corresponding amounts of money were fixed under the planned system. The extraction of resources from circulation would lead to the distortion of the chain of production plans they were related to. It follows that monetary units performed the functions of means of payment and of exchange only in a current, circular flow, and these functions could not be realised in time. Non-usage, or storage of money as past or future purchasing power, was senseless and impossible, since these monetary units were used only for instantaneous exchange. In other words, the function of money as a store of value, which directly points at money as a means of connecting past, present and future, was non-existent under central planning: credit was practically unknown in the CPE.

Planned exchange, an ineffective structure of production and the almost non-existence of money in an economic sense influenced the parameters of foreign trade in the USSR. The system was characterized by export aversion; exports were primarily treated as a means of getting currency for the purchase of deficit imports. Since socialist prices and money did not have much economic meaning, socialist currencies were inconvertible and exchange rates were meaningless.

Import tariffs and export subsidies are two mechanisms of fiscal policy. Since the state owned most of the economic resources in the country, profit, taxes, current and capital expenditures were transformed through the state budget. The division between state and enterprise financial resources was arbitrary, which implied that subsidies and taxes did not have much economic meaning under central planning.[2] A change in the price and volume of an import, as a result of a change in tariff rates, meant a change in the price and volume of domestic sales and production. But the latter could not happen as these parameters were fixed under central planning. Import tariffs were therefore meaningless. Enterprises could not be responsive to export subsidies either and the latter did not exist since, first, subsidies did not have much economic meaning under central planning in general and, second, the system was anti-mercantilist in nature.

Non-existence of tariffs and export subsidies does not mean, however, that the USSR's foreign trade was disorganized. Imports and exports were coordinated through administrative directives, generated by the Gosplan (the State Planning Commission) and branch ministries. It could be assumed that the whole system of foreign trade organization was a giant quantitative restriction. This would be an incorrect perception since the administrative mechanism covered not only imports but also exports. Neither made any impact on the domestic production since the actual transactions were performed by foreign trade corporations, which were divorced in economic terms from domestic enterprises.

With the transformation of ownership and the emergence of competitive exchange post-CPE countries inherited an ineffective structure of production. Additionally, the space that was once occupied by the plan is not immediately occupied by money. In macroeconomic terms, this is manifested in a very low level of monetization, which corresponds to the low value of money in instantaneous payment and exchange, and the lack of its function as a store of value under central planning. With the creation of competition and the liberalization of prices the low value of money, unnoticed under central planning, results in a sudden and dramatic fall in the purchasing capacity of money at all levels: public, enterprise and household. A massive decline of production becomes inevitable since there are no means to buy and no effective demand to sell products. This explains the abnormally low level of prices on goods in Russia, Belarus and Ukraine at the beginning of transition. In 1991, the price of gas in the USSR accounted for only 3 per cent of the world price; petrol accounted for 9 per cent and oil, 13 per cent.

These low levels of prices reflect the low added value of socialist production. For social and strategic economic considerations the governments of Ukraine, Russia and Belarus have maintained price controls for a decreasing range of goods. The maintenance of price control becomes impossible as the prices realized in revenues are not enough to enable the industrial purchase of input materials, whose prices have already been liberalized and therefore increased. This is aggravated by the inherited ineffective production structure, which additionally increases input costs. The price control of energy sources is the most vivid example of this. These commodities are priced in Belarus, Russia and Ukraine at a much lower level than in market economies in order to prevent the complete collapse of domestic industry and to provide minimum social security for households. On the other hand, these prices cover only part of producer costs, which results in very low wages, or their non-payment for months, and the bankruptcy of those industries whose products are used as factor input in other spheres. Periodically, states undertake indexation of prices. Until now, however, these controlled prices do not cover production costs: in 1999-2002 the price for railway services in Ukraine and Russia covered only 80 per cent of railway costs. Equally, as a result of domestic price control on gas and oil, these two industries accumulate extensive mutual payment arrears. For this reason, some of the enterprises of oil and gas industries in Russia recently made a decision to merge. The situation in gas and oil is more advantageous compared to other industries, which do not have much export possibilities and whose product prices are domestically controlled. Hydro-energetic industry is an example of this: this industry remains unprofitable despite recent Russian economic growth.

Soon after price liberalization, some domestic products reached the level of world prices and even exceeded it; this became the case with metallurgical production in Russia and Ukraine by the end of 1995. Although the labour force in Russia, Belarus and Ukraine has been extremely cheap, cheaper than in developing countries, the ineffective structure of costs caused many products to reach and even exceed the world price level by 1995.[3] For instance, in the metallurgical sector, the cost of energy consumption was 20 to 30 per cent higher, and labour productivity in this sector in Russia and Ukraine was two-three times lower, than in the West. Much of the production of chemical industries became unprofitable to export by the end of 1990.

The other main context influencing foreign trade in Russia, Belarus and Ukraine is regional and international pressures. After the collapse of the USSR, Russia, Belarus and Ukraine developed production structures that were mainly oriented to ex-socialist markets. From the economic point of view, this regional bias is explained by the low competitiveness of Soviet goods – their market was mainly the central planned or developing countries – and by the planned division of labour within the Soviet sphere of influence. After the collapse of the USSR, twelve of its former republics formed a free-trade area, established a free movement of goods between their territories. Relations between Russia and Ukraine and between Belarus and Ukraine are formed on these principles. Belarus and Russia have gone one step beyond this and have pursued a policy of re-integration: in 1995 they signed a customs union agreement.[4]

All three countries seek EU membership, with Ukraine being the most active as it adopted a number measures aiming to speed up its integration with the EU. In 2000, the Ukrainian President adopted a programme for Ukraine's integration with the EU; in 2001, a presidential decree on speeding up the accession to the EU was signed, and in 2002, and Ukraine started negotiations with the EU on establishing a free trade agreement. A top foreign trade priority for all three states is WTO membership. All of them applied for membership immediately after the WTO was established, and, since then, they have been going through accession negotiations. The WTO is a great influence not only on foreign trade, but also on many aspects of domestic policy since it imposes concrete and binding obligations on a wide range of domestic policy areas in acceding countries.

Foreign trade performance

Trade in value estimation: volumes and commodity composition

Belarus, Ukraine and Russia can be ranked according to the state of their foreign trade balance. Belarus has been experiencing a chronic negative balance over the years of transition; Ukraine managed a positive balance in late 1990s; and Russia has had a stable positive balance. The negative balance in Belarus, and until recently in Ukraine, mainly appears in trade with CIS, and is caused by Ukrainian and Belarusian dependence on Russian primary commodities, specifically energy sources. Ukraine's trade problems have been not as grave as Belarus's due to the relatively rich endowment of the former in non-energy mineral resources. This caused less import dependence and improved export performance (see below). In Belarus, however, about 40 per cent of imports are in the form of mineral products, ferrous and non-ferrous metals, which mainly come from Russia. Apart from causing a significant trade deficit, this led to trade dependence on Russia. Russia, in turn, is not dependent upon mineral resources; thus, those factors that played an adverse role in Ukrainian and Belarusian imports did not have any role in Russian imports.

Over the years of transition, a change of the share of imported goods in the domestic market took place in Russia, Ukraine and Belarus. This has particularly been the case with processing industries, whose prices were liberalized earlier than other sectors of the domestic economy. As a result of the continuous decline of domestic production, aggravated by high taxes, the products of the processing industries were unable to meet demand, which itself dropped considerably. Additionally, with price liberalization, the domestic prices of goods produced in Russia, Ukraine and Belarus started to exceed world price levels. In these conditions, it becomes cheaper to buy imported products. Whereas in 1989 the share of imported foodstuffs in Russia was not more than 20 per cent, in 1996 this level grew up to 50 per cent; in 1991 the share of imported television sets accounted for 8 per cent of domestic demand, in 1995 it accounted for 60 per cent; in 1991 the share of imported shoes accounted for 8 per cent, in 1995, 82 per cent (data from the Institute for the Economy of Transition, Moscow).

On the export side, goods with little added value have started to play a more important role in the trade of Russia, Belarus and Ukraine during the years of transition. The structure of exports reflects the structure of domestic production to a considerable extent. A structural shift in terms of an increase of goods with large added value in the domestic production and exports is an indicator of development. Such a shift is dependent on investment inflows into the economy beforehand. Since a lack of domestic finance, both in the form of long-term capital and immediately available cash, is an inherent feature of post-central planning transitional economies, a structural change underpinned by domestic investment sources is very unlikely to happen. As a result, domestically produced commodities, especially from processing industries, are declining in their competitiveness against foreign production. The share of machines and equipment in the merchandise exports of Russia decreased from about 20 per cent in the late 1980s to 9.8 per cent in 1994, and rose only slightly to 10.6 per cent by 2000 (IMF, 2001, p.108). Raw materials, having value in themselves, have little value added in the process of production. Therefore, the structural bias inherited from the centrally planned system, namely, ineffective costs of production, is present least of all in the products of extractive industries. This prompted a steady increase of primary products in exports. In Russia, the export share of fuel products (mainly gas and oil) ferrous and non-ferrous metals, precious stones and metals has been increasing and reached about 70 per cent of merchandise export by 2000. Ukraine experienced an analogous process as the share of ferrous and non-ferrous production in its export have risen from about 30 per cent in early 1996 to 40 per cent by 2001 (IMF, 2001, p.45-47).

Such export dynamics are possible only for counties richly endowed with natural resources, like Russia and Ukraine. Belarus, poor in natural resources, has been heavily dependent upon their import. Domestic industry and export principally involved the processing industries, which have constituted approximately the same proportion of all merchandise exports throughout the years of transition: 65 per cent. Without the possibility of developing industry technologically, these low quality and high costs products have been increasingly difficult to sell not only in the West but also in developing markets and the traditional one of the former USSR.

In conditions of extremely low effective demand in transitional economies, export becomes the key source of monetary (currency) inflow. This devolution of foreign trade composition, therefore, plays a somewhat positive role in Russia and Ukraine. In Russia, the oil sector provides 35 per cent of all currency revenues. Additionally, Russia has been getting a stable currency inflow from the export of gas, precious metals and stones, ferrous metals and non-ferrous metals. Similarly, ferrous and non-ferrous metals provide 40 per cent of Ukrainian currency revenues.

By ensuring monetary inflow into the economy, exports are a vital factor for increasing domestic demand and production, and enabling economic growth in Russia and Ukraine. A relatively swift increase in domestic production as a result of increase of demand is possible in transitional countries since they have large capacity reserves as a result of the years of massive production decline at the beginning of the transformation process. Between 1991-1998, the level of capacity utilization in these countries declined and reached 50-51 per cent. Demand, in turn, both household and industrial, has the potential to increase in these countries as a result of the dramatic fall of the purchasing capacity of consumers during the transition period. There is demand for the goods, but this demand is not effective due to the shortage of money. It can be concluded, therefore, that as a result of the severe deficit of money domestically, the possibility for growth in transitional countries is possible mainly through external factors: foreign investments or export earnings. The level of economic growth in Russia and Ukraine in 1998-2002 is principally rooted to the raw resource export, which is particularly evident in the case of Russia. The high price of oil during this period was extremely beneficial for Russia. It is estimated that Russian growth may continue even if the price of oil drops as low as US$13 per barrel (ABN, 2002). For Ukraine, the world market has been less fortunate as prices on its primary export commodities – ferrous and non-ferrous metals – have been unstable over the past few years, due to an increase in protectionism in the form of anti-dumping and safeguards measures elsewhere in the world, as well as a lifting of import duties in the US. In such circumstances, Ukraine's reliance on ferrous and non-ferrous metals as the principle export commodity makes its position worse than Russia's: the share of ferrous and non-ferrous metals in merchandise exports in Russia is half what it is in Ukraine. Apart from demand in overseas markets, the recent economic growth in Russia meant an increase of demand for Ukrainian products in Russia; this is important as 20 per cent of Ukraine's exports go to Russia. Thus, apart from its own export revenues from primary commodities, Ukrainian growth was also stimulated by Russian economic recovery, which started one year earlier.

The institutional and structural legacies of the central planning, in the form of monetary vacuum and low competitiveness of domestic production, were therefore compensated for in Russia and Ukraine by natural resources endowment, whose exports became the accelerator of growth. This picture sharply contrasts with Belarus, which does not have natural resources and therefore has no prospects for currency earnings. The only mineral Belarus is rich in – potassium salts – are produced and exported by one Belarusian enterprise, Belaruskali, which provides the lion's share of the country's currency earnings. As a result of a dramatic shortage of monetary resources in Belarus, a typical measure over the last few years has been administrative re-allocation of Belaruskali's currency earnings for the purchase of important goods.[5] Volumes and composition of foreign trade have been, therefore, influenced primarily by resource endowment and legacies of the central planning. If the latter created commonality between Ukraine, Russia and Belarus, the former has established differences. In the case of Russia and Ukraine, it has even become a factor of economic growth.

The geographical dimension of trade: directions and forms

As a result of the institutional legacy of central planning, Russia, Belarus and Ukraine were oriented towards trade within the USSR and to CMEA economies. This geographical scheme of foreign trade has undergone quite substantial modification in Ukraine and Russia, but not in Belarus. In the latter, the share of CIS exports and imports has constituted respectively over 60 and 70 per cent of its trade during the years of transition. A significant re-distribution of Belarusian exports within the CIS has taken place: Belarus has been increasingly dependent on Russian markets. In 1992, Russia accounted for about 40 per cent of Belarusian exports; in 2000, this rose to 55 per cent (Ministerstvo Innostrannykh Del RB, 2000, p.22).

Ukraine has pursued a policy quite different to Belarus. In Ukraine, the share of CIS countries it imports from, and exports to, has decreased respectively from 66 per cent and 56 per cent in 1994 to 53 per cent and 39 per cent in 2001. Both

Table 5.1 Volumes and regional structure of trade (US$ billions)

	1994	1995	1996	1997	1998	1999	2000	2001
Belarus								
Export		4.8	5.6	7.3	7.0	5.9	7.3	7.5
Import		5.5	6.9	8.6	8.5	6.6	8.6	8.0
Balance		-.7	-1.3	-1.3	-1.5	-.7	-1.3	-.5
With CIS								
Export	2.0	3.0	3.7	5.3	5.1	3.6	4.3	4.5
Import	2.9	3.6	4.5	5.8	5.4	4.2	6.0	5.5
Balance	-.9	-.6	-.8	-.5	-.3	-.6	-1.7	-1.0
Ukraine								
Export	11.4	14.2	14.4	14.3	12.6	11.5	14.5	16.2
Import			17.6	17.1	14.6	11.8	13.9	15.7
Balance			-3.2	-2.8	-2.0	-.2	.6	.5
With CIS								
Export			7.4	5.5	4.2	3.2	4.4	4.6
Import			11.1	9.8	7.8	6.7	8.0	8.8
Balance			-3.7	-4.3	-3.6	-3.5	-3.6	-4.2
Russia								
Export	67.8	82.9	90.5	89.0	74.8	75.6	105.5	101.6
Import	50.4	62.6	68.0	71.9	58.0	39.5	44.8	53.7
Balance	17.4	20.3	22.5	17.1	16.8	36.1	60.7	47.8
With CIS								
Export	15.7	16.9	18.5	19.0	15.7	11.9	14.2	15.1
Import	13.9	18.3	20.8	18.5	14.3	10.3	13.4	13.0
Balance	1.7	-1.6	-2.2	4.8	1.4	1.6	.8	2.0

Sources: data from Central Bank of the Russian Federation, Ministry of Statistics of the Republic of Belarus, National Bank of Ukraine, IMF (1999)

countries continue to depend upon Russian imports of energy and raw material supplies. Unlike Belarus, Ukraine, however, has managed to re-direct its exports considerably. The proportion of Ukrainian exports to Russia has dropped from 40 per cent in the early 1990s to 20 per cent today. Such a shift is possible for Ukraine because of the different domestic production and export commodity structures of the two countries, a result of different resource endowments. Of the increased Ukrainian exports to non-CIS countries, over 50 per cent are ferrous and non-ferrous metals.

The Russian strategy towards non-CIS countries is analogous to the Ukrainian one. In 1994, the share of CIS countries accounted for 27.7 per cent of the imports and 23.2 per cent of the exports of Russia; whereas in 1999 these numbers were 24.3 and 14.9 per cent respectively (see Table 5.1). As in the case of Ukraine, raw materials constituted most of its exports to non-CIS countries.

What is the reason for leaving familiar CIS markets and re-directing foreign trade, especially exports, towards Western markets, where competitors and consumers are less known, and where transitional countries are often the objects of dumping charges? One of principal causes is the low purchasing capacity or effective demand in transitional countries. As a result of monetary vacuum, consumers either cannot buy, or create indebtedness, or generate barter exchange. These problems have been affecting international and domestic trade at enterprise and state levels in all three countries throughout the years of transition.

Belarusian enterprises are heavily indebted to Russian energy sources. Although Russia supplies gas to Belarus at prices three times lower than the world market price (US$30 versus US$103) Belarusian enterprises are still unable to pay for Russian gas and have accumulated arrears of over US$230 million by 2001, mostly to the Russian enterprise Gazprom. In the same way, Ukraine is heavily indebted to Russian energy sources and is equally unable to pay. Ukraine pays a higher price for Russian gas – US$50-80 – but this price is compensated by Ukraine's illegal expropriation of up to 55 million cubic meters per day of Russian gas that is in transit through its territory.

Apart from payment arrears, another factor that has caused trade re-orientation and has it roots in CPE, is the spread of barter. Barter has made up a large proportion of foreign trade in Ukraine, Russia and Belarus since the early 1990s. In Belarus, 24 per cent of exports and 23 per cent of imports were in the form of barter in 1993. There were similar indicators for Russia and Ukraine. In the following years, some official indicators show even higher rates of barter. For example, in 1994 the share of barter in Ukrainian exports was 59.2 per cent and 29.4 per cent in imports. Some products were almost completely traded in barter: in the mid-1990s, 85 per cent of rubber and rubber products were traded for barter; about 70 per cent of Ukrainian agricultural exported was bartered (WTO, 1995a; WTO, 1997a). The increase of the share of barter trade by the mid-1990s, as compared to early 1990s, can be explained by the fact that until 1994 Russia, Ukraine and Belarus still maintained considerable elements of centralized import and export distribution, with specially authorized foreign trade companies, as was the case in the USSR. These forms of trade were non-monetary in effect (as money did not have much economic meaning under central planning) but they might have not entered official statistics on barter since they referred to a different institutional setting.

Barter takes place not only between enterprises, but also at the level of inter-governmental agreements. Usually the latter refers to a country's payment for energy resources. For example, in 1999 the Ukrainian concern Naftogas announced a tender on goods to Turkmenistan as a payment to gas imports. It was decided that 60 per cent of Turkmen imports were to be paid for by Ukrainian goods. In 2000, the Belarusian government made a decision to supply Belarusian trolley-buses as a payment for energy resources (Resolution, Verkhovnaya Rada of Ukraine, 21 June 2001, no.700; Resolution, Cabinet of Ministers of Belarus, 16 May 2000, no.689).

Barter is an ineffective form of transacting exchanges since there are no currency revenues, the value exchange is biased and the state loses on taxes. In spite of the attempts to constrain barter trade, it continued to play an important role in post-communist trade.[6] However, by the end of the 1990s, as a result of the geographical re-reorientation of foreign trade, the share of barter trade has significantly decreased in Russia and Ukraine. These trends are less obvious in

Belarus, since it does not have the structural advantages of Russia and Ukraine that allow them to re-orient their trade away from CIS partners. In 2000, the share of barter still accounted for 35.5 per cent of Belarusian exports (Ministerstvo Innostrannykh Del RB, 2000, p.24). Market economies, therefore, where export is paid for by currency, are more desirable as export destinations, even regardless of the fact that they often impose dumping charges on transitional economies. Dumping investigations became a chronic problem for Ukraine, Belarus and Russia in non-CIS markets. In 1995-1996, no less than 10 per cent of Russian exports to the USA were of commodities subject to anti-dumping restrictions (data from an interview with an official of the Ministry of Foreign Affairs of Russia, February 2000). In the following years, the amount of anti-dumping cases grew and reached 150, generating a loss of US$2 billion for Russia annually. A number of cases were also initiated against Ukraine and Belarus.[7]

The general reasons for Ukraine, Belarus and Russia selling at low prices can be traced back as to the Soviet period. The reason for low pricing in the USSR and in transitional economies remains broadly the same: ensuring currency or monetary inflow as a result of the very low level of monetization in the domestic economy. The sale of goods at lower prices happens, therefore, in structurally specific conditions. Low price sales happen primarily for the sake of earning currency; export increases take place against the background of domestic production decline. Dumping occurs not in conditions of domestic overproduction, but very often in the situation of unsatisfied domestic, or CIS, demand. Many of the goods going for export, including those labelled as dumped, are restricted in exports in order to secure their adequate supply in the domestic market. The usual way of defining a dumping margin is through the price in the internal market of the exporting country.[8] This is often an inapplicable method for transitional countries, as the latter remains lower than export prices due to the state-control of domestic prices. The usual assumption in this case is that domestic prices in Russia, Belarus and Ukraine are subsidized. If this is the case, investigation in to dumping should establish compensation for unfair export subsidies. In fact, and as we will see below, subsidies in Russia, Belarus and Ukraine are almost non-existent compared to the degree of state support in developed and even developing countries.

Since usual anti-dumping procedures are difficult to apply as a result of low domestic prices in Russia, Belarus and Ukraine, they were defined as 'non-market economies'. This allowed petitioners to use the costs of any market country in order to calculate the dumping margin of goods, and has been one of the most vivid examples of discriminatory treatment of Ukraine, Belarus and Russia in trade practices over the last decade.[9]

A regional, small-scale prototype of selling at low prices is the so-called 'shuttle trade'. This is a kind of shadow economy, in which individuals purchase and sell goods in large quantities, unofficially, avoiding taxes. Shuttle trade usually happens between neighbouring countries because of low transportation costs and relaxed migration policies. When a transitional country liberalizes its prices, they normally rise significantly as a result of the structural legacies of central planning. It then becomes beneficial to import goods from another transitional country, where price control is still in force, and prices, therefore, are much lower. Shuttle trade was particularly active in the early-mid 1990s in Belarus, Russia and Ukraine. Goods were normally supplied to neighbouring Poland, Turkey and China. Shuttle trade accounted for 5 per cent of Russian exports to and 22.5 per cent of its imports from the CIS in 1994. Domestic demand for some commodities was almost completely satisfied by shuttle trade. For example, in the mid-1990s, this form of supply ensured 70 per cent of the domestic textile clothing supply, 50 per cent of leather clothes, and 30 per cent of audio and video equipment (data of the Institute for the Economy of Transition, Moscow). In 1999, the share of shuttle trade in Russian exports accounted for 2.4 per cent and for imports, 23.2 per cent. The decrease of shuttle trade in export is the result of Russian price liberalization. Russian goods are unprofitable to export because their price equals, or sometimes exceeds prices in other countries. On the other hand, the share of shuttle trade in Russian imports has increased due to price controls on certain commodities in neighbouring countries.

It can be concluded that a noticeable regional re-orientation of foreign trade – from CIS to non-CIS states took place in Ukraine and Russia. This shift is necessary in all countries, since money earnings, which are vital for money-aggrieved transitional economies, come from outside of the CIS region. Due to different natural resource endowments, this shift was possible for Ukraine and Russia, but not for Belarus. Trade within CIS, in turn, has been characterized by a substantial share of barter and shuttle trade. Both result form the legacy of CPE, with shuttle trade also being caused by a varying speeds of price liberalization in neighbouring countries.

Regulatory mechanisms of foreign trade

Tariff regulation

Export tariffs A common feature of Russia, Belarus and Ukraine is an active use of export tariffs, especially in the early 1990s. In fact, export tariffs appeared earlier than import tariffs in these countries: import duties started to be applied from late 1992 at the earliest whereas export ones were in operation at least from the beginning of 1992. Goods that were subject to export duties were largely those whose domestic prices were state-controlled. In conditions where domestically controlled prices are much lower than world prices, and when producers strive to sell goods overseas in order to get currency revenues, a government, which introduces export tariffs, pursues two main objectives. First, it tries to constrain export for the sake of ensuring the supply of these goods in the domestic market. This was particularly important in the early 1990s, since as a result of the dramatic decline in production, the increase in export happened at the expense of decreasing sales in the domestic market. The second aim is fiscal; here tariffs, as compared to non-tariff restrictions, play a significant role. In the conditions of massive budget deficit caused by monetary vacuum in public finance, the state aimed to maximize its fiscal functions. In 1992, for instance, the Ukrainian government put into the planned budget for 1993 to collect 5 per cent of revenues from export duties only

(*Vedomosti Verkhovnoi Rady*, no.20, 1993). In Russia, the revenue share of export and import duties stood, respectively, as 3 per cent in 1994 and 6.7 per cent in 1995 (WTO, 1996b, p.3). To compare, in 1994, the share of tariffs in budget revenues accounted for 2 per cent in the United States and 1 per cent in Japan; and these revenues came from import duties (World Bank, 1997, pp.194-96).

The early 1990s saw the most active application of export tariffs. For example, until 1995, about 75 per cent of Russian exports were subject to the imposition of export duties: marine products, grain, metal ores, metal concentrates, oil, oil products, gas, metals, chemical products, fertilizers, animal products, paper products, and wood products, scrap of ferrous metals, weapons and so forth. In the same years, Belarus applied a tariff regulation similar to Russia's (WTO, 1995b, 110-1). A massive number of goods were covered by export duties in Ukraine as well, including agricultural commodities, raw materials, fibre, salt etc (Resolution, Verkhovnaya Rada of Ukraine, no.12, 1993). Rates of customs duties were quite high; many *ad-valorem* rates reached 30 per cent. It is noticeable that most of the export duties were expressed non-*ad-valorem* (or specific) in form. The usage of specific duties was explained by the fact that in the early 1990s, all economic categories of value (profit, costs and price) were still distorted in transitional countries. Exchange of many goods was still perceived more easily in physical volumes rather than in terms of monetary values, especially since a significant portion of domestic prices was state-controlled until the mid 1990s. For example, Belarusian export tariff as of 1995 was almost completely comprised of specific duties (Resolution, Cabinet of Ministers of Belarus, 29 September 1995, no.536).

From 1995-1997, with the liberalization of domestic prices and their reaching the level of world prices, export tariffs have been significantly phased out in Russia, Belarus and Ukraine. In 1999, however, some export tariffs were re-introduced in Russia as a result of 1998 default. These measures were implemented for commodities significantly oriented for export: export-oriented enterprises having large currency reserves found themselves in a very advantageous position. Duties were established on energy sources, ore and scrap of non-ferrous metals, leather. Recently Russian export duties started to be applied for exported goods to CIS countries, which violates the CIS free trade framework. Initially, it was planned to establish export duties for only six months, but this period was extended, with some duties to be even lifted later on: on marine products, on fertilizers, on raw oil and oil products; duties were introduced on plywood in 2000. Nevertheless, the abolition of export duties promises to be a dominant trend in 2002 and 2003 as their role becomes obsolete with the strengthening of the Russian currency and further price liberalization. Export duties were decreased on chemicals, liquid fuel, metal production, paper products, and metal products. In 2003, Russia plans to further decrease export duties with high value added and decrease those export duties, which do not bring considerable revenues.

As a result of the customs union agreement, export duties in Belarus have been identical to those in Russia. The compositions of these export duties poorly reflect economic interests of Belarus. Export duties on raw gas, oil, fish products, and ferrous and non-ferrous metals are only loosely applicable for Belarus as it does not produce and export these commodities. Here, as with the case of import tariffs (see below) Russia policy is prevalent. In 2001, Ukraine, in turn, has been applying a small list of export tariffs, mainly on flax and sunflower oil.

Import tariffs Under conditions where there was a sharp necessity for imported goods, aggravated by the lack of currency, the import regime in Russia, Belarus and Ukraine was bound to be exceptionally liberal in the early 1990s. Until the end of 1992, these countries did not maintain import tariffs at all. The legislative elaboration of import tariffs started in 1993, when a basic legislative law 'On Customs Tariffs' in Russia and Belarus (separately), and 'On the Unified Customs Tariff' in Ukraine were adopted. These acts established very broad principles of customs administrative regulations and tariff schedules and were subject to numerous changes over the subsequent years.

In 1993-1994, the level of tariffs was very low in all three countries. The weighted average tariff of Russia was 6.2 per cent in 1993 (World Bank, 2002c, p.350); in Belarus, it was 5 per cent in 1994. Equally, the rates in Ukraine were so low in the early 1990s, that later, in one of the WTO accession negotiations of Ukraine, WTO members advised Ukraine to implement those low tariff rates as a basis for further tariff regulation. The Ukrainian delegation replied that those were regulations related to central planning legacy, whereas Ukraine needed to build a market economy (WTO, 1997b). Protection was therefore not an important function in these years of transformation. The massive decline of domestic production, the necessity to secure continuation of inputs into the domestic production and the need for socially important goods caused a very liberal level of tariff protection in early 1990s. This feature of foreign trade regime in transition economies persisted in these countries for a few years. In late 1990s, in the framework of Russia's WTO accession negotiations, Russian officials' calculation of prospective levels of tariff protection on the basis of retrospective data suggested they had negative rates of tariff protection (data from an interview with an official of the Russian Embassy, February 1999, Geneva, Switzerland).

With the gradual liberation of domestic prices, the ineffective structure of production was expressed in high prices. By mid-1990s, many domestic prices in Russia, Belarus and Ukraine were already 70 per cent of the level of world prices. Consequently, in the following years, especially from 1995-1997, the level of import tariffs increased. The rates were especially increased on the processing industry products, mainly manufacturing, as they contain the highest ration of added value and reflect the ineffective costs structure most of all. In 1996, Russia increased duty rates on buses, lorries, freezers, machines, washing machines, aluminium products, and chicken meat; in 1997, on textiles, agricultural products and some raw materials.[10]

In the early-mid 1990s, Belarusian import rates were practically identical to Russian ones, although industrial goods, transport vehicles, leather, foodstuffs, building materials and wooden products were charged at rates higher than those applied in Russia; on raw materials rates lower than in Russia were used. The years 1997-2001 did not see much tariff increase; some of the rates were lifted and some decreased in Russia, Belarus and Ukraine. Tariff increase, with the aim of exercising fiscal functions has been remaining a structural necessity in these countries until recently.[11] This fiscal function has been caused by the structural specificity of transition, the lack of finance at a public level. In such conditions, governments exercise not so much stimulatory or protective, but mainly fiscal functions of tariffs. For example, the actual tax pressure in Russia in the mid-late 1990s was estimated at 60 per cent (Illarionov, 1998, p.24). Fiscal customs duty, as a tool of budget revenue, was therefore in line with the specificity of budgetary policy during transition. For example, in 1998 Ukraine lifted tariffs on 622 categories of commodities: TV sets, radio receivers, toys, household appliances, clocks and watches. Apart from the protection of the internal market, Ukraine also pursued a fiscal objective, aiming to collect 50 million Hrn (*Ukrainian Economic Trends*, April 1998). In 1998-1999, Belarus tariff rates were lifted on imported machines, chemicals. According to the Ministry of Foreign Affairs of Belarus, the main function of the tariff regime remained a fiscal one. However, with price liberalization, the protective role of tariffs has started to manifest itself as well. The ineffective costs of post-central planning production made imported commodities cheap, even after tariff increase in 1996-1997, and therefore more competitive compared to domestic production. One of the latest examples of protecting domestic industry in Russia is the increase of import duties on cars (Resolution, Government Russia Federation, 16 August 2002, no.10). Such tariff increases for the protection of domestic producers are practiced by all countries. For example, the US lifted its customs duties on steel production by 30 per cent in 2001; similarly, in 2002 the EU increased customs rates on rye and barley.

With the beginning of economic recovery, especially in Russia and Ukraine, a stimulatory function of tariffs started to become more evident. This led to tariff reductions, especially on semi-finished products and spare parts. In 1999, Russia decreased customs duties on some fish from (10 per cent to 5 per cent) wood (from 20 per cent to 10 per cent), and furniture products; duties were also decreased (from 30 per cent to 20 per cent) on technological equipment in about 300 positions. In the same way, with the aim of supporting the domestic automobile industry a wide range of goods relating to automobile spare parts was made duty free in Ukraine (Resolution, Government of Russia 1999, no.933; Resolution, Verkhovnaya Rada of Ukraine, 1 June 2002, no.737). Other factors influencing tariff decreases were of external origin: WTO accession or EU influence played particularly important roles. For example, in 2001, Ukraine made significant reductions on import duties for many textile goods – cotton yarn, jute yarn, cotton fabrics, threads, non-woven materials, clothes and knitted wear – to the level of the EU. Ukraine made these tariff reductions in exchange for EU cancellation of its quotas on the import of Ukrainian textiles.

In 2001, the weighted average import tariffs of Ukraine were 5 per cent whereas it was 12-14 per cent in Russia and Belarus. To compare, in the same year, the weighted average tariff was 1.8 per cent in the US, 2.0 per cent in Japan, 21.7 per cent in Brazil, and 41.7 per cent in Pakistan (World Bank, 2002c, p.350). Ukraine, Russia and Belarus have, therefore, started their import tariff policy from the opposite end to most states: from not having any import tariffs in the early 1990s to having increased them by the end of the 1990s, with Russia and Belarus reaching the average level of some developing countries. Ukraine followed the same path, although in a more liberal way until the late 1990s, when it undertook a considerable reduction, approximating its level of import tariff protection to that of the most developed countries. It is apparent that the average level of tariff in transitional countries is higher than in some developed, but lower than in developing, countries. Making a conclusion about the level of tariff protection in Russia, Belarus and Ukraine, three additional considerations need to be taken into account.

First, import tariffs reflect the protection of domestic merchandise production in these countries. The share of industry and agriculture in the GDP accounted for 46 per cent, 52 per cent and 53 per cent in Russia, Ukraine and Belarus respectively. In the same years, the share of these sectors constituted only 29 per cent of the GDP in the United States, and 34 per cent in Japan and Singapore (World Bank, 2002c, pp.208-10). There is no need for developed countries, with their economies in which the share of agriculture and industry accounts for a small part of the GDP, to protect goods, whose production has been declined in favour of service industries. In post-CPE countries, the structure of import protection reflects the over-industrialized economy inherited from central planning.

Second, industries that play an important economic or social role are subject to much stronger protection in developed and developing countries compared to Russia, Belarus and Ukraine. This is seen in the level of peak tariff rates on particular commodities. In some rare cases, the highest rates of tariff protection in Belarus, Russia and Ukraine reached 150 per cent. However, for most of the post-communist period, however, the maximum rate did not exceed 100 per cent. To compare, as a result of 'tariffication' (conversion of specific duties to *ad-valorem*) required by the WTO, the average weighted rate of imported agricultural products in Japan rose to 444 per cent (rice), and 193 per cent (wheat); in the US, to 93 per cent (diary products), and 91 per cent (sugar); in the EU, to 231 per cent (rice) 205 per cent (diary products) and 279 per cent (sugar) (Borzunova, 2000). One of the major reasons for low tariff peaks in Russia, Ukraine and Belarus has been that the tariffs schedule is for broad categories of goods. This is a legacy of the insignificant role of foreign trade and import protection (in the market sense) played under central planning. The insignificant role of foreign trade under CPE meant that the administrative side of foreign trade was very undeveloped.[12] For example, in 1996 the Belarusian tariff included only 789 items. This figure compares strikingly with the USA, for instance, which had over 10,000 tariff items, or Bangladesh, which had over 7,000 (OECD, 1999, pp.146-74). The poor differentiation of tariff items creates a situation where a tariff rate is applied regardless of whether all goods within a trade category are produced in the country in question or not. In this way, a country with poor tariff differentiation works both for and against its own trade interests at the same time.

Third, over the years of transition, Russia, Ukraine and Belarus have been applying a negligible share of specific duties. In fact, such import duties were non-existent in these countries up to the mid 1990s. This sharply contrasts with other countries. In 1999, the level of non *ad-valorem* duties in Switzerland was over 80 per cent; in the USA and the EU, over 10 per cent. Moreover, the share of US non *ad- valorem* duties on agricultural products was 40 per cent in 1999 (OECD, 1999,

66). The low share of non *ad-valorem* duties in Russia, Belarus and Ukraine cannot be attributed to the lack of expertise in these countries as specific duties were the principle ones used by all of them in respect for export tariffs starting from the early 1990s. The application of specific duties, whose level is difficult to estimate, is a way of protecting domestic producers. The insignificant share or even a lack of specific duties in Russia, Ukraine and Belarus can be attributed to the fact that over the years of transformation, the dominant feature of their tariffs was a fiscal rather than protective one.

Quantitative restrictions

Export quantitative restrictions As with tariffs, the most active application of quantitative restrictions (QRs) occurred in the early 1990s, and in the same way there were more QRs on export rather than on imports until the mid 1990s. The most widespread types of QRs were quoting, licensing, contract registration and the establishing of minimal export prices. Export QRs were broadly used for those goods whose domestic priced was controlled. The chief problem with QR as compared to tariffs is that it does not perform a fiscal function, which is one of the most important functions of trade regulation during transition. Russia, Belarus and Ukraine have partially overcome this problem by imposing fees for licenses and quotas. The advantage of QRs is that it is possible to provide a precise regulation of volumes of export and import. This is important for transitional countries, since their post-central planning economies, especially in early 1990s, were unreceptive to monetary value categories.

In order to prevent the exhaustion of the domestic market a list of goods eligible for export control was defined in Belarus, Russia and Ukraine as early as 1990 (for example, Resolution of the Council of Ministers of BSSR, 6 November 1990, no.275). The early 1990s saw the longest list of goods subject to QR in operation. In Ukraine, quotas covered a massive range of agricultural, chemical products, foodstuffs, gas and oil.[13] By 1995, about 50 per cent of the volume of Russian exports was subject to export contract registration. This included fifteen aggregated commodity groups: oil, processed oil products, natural gas, fertilizers, timber, agricultural products and so forth (WTO, 1997c, p.61). In Belarus, there were export restrictions on the export of oil, refinery products, fertilizers, ferrous and non-ferrous metals, waste and scrap (Resolution, Cabinet of Ministers of Belarus, 1 December 1994, no.213). In all cases, the aim of export control was mainly to ensure a sufficient supply of goods and prevent the disruption of domestic production and consumption.

By the mid-1990s, export QRs, in parallel with export tariffs, were gradually eliminated. In the same years, the centralized exports and imports of foreign trade were practically eliminated in Russia, Belarus and Ukraine. By 1994, the list of export QRs in the Ukraine was considerably smaller than in 1993 and covered grains, steel-making, pig iron, coal, wastes of ferrous and non-ferrous and noble metals. In 1995, export QR was eliminated for the export of wastes and the scrap of ferrous and non-ferrous metals, precious metals, pig-iron and grain. In 2002, Ukraine used quotas for ores and concentrates of precious metals, precious stones and coins. Maintenance of export restrictions on precious stones has been used in Belarus and Russia as well. The reason for this is that these goods are capital articles, able to ease the structural problem of the lack of finance in transitional countries. In WTO negotiations Ukraine, Russia and Belarus justified their position in respect of export control on precious metals and stones as necessary to prevent 'illicit capital transfers abroad', to form state gold reserves and to resolve balance of payment problems (see Resolutions of the Verkhovnaya Rada of Ukraine of 31 March 1995, no.222; 18 January 1995, no.35; 24 October 1994, no.734; WTO, 1995c; WTO, 1996b, p.50).

In mid-1990s, the application of export QRs started to decrease. The Russian system of export contract registration was abolished in 1996; in 1997, Russia abolished export QRs on silver, gold and other precious metals (Resolution, Government of Russia, 23 July 1997, no.767). The latter measure was superseded by the abolition of the state monopoly on gold, silver and other precious metals, and mainly resulted from the fact that state controlled prices on precious metals caused problems in the second and third working parties of Russia's negotiations with the WTO. The situation in Belarus was not as straightforward as that in Russia and Ukraine. Although quotas and licenses on oil products were abolished in 1996, and export restrictions on some types of fertilizers and saw-timber were abolished in 1997, Belarus maintained and re-introduced QRs on other goods (Decree, President of Belarus, 19 March 1996, no.108, Resolutions of the Cabinet of Ministers of Belarus, 1 October 1997, no.1348; 10 July 98, no.1091). By 2000, there was a considerable list of commodities that were subject to export licensing, export contract registration, and also goods subject to contract registration in regional (*oblast*) executive committees; this list remained practically unchanged until 2002. These massive export restrictions in Belarus are caused by the continuing decline of its domestic production, which necessitates prevention of the outflow of goods that are scarce in its internal market.[14]

Import quantitative restrictions The peculiarity of import QRs in Russia, Belarus and Ukraine is that QRs did not exist until the mid-1990s due to the massive decline of domestic production in the first years of transition. This is particularly noticeable if we recall the very long lists of export quantitative restrictions that existed in these countries up to the mid 1990s.

In 1994, Ukraine introduced import quotas on meat, milk, cereals, oil, butter, machines and equipment. Import licenses applied to metal strap, plant protection and veterinary chemicals. Compared to Russia and Belarus, Ukraine remained the most liberal of the three countries, applying only a very limited list of import QRs. In 1996, it restricted only herbicides, pesticides, pharmaceuticals, veterinary medicines and other goods, threatening health levels and the ecological balance in the country (Resolutions of the Verkhovnaya Rada of Ukraine, 17 December 1993, no.1046; 12 December 1996, no.1590). This liberal application of QRs has been in line with Ukraine's liberal policy, which, as we saw, was reflected in very low import duties.

In 1994, less than 1 per cent of the value of Russian imports required licensing or other authorization (in addition to the payment of import duties) (WTO, 1996c).[15]

In 1996, however, Russia maintained quite a wide list of import QRs, many of them going beyond purely health, security or environmental considerations, and including a number of chemical products, raw materials, and industrial goods (WTO, 1996e). The reason for the increased application of import QRs is similar to that of import tariffs in the same years: it aimed to protect domestic industry, whose low competitiveness becomes more apparent in the conditions of price liberalization. In 1998-2002, Russia reduced the list of import quantitative restrictions, mainly applying them to colour plant protectors, TV sets and carpets (Resolution, Government of Russia, 11 December 1997, no.1549). The Belarusian policy on QRs was almost identical to the Russian one during these years.

The application of import QRs on industrial goods, as in Belarus and Russia is not a rare phenomenon in international trade, even regardless of WTO limitations. In Turkey, for example, import restrictions apply to electrical apparatuses, telephone answering machines, machine tools, vacuum cleaners, tractors, motor-cycles, various vehicles, various liquids and oils for industrial needs, and fertilizers. In Singapore, in which the share of contribution of the manufacturing industry to the GDP is far less than in Russia, Belarus and Ukraine, there are import licences on videotapes, disks, fruit or jackpot machines, and controlled telecommunications equipment. Restrictions on the import of raw materials as practiced in Russia are also applied in the US for natural gas (WTO, 2000a and 2001).

A common feature of the economies of Russia, Belarus and Ukraine has been the maintenance of import QRs on alcohol and tobacco products over the years of transition. Moreover, different sorts of government control applied to domestic production and distribution and include licenses on the production and circulation of tobacco and alcoholic products, the establishment of quotas for production and wholesale and so forth. The reason for such control over alcoholic and tobacco products is mainly revenue considerations: these products usually provide a stable income for the state budgets. For the same reason, import control over tobacco and alcoholic products is popular in other counties as well. For example, import restrictions apply to wines, malt, beverages, distilled spirits or alcohol for industrial use, tobacco products in the US (WTO, 2000a).

The feature that unites Russian, Belarusian and Ukrainian economies into a category of countries, as far QRs are concerned, and distinguishes them from many developed, developing and newly industrialized is the almost non-existence of import restrictions on agricultural commodities. Quantitative import restrictions on agriculture are not actively applied in Ukraine, Russia and Belarus as a result of the massive decline in the domestic production of these products, caused by the institutional and structural specificities of transition. Here a contrast with other countries is apparent. The overproduction of agricultural commodities and foodstuffs in the EU, for example, leads it to employ remarkably active import restrictions on these products. Imports of diary products are also restricted in the United States. In Singapore, licences exist in respect of vegetables and fruits, meat, fish, sweeteners; in the EU, licences and tariff quotas are applied to a large range of foodstuff (WTO, 2000a, 2000b, 2001b).

We can see, therefore, that along with an increase of market elements in the economy, a gradual abolition of export QRs in Russia, Ukraine and Belarus took place. On the other hand, in mid-end 1990s, a protection function of import QRs started to play a role. This resulted in an increase of the application of import QRs in these years. The difference in the degree and length of application of import and export was caused by different speed in economic recovery and price liberalization. Some elimination of QRs was also made under the influence of the WTO.

Export subsidization

The word 'subsidy' should be applied to resource redistribution under CPE only with substantial reservations. Export subsidies were particularly alien to the central planning system in the economic sense as the system suffered from export aversion. We might expect, therefore, that export subsidies as an element of the market economy should start to play an increasing role in economic life along with import tariff duties and quantitative restrictions, as transition progresses. Formally speaking, this was the case since transitional economies became responsive to the market notion of subsidy with the introduction of elements of market economy. But in actuality, the amount of subsidization has remained so insignificant that until now there has not been much ground to talk about exports subsidy in Russia, Belarus and Ukraine.

The ability of a state to subsidize depends upon its public finances. As a result of monetary vacuum, the budgets of transitional countries became so small that instead of subsidization and favouring domestic industries, states tried to increase fiscal pressure on them. It is not surprising that in WTO negotiations, Russia, Belarus and Ukraine emphasized the lack of any export subsidies. WTO negotiations, however, always have some political flavour as countries strive to hide strategic information. Therefore, it is useful to see whether Russia, Belarus and Ukraine are able to carry out substantial subsidization in general. This would give an indirect picture of their potential for export subsidization.

A substantial ratio of state support in Russia falls to the coal sector and agriculture, which, incidentally, have not been export-oriented sectors. In 1997, 87 per cent of the total budgetary expenditures appropriated to enterprises and organizations in Russia were given to the coal industry (WTO, 1997d). The 2002 budget of Russia estimated the amount of subsidies for the coal sector at US$144.8 million. In Ukraine, a substantial share of the public finance was allocated for the development of machine building and the reconstruction of metallurgical enterprises in 2001. All together, these received US$4.5 million. In Belarus, 'Industry, energy and construction sectors,' were estimated to receive approximately US$17 million in 2002. These measures are insignificant compared to those in developed countries and even some developing countries. In the case of EU countries, EU-level subsidy programmes alone for various agricultural, industrial and other programmes accounted for ECU90.7 billion in 1998. In the USA, many subsidy programmes are estimated in *hundreds of millions* of dollars. In Brazil, the 'Export Financing Programme', one of several subsidy lines, was estimated at US$844 million for 1999, which is well above the total level of subsidization in Belarus, Russia and Ukraine (WTO, 1998, 1999 and 2001c).

Agriculture is probably the most sensitive item in WTO negotiations. If there is any state assistance in Belarus, it is primarily directed to this sector. Russia has the greatest capacity for subsidization as a result of its oil export revenues and improved economic performance. Nevertheless, as a result of the lack of money, some state assistance for agriculture has been provided not in money, but in credit in kind in the form of fuel and lubricants. It was estimated that in 2002 in Russia the level of support of agricultural producers per hectare of arable land is forty times lower than in the EU (RTR-Vesti, 2002). With such poor possibilities of domestic support for agriculture, there is even less possibility of export subsidization. The lack of export subsidies for agriculture was reported in WTO negotiations by all three countries in our analysis. Only in 2000-2002, after two years of economic recovery, did the Russian and Ukrainian governments start to plan export programmes for agriculture. So far, these plans principally refer to public discussions and not to actual measures. This implies that the dramatic economic decline in the 1990s prevented them from subsidizing this area for export purposes. In Belarus, no serious discussions about agricultural export subsidization have occurred. The extremely low, or virtually non-existent, level of subsidization results not so much from an ideological or political commitment to a certain policy stance, but from the actual impossibility of subsidization, which is one of the most distinctive structural features of transition. This is particularly demonstrated by the domestic discourse in Ukraine, a country that started to consider the possibility of export subsiding regardless of her quite liberal economic policy over the past few years.

The importance of export for transitional countries is, however, difficult to overestimate due to the vital role of currency inflows into transitional economies that are experiencing dramatic monetary deficits. There have been *ad hoc*, non-monetary attempts to stimulate exports in Russia, Belarus and Ukraine. For instance, discriminatory application of excise taxes has been practiced in all three countries (i.e. imported goods were charged at higher excise tax compared to goods produced domestically). Apart from supporting domestic industry, these measures had a considerable fiscal role. In Ukraine, for example, although the rates of excise tax on imported alcohol and tobacco were several times higher than the ones applied to domestic production, the latter was also a charged with high rates: 100 per cent tax was applied on wines, 60 per cent on cognac. However, this did not last long due to IMF and WTO pressure. In 1995 in Ukraine, and in 1997 in Russia and Belarus, discriminatory excise tax application was phased out.

An unusual measure of export promotion was granting preferences to those enterprises that conducted exports in exchange for currency. Such measures were applied in Belarus and in Ukraine in 1997. The peculiarity of this measure was that the preference was granted not so much upon the expansion of exports, but upon the receipt of currency. This was aimed at easing the problem of monetary vacuum inherent in transitional countries. Exports are perceived mainly as a resource for the import of economically and socially important commodities. Other measures of state export promotion, such as government guarantees and insurance, only started to appear in the mid-late 1990s in Russia, Ukraine and Belarus. For example, in 1996, the Russian government introduced a system of government insurance for exports. This measure, common in other market countries, has been hard to introduce in financially aggrieved transitional countries. For some time this state insurance had only one active element, the Russian export-import Bank (Roseximbank) while the other element of the system, export-oriented loan insurance, remained on paper. Finally, there were attempts to apply measures of import substitution in Russia, Belarus and Ukraine. As a result of the impossibility of providing financial resources, these initiatives have been empty gestures in practice or have, as in the case of Belarus, been ordered through administrative fiat in the absence of economic resources to back them up. For example, in 2002 public transport was ordered by government resolution to use only domestically produced vehicles (Resolution, Cabinet of Ministers of Belarus 30 June 2002, no.1117).

Export subsidization has thus been practically non-existent in Russia, Belarus and Ukraine. This reflects the fact that there are in general very limited possibilities for any subsidization in these countries. Monetary subsidies are miserable in amount due to the monetary vacuum inherited from CPE. Non-monetary export subsidies are practically non-existent as well. The question of whether or not there is non-monetary subsidization domestically goes beyond the scope of this chapter. But in light of the legacies of the central planning and the character of export subsidization, it is possible to speculate that non-monetary subsidies in Russia, Belarus and Ukraine result not from a desire to hide strategically important economic policies, but from the impossibility of monetary subsidization.

Other measures of export and import regulation

During transition, Russia, Belarus and Ukraine have maintained various mechanisms for extracting currency revenues from exporters. The purpose of these measures was not to restrict export, but to obtain monetary or currency resources for public needs. However, as such methods put exporters in a disadvantageous position compared to domestic traders or importers, obligatory currency sale can in effect be considered a measure restricting exports. This measure is a direct result of transitional countries public finance problems, their lack of monetary, and therefore currency, reserves. In 1990-1991, urgent measures were adopted in all three countries to establish currency reserves. In early 1990s, a tax on currency revenues and later a requirement for enterprises to keep their currency earnings in national banks were imposed. The aim of these measures is to collect and to keep currency within country. The longest and most popular measure has been 'mandatory currency sales.' In 1991, in Russia, enterprises, organizations, physical persons had to sell 40 per cent of currency they earned from exports of goods and services to the Russian Federation Reserve at a special rate of exchange. In 1992, this measure was substituted by a mandatory sale of 50 per cent of foreign currency receipts from goods and services (Decree, President of Russia, 14 June 1992, no.62). The same measure was established in Ukraine and Belarus. Over the years of transformation, the amount of mandatory currency sale has generally between 30-50 per cent in Russia, Belarus and Ukraine.

Another specific measure of foreign trade regulation of Russia, Belarus and Ukraine has been the classification of imports as essential, non-essential and critical. This hierarchy of imports has been necessary due to the shortage of currency resources, which makes it necessary to determine which imports are of social or strategic importance. These import classifications have been imposed differently in each state thanks to the differences in each country's revenue raising powers. In Belarus, these measures were longer and more comprehensive in application than in Russia, with Ukraine occupying the middle ground. Critical or essential imports usually refer to commodities of strategic or social importance: raw materials, agricultural production, and medicines. The remaining elements of the centralized imports (until the mid-1990s) broadly covered these types of goods. With the abolition of all centralized central planning foreign trade operation, the import of these commodities usually enjoys various tariff and non-tariff preferences. Non-essential imports are usually denoted as those commodities that are produced, or can potentially be produced in the domestic market. Import of such commodities is discouraged through the application of various restrictions like contract registration, licensing and so forth. In 1997, the share of non-essential imports accounted for 20 per cent of all Ukrainian imports. In Belarus, the list of non-essential goods includes tyres, confectionary, beverages etc (WTO, 1996b, p11; Resolution, Cabinet of Ministers of Belarus, 10 October 1997, no.1348).

Conclusion

The structural and institutional composition of foreign trade in Russia, Belarus and Ukraine are primarily influenced by three sets of factors: the legacies of CPE; raw resource endowment; and regional/international influences, underpinned by domestic political commitments.

The legacy of CPE unites Russia, Belarus and Ukraine in a homogenous group of countries that are different from developed and developing market economies. On the structural side, the legacy of the central planning caused low competitiveness for the products of processing industries and primary commodity export specialization, especially in Russia and Ukraine. On the institutional side, the legacy of CPE is manifest in the small possibility of export subsidization and a high ratio of 'shuttle' and barter trade. Other commonalities caused by central planning legacies can also be found in particular years. Up to the mid-1990s, Ukraine, Russia and Belarus were characterized by non-existence of, or very low, customs duties and quantitative restrictions on imports. At the same time, considerable tariffs and qualitative restrictions on exports were in place. In the mid to late 1990s, a common feature was the gradual abolition of export regulation and an overly fiscal function of import duties.

The influence of the WTO is another factor that causes similarities in Russian Ukrainian and Belarusian foreign trade regulation. All three have been striving for full membership of this organization. Liberalization of tariff and non-tariff measures in late 1990s was partially caused by this effort. The end of discriminatory anti-dumping investigations against Russia, Belarus and Ukraine is seen as an important benefit of WTO membership.

The differences between the countries are caused, first, by different resource endowments and, second, by regional influences, underpinned by domestic political commitments. In the first case, the rich mineral resources of Russia and Ukraine were the principle reasons for their re-orientation of exports towards non-CIS countries, positive foreign trade balances and, to a considerable extent, for their economic recovery in 1999-2002. This picture contrasts with Belarus, which, being poor in natural resources, has been locked in to trade dependence with the CIS and especially Russia. It has had a chronic negative foreign trade balance, and no economic improvement over the years of transformation.

Regional factors have also affected the three countries in various ways as well. Belarus and Ukraine present a contrast in terms of their relations with Russia. Belarus, being bound by its commitment to the customs union, finds itself in following the unilateral policy of the strongest customs union partner, Russia. Ukraine, on the other hand, has been actively striving to integrate with the EU, and has significantly liberalized its foreign trade regulation.

Notes

1   Russia has 90 per cent of the gas, 75 per cent of the coal, 90 per cent of the oil, 90 per cent of the timber and 60 per cent of the ferrous and non-ferrous products of the CIS. Russia is also rich in precious metals (gold, silver) and precious stones (diamonds). The main resources in the Ukraine are ferrous and non-ferrous metals, coal and fertile land. Belarus is poor in natural resources, except potassium salts – it has the second largest deposit in Europe.

2   The economic indicators of an enterprise were divided into direct costs, taxes, various deductions and profit. Direct costs were formed by current and fixed capital costs, which were covered by the state and could not be modified by an enterprise. Taxes, payment for credits, and state guarantees were fixed in the plan as well. The deduction of these costs from the gross income of an enterprise gave profit. Profit, in turn, was divided into: payment for funds, fixed and rent payments, 'stimulation' funds, payment for bank debts, increases in current internal assets, and free disposable income. All these proportions were defined by the state. The only two elements, which could potentially offer room for an incentive mechanism, were 'stimulation funds' and free disposable income. However, they did not play an incentive role. First, they both occupied a minor role in profit. Second, the stimulation fund was calculated according to a complex formula and depended upon indicators like the volume of realization, the increase in labour productivity, and the costs of production, as a result of which it could happen that profit increased and the stimulation fund decreased. Third, free disposable income was expropriated by the state. Collectively, this meant that the state effectively imposed a 100 per cent tax on enterprises (Shmelev and Popov, 1989, pp.205-59).

3   In 1994, average monthly salaries in Belarus, Russia and Ukraine were US$26.8, US$99.1 and US$30.3 respectively. In the same year, the monthly average salary in Turkey was US$394.0 and in Germany, US$941.4. In 2000, monthly salaries were US$89.0 in Belarus, US$80.2 in Russia, US$42.5 in Ukraine, US$811.1 in Germany and US$722.7 in Turkey (IMF, 2002, p.20).

4   In the same year, it was also signed by Kazakhstan, Kyrgyzstan and three years later, by Tajikistan. The customs agreement is in the initial stage of development. Members of the customs union have different tariff and non-tariff regulation and there are many exemptions from the customs union and the free trade agreement. In 1998, Kyrgyzstan joined the WTO, violating the principles of the customs union.

5   Belneftekhim, a union of enterprises of oil and chemistry industries, of which Belaruskali is a member, has been providing up to 40 per cent of all currency revenues of Belarus. Apart from Belaruskali's revenues, most of the rest export earnings come from oil production exports: about 60 per cent of Belarusian imported oil is re-exported as refined products. This export income is unstable and is likely to fade out significantly since it is based on Russian cheap oil imports; over the years of transition Russia has been striving to direct its oil towards more profitable non-CIS purchasers (data from an interview with an official of Belneftekhim, February 2000).

6   The Russian government obliged barter traders to obtain 'passports' for their transactions from the Ministry of Foreign Economic Relations and fulfil various formalities (like dates of delivery of goods). In Ukraine, a system of 'import deposits' was operated: it required traders involved in barter operations to open a preliminary import deposit account. Belarus maintained charges on barter operations.

7   The following examples illustrate anti-dumping duties, introduced on Russian, Ukrainian and Belarusian commodities: 1996, anti-dumping cases were initiated against Russia on potassium chloride (EU) and on polyester staple fibre (EU); 1997, polyester filament tow (EU); 1999, on metal production (Mexico) steel (Indonesia) diamonds (South Africa); 2000, on Vitamin C (India). By 2002, Ukrainian exports were subject to anti-dumping charges on steel wire rods (US, Canada); ammonium nitrogen fertilizer (Brazil) rubber (US, Canada, ammonium nitrogen (US, EU) urea (US, EU); urea mixture (EU); pipes (Russia). In 1992, the EU introduced anti-dumping measures against Belarusian chlorine potassium and in 1994 it made these measures more severe.

8   According to Article 2 of WTO 'Agreement on Implementation of Article VI of the General Agreement on Tariffs and Trade', the principle approach to dumping in the WTO is 'a product is to be considered to be dumped ... if the export price of the product exported from one country to another is less than the comparable price in an ordinary course of trade, for like products when destined for the consumption in the exporting country'.

9   In 2002, Russia was granted market economy status by the EU and US; recent talks between Ukraine and the US also opened the possibility of granting it the same status. In 2002, the EU undertook amendments to its anti-dumping regulations so that world prices will be taken as a point of reference in the case of domestic prices being much lower than world prices. This means that as before, dumping margins will be calculated using a third country. This clause contradicts WTO rules and Belarus, Russia and Ukraine see WTO membership as an important remedy against discriminatory anti-dumping practices.

10   In the case of aluminium products, the raising of tariffs was caused by a decrease in prices of aluminium in the world markets, increase in prices of alumina on world markets and increased energy prices in Russia. Together these made Russian aluminium higher in price than imports. It is noticeable that although external markets played a considerable role in the decreased profitability of aluminium, the structural legacies of central planning were nevertheless an important factor. Extremely cheap labour and low domestic energy prices were not enough to compensate for the production costs inherited from central planning. Hence, adverse changes in the world aluminium markets immediately made domestic prices for aluminium production

higher than world prices. Data of the Institute for the Economy of Transition, Moscow; see also Resolution, Government of Russia, 11 April 1996, no.413.

11 An official of the Ministry of International Economic Relations of Belarus observed in an internal note in 1997 that the tariff system: '[provided] the solution to short-term fiscal problems, filling the budget with revenues, whereas the protectionist function – the defence of the interests of producers – [was] not practically fulfilled although the law on "Customs Tariff" allowed for the imposition of protectionist measures on imported products. Nowadays there is a necessity to introduce measures aiming to protect the national market against some types of agricultural, industrial, chemical and textile products. There is a need to create a system of protection, corresponding to the norms of international standards'.

12 For example, only in 1989 were ministries of the USSR asked to elaborate and enforce statistics on foreign trade.

13 These included: types of grain, horses, animals, rape, sunflower, and flax seeds, rice, ethyl alcohol, medicines, butter, sugar, leather, textiles, fibre, chemical fibre, raw oil, gas, paraffin, oil products and so forth.

14 For example, in 2001, export quotas were re-introduced on fertilizers in Belarus with the aim of securing supply to the domestic market. See Resolutions of the Cabinet of Ministers of Belarus 21 Arpil 2001, no.579; 29 December 2001, no.894; 25 April 2002, no.529; 28 June 2002, no.875; 29 December 2001, no.1894. It should be noted that not all QRs on export were motivated by the need to insure an adequate domestic supply. Some of them were subject to voluntary agreements concluded with other countries and the European Union.

15 Russia has emphasized the lack of import QR in WTO negotiations: 'Russia remains one of the few countries which have not imposed QRs or other measures of non-tariff control over import' (WTO, 1996d).

Chapter 6

Path Dependency, Global Economy and Post-communist Change

Neil Robinson

Introduction

Continuity, as much as change, has marked the political economy of the former Soviet states within the Commonwealth of Independent States (CIS). Empirically, the tendency toward continuity is easy to record, since it can be seen in the delays and failures of marketization that are recorded in Chapters 2-4. Accounting for continuity is harder. Political factors have increasingly born the main weight of explaining why some states have lagged in the process of transformation. Whilst this a welcome development, the conception of politics and the range of variance explained leave much to be desired. Where comparison covers both Eastern Europe and the CIS, politics is reduced to institutional design – the executive/legislature design and electoral rules – and it is assumed that path dependence follows from choices made at the onset of reform path (Hellman, 1998; Fish, 1998). This discounts the influence of the communist past and the importance of political factors beyond the organization of central government, particularly the influence of structural factors and the incentives that they create. Alternatively, small-N comparative studies generally do not cover both Eastern Europe and the CIS since they concentrate on clusters of states such as Poland, Hungary and the Czech Republic, or single case studies (cf. Stark and Bruszt, 1998; Burawoy and Verdery, 1999). The result of this is often that the past is often seen in very one-sided terms. Comparison of similar systems can often lead to structural phenomena being underanalyzed – again – since they are held to be constant across the small range of cases and are seen additions to the complex local patterns of interaction and power, rather than factors that might shape such interactions. The way that small-N comparisons of path dependency write phenomena such as global economy and the state out of the picture make it difficult, as Böhle (2000, p.246) has argued, to be sure that small-N path dependency arguments have properly identified 'which elements of the past matter, and exactly how they matter'.

This chapter does not dispute the crucial importance of politics in explaining the variety of post-communist outcomes, and in particular, the relative backwardness of the CIS in comparison to Eastern Europe. However, it argues that what constitutes political influence upon post-communist political economy needs to be broadened out. It argues that a crucial factor influencing reform has been the type of state formed by the interaction of communist system and the international economy before the collapse of communism. The chapter defends this position by first, defining ideal-type classifications of state that can be used to distinguish between the classic Stalinist system, the evolving communist state, and the object of market reform. It argues that different forms of state emerged during the communist period as elites tried to balance the failings of central planning and the classic form of communist state with external assistance. Some of these forms of communist state produced conditions that made them amenable to marketization through their interaction with the global economy. These conditions were more prevalent in Central and Eastern Europe than in the CIS. As a result, the possibility of market change has been greater there than in the CIS since elites are more vulnerable to pressure from their domestic populations and external agencies, and have incentives to lead reform. In the CIS, where the state evolved more slowly, change has been more sluggish. Although there has been variance in patterns of change across the FSU, the lack of evolution in the past has enabled a far greater degree of continuity at the expense of economic and political pluralism.

Ideal-types of state, communism and the post-communist policy agenda: property states, rentier states and tax states

Although the importance of the state in transition has become increasingly apparent over the last decade, conceptualizations of the communist and post-communist state as an explanatory variable have not been developed. One reason for this that the classificatory schemas of communist studies were concerned with regime definition, rather than with the power of the state *per se*. The usefulness of concepts derived from communist studies is therefore purely historical since they do not describe variance over any longer time; once the regimes that they described collapsed so did the explanatory potential of concepts from communist studies as diverse as totalitarianism (at one end of the spectrum) and institutional pluralism (at the other). Concepts of state and state power that can help to re-establish the state as a conceptual variable must be able to work across the historical divide to account for both continuity and change.

Given the changing nature of institutions and purposes, the best way to look at change over time is to concentrate on functions of the state. These can be divided up in many ways, but its most direct economic functions are redistributive and involve taxation and resource allocation. Taxation and resource allocation can be achieved in a variety of ways and through a variety of mechanisms. In essence, these can be reduced to revenue generation through the general taxation of independent economic activity, or through appropriation of revenue taken by the state by right due to ownership. The latter type of revenue collection can take two forms: it can either be taken directly from the appropriation of revenue from domestic producers who work the economy on behalf of the state, or it can come from external sources. These external sources can be trade revenues from the sale of resources owned by the state, or grant aid from other states.

Table 6.1 State types

State type	Main source of revenue	Autonomy	Constraints on revenue generation
Property	State-owned property	Formally high, actually low	Formally low, in practice high due to control problems
Rentier	External sources	High	Externally generated
Tax	General tax of independent economic activity	Embedded and relative	Political as well as economic

The latter distinctions are fundamental to the form that the state takes and correlate significantly with the form in which revenue is taken. These are summarized as ideal types in Table 6.1. Ideal-typically, states that take revenue as property-owners from domestic economic activity are property states. States that take revenue from external sources are rentier states, although there is an important distinction to be drawn between those that take rent from the sale of commodities that they own, and those that take rent through aid and external subsidy and are therefore constrained by the wishes of their benefactors. States that take revenue from independent economic activity in monetary form are tax states.

Rentier (especially the commodity traders) and property states are alike in that they have a high degree of autonomy from the societies that they govern by virtue of their taking revenue as a right. However, under certain conditions, the autonomy of rentier states is higher than that of property states and the rate of taxation that they take from domestic sources is lower. Where rentier states take rent from the export of a small range of commodities, they are more minimally involved in the production systems of their domestic economies, and classically, as result of low domestic taxes, are not responsive to domestic pressure. Indeed, society is a supplicant to the state since access to external rents is conditional on access to state institutions. This leads to patron-client relations as officials use externally generated rents to ensure political loyalty and create forms of patrimonial regime in which office holding is proprietary. The interest of officials in the future of the domestic economy is also minimal since extracting resources from society is not the chief means that the state has of gaining resources that can be used to barter for political support. There is, as a result, a tendency in rentier states to allow domestic economy to stagnate relative to economic competition. This has relatively little impact on the state's ability to collect resources. The constraint on revenue collection for rentier states is set externally, either by market prices for the resources that they sell, or politically by the willingness of other states to transfer resources to them in the form of aid and loans (Crystal, 1990; Ross, 2001, pp.329-32; Shambayati, 1994; Yates, 1996).

Property states, on the other hand, are autonomous in that they take revenue as a right, but are faced with principal-agent control problems. Property states are desirous of fostering economic growth in order that they may increase the surplus that they take from society. This growth may be insured by coercing agents that manage property to use it in ways that produce growth. This imposes a limit to growth since the costs of regulation may be high and coercion can have a negative effect where it destroys trust and heightens uncertainty. The alternative is for the state as principal to negotiate for political support from its economic agents. These negotiations weaken the autonomy of property states in practice in the economic sphere since they restrict the demands that it can make. The autonomy of tax states is always relative since the state is too a greater or lesser extent embedded in the community that it governs; the tax state 'can never be its own end but only a machine for those common purposes' that individuals 'are unwilling or unable to take over' (Schumpeter, 1991, p.110). All forms of state have limits on the amounts of revenue that they can raise (Olson, 2000). In the tax state, these limits are not just economic in that both indirect and most direct taxes have a maximum yield beyond which the revenue of the state will fall, but political, in that the state's coercive power to extract will be limited by its regard for others' property rights. Where this respect is breached, the state's tax base will shrink, as economic activity will decrease. The tax state is thus the antithesis of the property state. Where the property state fuses economy and politics so that politics drives economic activity and sets it objectives directly, the tax state regulates economic activity indirectly through the system of revenue collection and under political constraint.

Central planning created the closest thing in the modern era to an ideal-typical property state. Revenue was derived from property owned by the state in the form of profits from state-owned enterprises and kept high through the regulation of wages and consumer prices by the state; the government basically and according to need set the price of goods higher than money wages and took the difference as tax (McKinnon, 1992; Olson, 2000). Tax payments were thus made between branches of the state in the main; the fiscal survival of the state did not depend on the state's capacity to appropriate surplus through taxes on the private sector. The system of taxation in the Stalinist system was thus largely implicit and potentially the state was able to manipulate prices and wages to generate high revenues. The fact that money did not play a true accounting function as prices were arbitrarily determined by central planners and there were strict political limits to what could be done with money generated by enterprises and individuals contributed to this significantly by enabling a greater manipulation of wages and consumption. This form of taxation generated a large amount of revenue and investment for a time, but at the cost of low total factor productivity. This low total factor productivity, and the other problems associated with planning, meant that overtime the economy stagnated so that the state's ability to generate large amounts of revenue declined. This tendency of revenue to fall overtime was compounded by collusion between bureaucrats and the existence of soft-budget constraints, both of which negatively affected state finances by creating a situation in which a high level of revenue had to be diverted to combat the misappropriation of state resources, or by preventing the maximization of revenue generation through the promotion of efficiency (Urban, 1985; Kornai, 1986). Coercion protected the state's ability top extract resources, but it was not enough to resolve all of the principal-agent control problems created by the vastness of the state's holdings. As a result, not all decisions that were made in the economy were economically rational. The setting of prices and the shortages that resulted from this and from breakdowns in production lead to administratively generated rents, which could be used to buy political support at the cost of economic efficiency (Lazarev and Gregory, 2003). This was, however, self-defeating. The inefficient allocation of resources meant that growth slowed and the amount of resources available for reallocation shrank relative to demand. In turn, this threatened a net reduction in political loyalty amongst the population at large. Moreover, those actors who did not share in the exchange of gifts for loyalty tried to appropriate a part of administratively generated rents for their own use. Both of these problems exacerbated the problem of investment hunger that was intrinsic to the communist order due to its desire for modernization and the absence of self-restraint on demands for investment such as exist in capitalist economies where investment, in the form of borrowed money, has to be repaid through the generation of profit (Kornai, 1992, pp.162-3). As was noted in Chapter 1, the shortage of investment resources delayed the completion of investment projects and led to high investment levels at the cost of consumption and general economic performance.

Problems of control and associated economic dysfunctions led the communist state to evolve, a point we will return to below. However, even when there was evolution, the fact that central planning remained the main mechanism for distributing resources and collecting revenue meant that communist systems never totally escaped from some conformity to the property state ideal. Ending central planning and recreating private enterprise after the collapse of the party-state as a political regime meant creating a new form of state and revenue collection. Creating the outlines of a tax state has been an aim and aspiration of reform policies in the post-communist world. This desire was heightened by the aspiration to democracy, since the consolidation of democratic governance requires economic pluralism to support political pluralism (Linz and Stepan, 1996, pp.11-13). Property and most forms of rentier state do not support economic pluralism, since the distribution of resources is dominated by political forces and pluralism is consequently curtailed. Tax states may also have considerable resources to distribute, and this may have major economic affects. However, this tends not to inhibit economic pluralism since the amount of revenue that they can take and hence redistribute, is constrained by the effect that tax has on private economic activity. Finally, moving toward creating tax states was a strategic matter for post-communist politicians. Collecting revenue in the form of money raised from private economic activity instead of from ownership meant changing the relationship that money had to economic activity under central planning. Collecting revenue from private economic activity involves the creation of money as a universal, transferable, transparent means of exchange, and erodes soft budget constraints and the use rights to property that managers and political appointees hold because of their office. Moving toward the tax state ideal thus involved breaking down the power of old elites to some degree, and at least as a construct of economic culture, and counterbalancing it with both new social groups who had access to money, and the state, which controls the production of money and its use through taxation (Woodruff, 1999). Redistribution of resources would not be achieved by manipulating prices as under central planning, but could be either direct, through state expenditure on welfare etc, or indirect through the setting taxes, interest rates and exchange policies. The constraints on political power and the revenue generating power of the state would thus change. Instead of being constrained by the problems of principal-agent control, the state would be constrained by the rights of economic agents to hold property (which sets an absolute level to taxation after all), and by the demands that would be made on the state by taxpayers for public goods.

Ability to move from something approaching the property state ideal after communism to something approaching the tax state ideal was influenced by the extent to which the property state was undermined by the development of rentierist elements. The combination of property state and rentier models under communism created constraints on post-communist elites and incentives to change. The greater the extent of rentierism underpinning the property state, the more elites were dependent on maintaining resources flows from abroad to maintain social peace. This made maintaining the credibility of economic reform important so that access to aid and investment was not compromised. Moreover, the fact that rents were earned on a broad selection of goods in Eastern Europe provided for some basic economic pluralism. The more sources of rent in a country, the more they are likely to balance out patrimonial tendencies built on control over a single rent source. The more diverse trade was, the more competing sources of power emerge. Diversity also creates incentives to co-operate, insures a level political playing field in which the state provides public rather than private goods. Such a political arena can reduce the vulnerability of economic agents to changes in international markets and demand for their goods. The provision of public goods such as low inflation, efficient and equitable economic arbitration etc can help to balance international with domestic demand by creating conditions for domestic economic growth. The same is true of rent gathered in the form of loans and aid. The use of these is constrained, first, by lenders setting conditions of use and by their often-public nature. Public claims on these may not always be honoured or effective due to asymmetries in information and influence, but they provide more scope for the balancing out of patrimonial interests than rent from the trade of a narrow range of commodities. Second, elites are constrained in that they frequently need to be able to roll debt over or defer repayment. Consequently, they need to insure a degree of stability in order to avoid default. Finally, the liberalization of trade controls can amplify these effects. Those sectors of the economy that did not enjoy access to foreign markets were desirous of sharing the resources and potential to increase consumption that openness might bring. The prospect that they might lose through increased liberalization both through competition and because of the end of implicit subsidies provided via the redistribution of rent by central planners was hidden by the manipulation of domestic prices before the introduction of stabilization policies. The fact that there might be some penetration of international price incentives in to domestic economy would also lend weight to moves to collect taxes in money and the creation of money as a universal, transferable, transparent means of exchange.

Rentierism therefore created something akin to domestic constituencies for change and as a result neutralized the collective action problems of reform.[1] As a result, it also created the potential not only for moving beyond some approximation of the property state, but also for its own demise. Where rentierism was extensive and involved a mix of commodities and debt/loans, reform could be locked in as both state actors and economic agents would be unable to perpetuate rentierism as a source of patrimonial power. In this co-operation and in the breakdown of patrimonial power that it entailed, lay the seeds of new tax states. The demise of patrimonial power and the willingness to cede decision-making to the state in the hope that it might provide stability and insure access to resources were essential to the construction of state autonomy within new political limits. Material incentives created by the undermining of the property state form embedded the new state autonomy in social consensus – no matter how rudimentary – about change, and connected that consensus to material as well as emotive, anti-communist interests. Where development of rentierism was low or skewed towards rent from the sale of a single or small number of commodities, incentives are more likely to be to extend some form of patrimonialism in order to protect the riches that accrue from trade by buying loyalty. This was the case in parts of the FSU, although the fragmentation of the Soviet economic space has meant that there has not been a straightforward course to rentierism across the region, a point that we will return to below.

The evolving communist state: the property/rentier mix and the basic differences between Eastern Europe and the USSR

In terms of structural economic problems, the evolution of the communist state was uniform in origin but diverse in outcome. Evolution was stimulated by internal factors, the failings of central planning as a system of control, the buy-offs and inefficiencies that resulted from this, and in the case of the USSR in particular, the exigencies of military competition. Communist leaders were constrained both to maintain high levels of investment to maintain growth and to fund growth in consumption. The latter was necessary both for ideological and practical reasons; as socialism was constructed and consolidated, there had to be a material pay-off for to the population; practically some increase in the amount of resources allocated to consumption was necessary to create incentives, and in Eastern Europe in order to maintain social control (Bunce, 1985, pp.8-9).

The combination of investment hunger and pressure to raise levels of consumption meant that some way of compensating for the shortcoming of the property state model had to be found. Reform was one solution. This, however, was complicated and politically difficult, as first Khrushchev and later Gorbachev discovered. In between these efforts at change, it was administratively much easier to develop aspects of rentierism in parallel with the property state. This was administratively easy because of the way that the party-state controlled the articulation of their domestic economy with the global economy (Evangelista, 1996). The centralized nature of foreign trade administration meant that communist states automatically acted as rentier states, no matter what the structure of their trade with the outside world. Revenue from export sales went to the central foreign trade organization, with the government then deciding what to redistribute to producers. The potential for raising revenue through exports was also great because of the state's control over prices. This enabled them to manipulate the domestic costs of production to effectively dump goods on the world market and secure export income. Communist rentierism was very varied, however. There were differences in what was traded, and differences in the forms that rent took, with some state receiving both rent from ownership and substantial rent from aid and subsidies, and differences in security rents. Finally, communist states dealt with the problems caused by rentierism in different ways. These different strategies combined with the different forms that rentierism took created different social pressures and opened them up to different external pressures. In nearly each case, the major dividing line was between the USSR and the rest of the bloc.

The most obvious of these differences were in the rents generated by trade and security. All of the states of Eastern Europe took security rents from the USSR in that they did not pay the full costs of protecting themselves from the external security threat of capitalism. These security rents were generated by accident and design. Eastern European states had no incentive to contribute towards defence, and to structure their collection of revenue accordingly, since the USSR spent in excess of what was necessary to provide for security and because the system of collective security was imposed by the USSR. Moreover, Eastern European states could save on defence expenditure and take rent from the USSR in order to fund domestic consumption to avoid social unrest. They could therefore play off the USSR's contradictory desires for bloc security through military might and bloc security through systemic stability (Eyal, 1992, p.44; Bunce, 1992, p.14).

Differences in trade rents between the USSR and Eastern Europe were equally great. All communist states, by virtue of their ownership of production and control over domestic prices, took rent from foreign trade no matter what the commodities and the value added to them in production. However, there were very great differences in what states took rent on and the contributions of rent to national income. The first difference is that the USSR was a source of rent for Eastern Europe. The extent to which the USSR subsidized its trade with Eastern Europe is contentious, but the USSR began to provide subsidies from sometime in the late 1950s as it charged low prices fro energy exports and allowed its terms of trade with Eastern Europe to deteriorate (Smith, 1992, pp.86-89; Bunce, 1986, p.12). Even when Soviet terms of trade with Eastern Europe improved in the late 1970s as the prices of energy rose, the USSR still charged under world market prices for exports to Eastern Europe (on average about 70-80 per cent of OPEC prices) (Bunce, 1986, p.17).

The second main difference between the USSR and Eastern Europe was in the structure of trade and its importance as a source of rent. These are summarized in

Table 6.2 Exports to the West in 1990 (% of total trade)

Commodity group	USSR	Eastern Europe
Primary Products	23.1	28.5
of which:		
Food	2.4	16.9
Raw materials (excluding fuels)	8.9	5.1
Mineral fuels	56.5	10.7
of which:		
Oil	40.6	5.6
Gas	11.7	0.1
Manufactures	14.4	60.0
Semi-manufactures	9.5	21.4
of which:		
Iron and steel	2.6	7.2
Chemicals	4.4	9.3
Machinery and transport equipment and goods	3.4	13.6
of which:		
Road vehicles	1.6	1.6
Transport equipment	1.0	6.8
Specialized machinery	0.7	4.8
Industrial consumer goods	1.5	25.0
of which		
Textiles	0.4	3.4
Clothing	0.0	9.8

Source: Lavigne (1999, p.85)

Table 6.3 Exports and national income under central planning (%)

	USSR	Bulgaria	Hungary	Poland	Romania	Czechoslovakia
1967	3.9	28	40	20	17	30
1980	8	40	54	31	27	29
1986	8	42	58	32	20	32

Source: adapted from Lavigne (1991, p.14)

Tables 6.2 and 6.3. The USSR's external trade was relatively uniform in that the bulk of its exports were and export revenue derived from the sale of energy abroad. As we saw in Chapter 1, the USSR had traded raw materials, particularly oil, for foreign currency revenue almost from its inception, but the extent of this trade was small until the 1970s. Then, as trade between the USSR and the outside world grew spectacularly, the USSR took advantage of high oil prices after 1973 to reap huge profits, using this money to fund consumption rises and cushion industry from change. Trade between Eastern Europe and market economies played the same function, but was of a very different structure, magnitude and impact. As with the USSR, the extent to which eastern European states traded outside of the communist bloc increased in general from the 1960s onwards. This was in part inspired by the USSR, which wanted to decrease the costs to its economy of subsidizing the economic systems of Eastern Europe. As Table 6.3 shows, the amount contributed to national income by exports rose significantly across the region in the 1970s, but with a marked difference between the USSR and Eastern Europe in terms of its contribution to national income (see also Collins and Rodrik, 1992, pp.31-3). The structure of trade was very different to that between the USSR and industrialized market economies. As Table 6.2 shows, the spread of traded goods was much broader in Eastern Europe, although with intra-regional variation, than for the USSR. Hungary, Czechoslovakia and Poland had relatively diverse trade structures, with a balance between the exports of consumer, machinery, raw materials and semi-manufactures, and agricultural goods. Bulgaria and Romania were more similar to the USSR in that their export trade outside the socialist bloc was more dependent on primary goods and was relatively uniform in structure.[2] As a result, the degree to which their economies were penetrated by external economic forces was more limited. Overall, however, the impact of foreign trade on Eastern Europe was much greater than it was in the USSR, as Table 6.3 shows. This combined with the structure of commodities traded, made Eastern European economies far more vulnerable to changes in world markets. Although they spread the risk far more than the USSR did with its energy dependent trade, the terms of trade for Eastern European states were much worse than for the USSR in the late 1970s. Economic downturn in the West after 1973 and the rise in oil prices meant that the USSR's terms of trade improved by over 100 per cent between 1974 and 1980, whereas for Eastern Europe they deteriorated by 20-25 per cent (Lavigne, 1991, p.41).

The centrality of exports to national income in Eastern Europe and the decline in the terms of trade in the 1970s exacerbated the systemic tendency for trade between communist and capitalist states to lead to the former's indebtedness because of the low quality of production in communist states and the hunger for imports caused by investment shortages (Kornai, 1992, pp.349-50). As the terms of trade declined, trade rents were increasingly buttressed by loans from capitalist states. The growth of loans was rapid in the 1970s, rising from US$6.5 billion in 1970 to US$88.1 billion in 1981 (Bunce, 1985, p.38). The spread of the debt burden was very uneven as can be seen in Table 6.4, with Hungary and Poland particularly hard hit. The USSR's foreign debt also grew rapidly during this period, but proportionately it was much less than the debt of nearly all the Eastern

Table 6.4 East European debt

	Net debt[a]		Debt-service ratio[b]	
	1982	1989	1981	1989
Bulgaria	3,912	7,957	21	48
Czechoslovakia	4,097	5,724	17	23
Hungary	10,344	18,015	42	49
Poland	27,033	35,890	163	76
Romania	9,581	-1,254	36	19

[a] US$ millions at 1989 exchange rate
[b] Debt-service ratio: all interest and amortization on medium and long-term debt as a percentage of one year's exports

Source: Baylis (1994, pp.251-22)

Table 6.5 Property/rentier state mixes

Property/rentier state mix	Characteristics
High	Predominately high ratio of exports to national income; high debt and debt-service ratio; high penetration of economy by rentierist elements through export trade diversity.
Medium	Mixture of high and low ratio of exports to national income; debt and debt-service ratio; penetration of economy by rentierist elements through export trade diversity.
Low	Predominately low ratio exports to national income; low debt and debt-service ratio; low penetration of economy by rentierist elements due to limited export trade diversity.

European states through the period, and was actually a smaller amount than Poland's debt (Lavigne, 1991, p.344). As Table 6.4 shows, debts for the most part continued to grow in the 1980s, and ability to service debt declined as debt-service ratios grew. Again, the USSR bucked the trend, its debt-service ratio being below 5 per cent for the period (Lavigne, 1991, p.328).

The forms of external rent taken across the communist world to shore up their economic systems were thus very different. Differences in how rentierism developed was linked to the different strategies that emerged for dealing with its problems. In some cases, strategy and the development of rentierism went more or less hand in hand; the development of relative economic liberalism in Hungary from the late 1960s and the expansion of its trade and debt over the course of the

Table 6.6 Property/rentier state mixes at the end of communism

	Export/ national income ratio	Debt	Debt-service ratio	Rentierist penetration of economy through export trade structure	Property/rentier state mix
Bulgaria	High	Low	High	Low	Medium
Czechoslovakia	High	Low	Low	High	Medium
Hungary	High	High	High	High	High
Poland	High	High	High	High	High
Romania	Low	Low	Low	Low	Low
USSR	Low	Low	Low	Low	Low

1970s would be a case in point. In other cases, strategy developed haphazardly, as in Romania where loan rents were foregone in favour of trade rents that could reduce debt, albeit at the cost of domestic consumption in the 1980s. The mix of strategies that emerged complicates the nature of the property/rentier mix in Eastern Europe as communism moved to its terminal stage in the late 1980s since it created different foreign trade regimes in the region, with some states moving toward decentralization. However, we can classify the property/rentier state mix in across the region by comparing the degree to which rentierism had become a vital part of the economic systems of the states of Eastern Europe. This classificatory schema is laid out in Table 6.5. The property/rentier state mix can be high, medium or low, according to the balance between the ratio of exports to national income, debt and debt-service ratio, and the degree to which the economy was penetrated by the global economy though a state's possessing a relatively diverse and balanced commodity export structure.[3]

How states in the region actually mixed the two ideal-type forms is listed in Table 6.6. The USSR and Romania had a low mix of rentier and property state forms, with relatively uniform sectoral exports that insured that the degree to which their economies were penetrated by rentierist elements was insignificant. Poland and Hungary, with their high levels of debt, debt-service, exports to national-income ratio and decentralized foreign trade regimes were at the other end of the spectrum and had diverse and relatively balanced foreign trade commodity structure that insured a wide domestic interaction with the global economy. Bulgaria also had a high degree of rentierism, but without the support of a diverse and relatively balanced foreign trade commodity structure so that although it demonstrated high rentierist elements its domestic economy was relatively isolated from global influences. Czechoslovakia mixed elements of both property and rentier forms, but unlike Bulgaria, this was more balanced by its more diverse and even sectoral trade patterns.

There is not space here to go through the various ways in which the different patterns of interaction with the global economy and property/rentier state mixes

Table 6.7 Property/rentier state mixes at the end of communism and initial post-communist economic performance to mid-1995

Property/rentier mix and trade structure	EBRD reform indicator average[a]	EBRD measure of trade and foreign exchange liberalization[a]	Private sector share of GDP (%)
Low and uniform			
Russia	2.55	3	55
CIS average	1.97	2.6	27
Romania	2.44	5	40
Medium and uniform			
Bulgaria	2.55	4	45
Medium and diverse			
Czech Republic	3.66	5	70
Slovakia	3.44	5	60
High and diverse			
Hungary	3.66	5	60
Poland	3.55	5	60

[a] Scale of 1 to 5, with 5 as the highest

Source: calculated from EBRD, (1995, p.11)

worked themselves out case by case. We can see, however, the basic outcomes that they helped to generate. A high or medium mixture mix of rentierism with property state forms was not in and of itself enough to guarantee a more rapid movement towards reform. Although rentierism was important in breaking down the property state, it was only effective as a support for reform where there was a diverse set of sectors involved in exports so that there was penetration of the domestic economy across a broad front. Czechoslovakia was thus in a better position than Bulgaria. Bulgaria, due to the low degree to which it was actually penetrated by rentierist elements, had more in common with Romania. The transition was much smoother in Bulgaria, where the property state form was more compromised, than in Romania, where it was stronger, but both had relatively uniform sectoral export structures so that collapse was not followed by rapid reform progress. Poland and Hungary, and the more penetrated Czechoslovakia were thus in the best position to implement reforms, whilst the Soviet successor states and Romania had less to support a reform drive.

The overall patterns of economic change can be seen in Tables 6.7 and 6.8. Table 6.7 shows how a high rentier/property state mix, or a medium mix with a diverse trade structure eased the path of reform in the first years of transition (until mid-1995 in table 6.7). Poland, Hungary, and the Czechoslovak successor states scored more highly on reform indicators such as the European Bank for Reconstruction and Development measures reported in Table 6.7, were more open and privatized than states with low property/rentier mixes, or low penetration by

Table 6.8 Post-communist government balances (% of GDP)

Property/rentier mix and trade structure	1990	1991	1992	1993	1994	2000
Low						
Armenia			-37.6	-48.2	-16.1	-6.3
Azerbaijan			2.8	-13.0	-18.0	-0.6
Belarus			-1.6	-8.3	-1.5	0.3
Georgia			-3.0	-28.0	-34.0	-4.1
Kazakhstan			-7.3	-1.2	-6.5	-1.0
Kyrgyzstan			-17.4	-13.5	-8.4	-9.6
Moldova			-23.4	-8.8	-8.0	-2.6
Romania	na	-1.9	-4.4			-3.7
Russia			-31.0	-18.8	-7.6	3.0
Tajikistan			-29.9	-24.7	-6.4	-0.6
Turkmenistan			13.2	-0.5	-1.1	0.4
Ukraine			-30.4	-10.1	-8.6	-1.3
Uzbekistan			-12.0	-20.0	-2.0	-1.2
Medium and uniform						
Bulgaria	-12.8	-14.7	-15.0			-1.0
Medium and diverse						
Czechoslovakia	0.1	-2.0	-3.3			
Czech Rep						-4.2
Slovakia						-3.6
High and diverse						
Hungary	0.5	-2.2	-5.6			-3.3
Poland	3.1	-6.5	-6.7			-3.2

Sources: EBRD (1995, pp.188-211); EBRD (2002, pp.117-217)

rentierism. In Russia, the CIS, Romania and Bulgaria, with their low mixes, or weak penetration by rentierism, progress towards reform was slower, although the latter two states opened up their economies more speedily than Russia and the CIS. Constructing a tax state requires a broad array of reforms to be implemented in both the economy and the political system. However, we can get some idea of the success in moving from one state form to another by looking at the general stability of government finances, which with some caveats can be taken as a proxy measure of progress towards the tax state ideal. Table 6.8 shows progress towards stabilization of government finances. Where the property/rentier mix was low, or was medium but with little depth, government finances suffered greater deficits in the early years of reform (1990-1992 in Eastern Europe, 1992-1994 in the CIS), than they did where there was a high property/rentier mix, or where the mix was medium but deep. In the latter cases, state finances have been relatively steady, with moderate deficits across the reform years. The absence of great shocks despite the experience of transitional recession highlights the ability of these states to take resources relatively effectively despite change in the economic system. Elsewhere, however, the picture is very mixed. States that had energy resources suffered less than states that had a weaker resource base. Hence, Romania fares better Bulgaria, Kazakhstan and Azerbaijan better than Armenia, Georgia and Tajikistan. In certain cases, at the end of the 1990s, government balances were even positive where the price of energy boosted economies (as in Russia, see Chapter 2). This does not signify that there has been progress, however, but that these states have been able to control energy rents in new rentier forms that have pushed aside remnants of the old property state form without giving birth to new tax state forms.

Patterns of post-Soviet rentierism

The acceleration of economic crisis under Gorbachev increased Soviet interaction with the global economy, but they did not touch the economy of the post-Soviet state uniformly. As oil prices fell in the late 1980s and import prices remained stable, the central state budget was heavily squeezed. The Soviet state was running a yearly budget deficit of about 9 per cent of GDP in the late 1980s (EIU, 1991, p.37). Foreign borrowing –'chaotic and large-scale' during this period – covered some of the central state's revenue shortfall as the USSR's short-term foreign debt doubled between the end of 1987 and the end of 1989 alone (Lushin and Oppenheimer, 2001, p.288; IMF et al, 1991a, p.40). Gorbachev further tried to alleviate crisis by opening up the Soviet economy, but as we saw in Chapter 1, the results were not impressive. These reforms did not fundamentally alter the property/rentier mix, therefore, and as a result, there were no powerful new incentives structures that might have strengthened pressure for change from either below or from within the state. Post-Soviet leaders were not faced with the same external and internal constraints as their counterparts in Eastern Europe. There was only weak involvement of outside parties, whether international financial agencies or private economic actors in the USSR at the start of the post-communist period.

In the absence of strong pressures to change, the most powerful incentives were to insure continuity. There were exceptions to this for some state actors, most notably the Russian effort at reform in 1992. This exception proves the rule, however. Russia's drive towards the market through shock therapy was a response to the weakness of the Yeltsin government in the face of domestic economic forces and an effort at reconnecting with the global economy to balance out domestic producers' power (see Chapter 2). The failure of this dash to the market, and the subsequent reconciliation of the Russian government with a part of the economic elite and transfer of energy resources to them, showed that there was not a domestic constituency in the Russia large enough to support market reform in the first instance. Moreover, exogenous economic agents, private and supra-governmental, did not have the same amount of leverage on the Russian government that they had elsewhere, especially since Russia was able to secure resources from the international community for foreign policy reasons (Stone, 2002).

Outside of Russia, insuring continuity was less controversial from the onset of independence. Independence, and the consequent fragmentation of the old Soviet

Table 6.9 Energy exports and rents, 2000

	Oil and gas export as % of total exports	Oil and gas export as % of GDP	Oil and gas as % of total government revenue	FDI in oil and gas as % of total FDI	Energy rents 1992-2000 as % of GDP
Azerbaijan	85.2	30.5	36.2	80.5	50.2
Kazakhstan	46.8	24.7	27.5	69.7	20.9
Russia	50.4	21.5	30.1	10.7	26.0
Turkmenistan	81	69.7	42.0		44.4
Uzbekistan	12.3	4.3	14.8		39.5

Source: Esanov et al (2001, pp.4, 5)

pattern of interaction with the world economy, meant that insuring continuity was going to be difficult, however. The collapse of the system for redistributing the USSR's trade rents was not accompanied by end of the requirement to channel resources to society. Unlike model rentier states, the new rulers of the CIS could not buy-off their populations through low tax policies coupled with selective distribution of resources in the form of patronage to elites. Social peace was not maintained by the state standing apart from private economic activity and taking little form it in the way of tax, but through the state providing basic welfare. Post-Soviet rulers thus had a difficult balancing act to achieve if they were to buy-off both elites and their populations. To achieve this they consolidated aspects of the communist rentier state model, albeit with new regional variations.

The chief variation has been in the depth to which rentierism has taken hold and the degree to which it has structured government. The first divide is between those states that have complex economies and are not reliant on one or two key imports, and those states that are more classic rentiers in their dependence on energy and primary product sales. The latter have developed patrimonial and personalistic regimes to a greater extent than the former. Energy rents have been the main source of patrimonial and personalistic power, although in some states, most notably Turkmenistan and Uzbekistan, considerable rents have accrued from cotton as well, or from other forms of mineral wealth such as gold in Kyrgyzstan. States where energy rents have played a significant role are listed in table 6.9. There is obviously a high degree of variance between the extents that energy sales contribute rent across the CIS. In Azerbaijan, Turkmenistan and Uzbekistan, energy rents have been very high as a proportion of GDP. In Azerbaijan and Turkmenistan, these rents have gone to government directly and then been redistributed (sometimes). In Uzbekistan, where large rents were also available from the cotton sector, they have been used to give subsidies to consumers, rather than accumulated as direct revenue flows to the state. Kazakhstan has taken revenue less from exports, but has compensated by allowing large FDI inflows into the energy sector. This strategy, shared by Azerbaijan, was a response to political threats, particularly regional divisions, and a lack of alternative rent sources. In order to quell potential threats and stimulate a rapid inflow of some resources from the one rent source that they had, Kazakhstan and Azerbaijan privatized their energy sectors to create short-term rent flows that could more immediately be used for patronage (Jones Luong and Weinthal, 2001).

No matter how rent has been taken, the effect, roughly, has been the same: personalistic regimes have developed based on patrimonial power. The extent of personalistic regime development has varied. Where there has been more state control and less privatization, the degree of authoritarianism has been more extensive. This pattern has produced authoritarian regimes in Uzbekistan and Turkmenistan, whilst the opening up of the economy and competition over resources has produced illiberal, but not fully authoritarian, regimes in Azerbaijan and Kazakhstan.[4] Case by case, how rents have been used to buy-off opposition has varied. Uzbekistan, Turkmenistan and Kazakhstan have cushioned their populations against GDP falls. The estimated GDP ratios in 2001 compared to 1989 of in the three states was respectively 105, 96 and 84 per cent; the CIS average is 64 per cent (EBRD, 2002, p.58). Azerbaijan, on the other hand, has not cushioned its population in general from falling GDP, but has channelled the money to economic elites by keeping enterprises profitable, despite high falls in production; it has one of the lowest rates of enterprise unprofitability in the CIS, second only to Uzbekistan (Statkomitet SNG, 2002, p.215).

Some small energy rents have accrued to other post-Soviet states, in particular through control over pipelines and transport routes. However, these generally make only a minor contribution to state budgets. More important in the absence of great mineral wealth or saleable commodities, have been the perpetuation of elements of rentierism by resource transfer from Russia in the form of security rents and subsidies.

Russia's role as regional hegemon in place of the USSR makes it a source of security rent. The ability to take this rent is not universal in that Russian military involvement in some parts of the CIS is far from benign (Georgia, for example). The system of security rents is not institutionalized in the same way that it was for the Warsaw pact. The CIS collective security arrangements have been far less successful or extensive than the old alliance system with the outer empire. However, post-Soviet states have benefited from, first, guarantees about the stability of borders made as the USSR collapsed between the new partner states of the CIS, and second, from security cover and bilateral treaties with Moscow. Sometimes these arrangements have been explicit, as with the Russian presence in Tajikistan, the CIS agreements on collective security and peacekeeping, or the bilateral agreements with Belarus or Kyrgyzstan enabling Russian military use of facilities. However, even where there were no formal agreements, many post-Soviet states rested under Russia's security cover because Russia has continued to be a regional hegemon sufficiently strong to prevent threats from other states, if not from small-scale insurgency. The extent of security rents, and what there removal might mean, is hard to gauge. However, elsewhere in the world the *de jure* recognition of statehood independent of a state's ability to defend its sovereign status has clearly been related to a decline in economic regulation by elites. Where there is no military imperative to accumulate resources, elites are able to deploy rents that they control to private ends and need not involve themselves in developing other resource streams (Bates, 2001). Security rents therefore magnify the effect of rentierism and make its demise less likely.

Subsidies have taken various forms. A one off subsidy was the gradual Russian shouldering of the USSR's external debts. These had been shared out by CIS states in March 1992, but Russia took over responsibility for the debt to secure political goals in the CIS over the next few years. Like Eastern Europe before them, Russia's energy exports to the CIS were heavily discounted. Energy exports consistently make up 40-50 per cent of Russian exports to the post-Soviet space (Goskomstat, 2000, pp.582, 587). In the first years after independence, they achieved only 30-40 per cent of the world market price. The net result was a loss to Russia of about 12 per cent of GDP. Russian subsidies in total amounted (at the lowest estimate) to 50 per cent of CIS countries' GDP and cost US$17 billion (the highest estimate was US$67 billion). Further subsidies came through the rouble zone and bank credits from the Russian Central Bank. These were very significant, ranging from 90 per cent of GDP in the case of Tajikistan to 10 per cent of GDP in Belarus (*Ekonomika i zhizn'*, 1996, 16, p.1; Åslund, 1995, p.123; van Selm, 1997, pp.108-10). Subsidies have not been provided as smoothly overtime to all post-Soviet states as they were to Eastern Europe due to breakdowns in relations and crisis in the Russian economy, and as the Russian government tightened the emission of credit to other CIS states through the Russian Central Bank. As some forms of subsidy have declined, post-Soviet states have replaced them with transfers from foreign lenders. This has lead to a massive build-up of debt as on average, external debt as a percentage of GDP and relative to exports has doubled in the post-Soviet states, especially since 1994 and the decline in resource transfers from Russia (EBRD, 2002). These debts have grown up as the decline in intra-regional trade has been replaced by imports from the west. States' capacity to maintain this trade is, however, itself dependent on subsidy from abroad in the form of cheap energy imports from Russia. The cheapness of energy inputs and unpaid bills enable foreign trade and its taxation. Ukraine, for example, owed Russia some $3.5 billion in trade debt by February 2000, with most of this outstanding amount being owed for gas imports. This unpaid fuel bill is a major factor that enables Ukraine to continue trading with the rest of the world: if fuel costs were paid, many Ukrainian exports would become uneconomic and unsaleable (von Zon, 2000, pp.113, 117). Although the Ukrainian state is not efficient at taxing trade, it does raise revenue from exports, particularly through licences and the arms trade. To an extent then, Ukrainian, and other states', ability to take tax from foreign trade results from Russian support, and as we saw in Chapter 5, they have put policies in place to extract resources to fund public works. This, of course, is not dissimilar to the position that Eastern European states were in before 1989.

Only one state, Belarus, has been able to use both security and trade subsidies to buffer its population to a great degree against the economic downturn associated with transformation from the property state model. It was able to do this because of the degree to which its economy, in particular its military industrial complexes, was integrated with the Russian economy before 1991. Belarus has maintained its trade links with the CIS and in particular Russia; 60 per cent of Belarus's exports were to the CIS in 2000, compared with an average for the whole CIS of 34 per cent; 89 per cent of these exports went to Russia. The bulk of Belarus's imports came from the CIS and Russia too (Statkomitet SNG, 2000, pp.70-1). This has helped Belarus maintain one of the few positive balance of payments amongst non-energy producing post-Soviet states. This has helped to keep its GDP high relative to the communist period and the energy producing states; in 2001 estimated real GDP was 91 per cent of 1989 real GDP, against the CIS average of 64 per cent (EBRD 2002, 58). This has also meant that Belarus has been one of the few states not to witness a massive build-up of foreign debt (see also Chapter 4).

There has therefore been great variance between both energy dependent and non-dependent states. There has been a tendency for resources to strengthen patrimonialism, but this need not be the case (as Belarus, where trade stands in for resources, demonstrates). Most non-energy dependent economies have been able to preserve some aspect of rentierism sufficient to keep the social peace, avoid harsh reform decisions and maintain some degree of elite continuity, but, like Eastern Europe before them have done so in large part thanks to the transfer of resources to them from Russia. The difference this time is that the source of rent, Russia, is not markedly different in the form that its relationship to the global economy takes than some other states. Although Russia has significant energy rents, these are not fully under the state's control and as a result, they cannot be used to hold old patterns of rentierism and patrimonial politics in place over the longer term. The reason for this is the way in which Russia privatized its energy industries and allowed private rent seekers to replace the state as the beneficiary of export rents. This was done in response to the failure of the first round of reform. As we saw in Chapter 2, this failure meant that Russia was left with an unreformed industrial sector and a growing budget deficit that could not be funded by energy rents alone, especially as pressure from below was undermining tax gathering and perpetuating subsidies to industry. The only way out of this for the government in the short-term was to trade control over oil rents from banks in the form of direct loans and short-term debt issues. Russia's considerable energy rents were not, as a result, directly under the control of the state in the 1990s, even though the revenue that it took from oil sales grew at the very end of the decade as the price of oil rose. This is still a long way from the tax state ideal, but it at least shows the hopeful sign that rentierism has not so far stabilized in Russia to the same extent that it has elsewhere in the FSU, even if the state has become more dependent on energy revenues, and is seeking to increase its share of them.

Conclusion

Patterns of change have been very different between Eastern Euope and the CIS and these differences are rooted in the past, in the way that there were seeds for change under communism in Eastern Europe that were missing in the USSR. Relations to the global economy were important to this process since they changed aspects of the classic communist state and created constituencies for change across the state/society divide. This was uneven and far from complete by the time that communism collapsed in Eastern Europe, but it gave governments resources that they did not have in the CIS and created incentives for economic actors to co-operate with reform, even if it was not in their short-term interest. Incentives and resources for change have continued to be missing in parts of the USSR, although this is not uniform. Where they have been missing continuity in elites and anti-democratic government has often been based on the intensification of rentierism at the cost of development. Some resource rich states may be able to sustain this pattern for a long time. However, the weakness of rentierism in other states, like Ukraine, means that they are likely to be prone to crisis, or held hostage to Russia's ability to provide subsidies and security rents. They lack the resources to ride crisis out without help from Russia, import crisis from Russia, and at the same time do not have the means to foster development and break their dependency. Russia itself, whilst displaying some elements of rentierism, has a diverse structure of ownership in the energy sector that has helped to remove part of the potential for rent from politicians' hands. This has not yet created something approaching the tax state model, but it has at least raised the political costs of moving toward rentierism in Russia, and this, together with its fragile political system and electoral cycle, have helped to keep it a low-level functioning democracy, although not a consolidated or secure one. Given Russia, and the region's past and sometimes present, this represents progress of a sort.

Notes

1   On these see Hellman (1998); Robinson (2002).
2   The structure of east European trade is difficult to compare since different national agencies used different categories. However, the statistics are indicative of certain essential differences between states with trade uniformity and states with trade diversity. Hungary's exports to developed states were evenly divided between machinery (27.1 per cent), raw materials and semi-manufactures (33.8 per cent), consumer goods (16.1per cent), food and agricultural products (20.7 per cent). Czechoslovakia's exports to non-socialist states were likewise evenly divided between machinery (23.8 percent), fuels, minerals and metals (20.3 per cent), chemicals (13.5 per cent), raw materials and semi-manufactures (33.8 per cent), consumer goods (20.3) and food and agricultural products (8.2 per cent). Poland demonstrated the most diversity with fuel and energy accounting for 13.8 per cent of exports to developed states, metallurgy 12.2 per cent, engineering 23.0 per cent, chemicals 11.5 per cent, light industrial goods 8.1 per cent, processed food 12.9 per cent and agricultural products 6.5 per cent. Romania and Bulgaria on the other hand displayed less diversity. Romania's commodity structure of convertible currency trade was dominated by fuels, minerals and metals, which accounted for 47.8 pr cent of export trade; the same sector accounted for 36.8 per cent of Bulgaria's trade to developed states, with a further 19.6 per cent accounted for by raw materials and agricultural products. Romania and Bulgaria therefore show a degree of uniformity in the commodity structure of their trade in comparison to the other CEE states. All figures are for 1988, except

for Bulgaria, where the figures are for 1990. Sources are EIU country profiles, 1990-1991 and OECD (1992).

3   Security rents and trade subsidies are left out since they were imposed and uniform, and they predated the evolution of the communist state in most of the area.

4   For a fuller analysis of regime types in Central Asia, see Ishiyama (2002).

Chapter 7

From 'Transition' to Dependent Development:
The New Periphery in Global Financial Capitalism

Anastasia Nesvetailova

Introduction

In 2004, several of the formerly socialist economies – the Czech Republic, Slovenia, Poland, Hungary, Lithuania, Estonia and Latvia – are to join the European Union (EU). A decade after the fall of the Berlin Wall, the international community already acknowledges these states as competitive democracies; and their economic systems are classified as market economies. By 1998, official measured GDP in Central and Eastern Europe (CEE), had bounced back from a transition recession, recovered its 1990 level, and exceeded that level by 6 per cent in 2000. Such results stand in sharp contrast to the decade of 'transition' in the other part of the former communist bloc, the Commonwealth of Independent States (CIS). GDP in 2000 in the CIS stood only at 63 per cent of its 1990 level. While in Poland – the most populous country of the former socialist region – GDP increased by more than 40 per cent between 1990 and 1999, it shrank by 40 per cent during the same period in the Russian Federation, the most populous country in the CIS (World Bank, 2002b).

On 29 May 2002, the president of the European Commission officially announced Russia's status as a 'market economy'. However, this step is considered by most analysts as little more than a symbolic gesture rewarding President Putin's attempts to cooperate with the West following 11 September 2001; or EU's ambition to steal a political march over the USA (*Financial Times*, 31 May 2002). The political, economic and social crises that have overwhelmed the successor republics of the USSR persist, and despite Russia's post-crisis economic recovery, much of the country's problems remain unsolved. Spectacular economic growth in 2000-2003, averaging 4-5 per cent per year, is mostly accounted for by the devaluation of the rouble after the financial crisis of 1998 (see Chapter 2). In addition, boosted oil revenues, thanks to high world oil prices, provided Russia with large current account earnings. Yet at the same time, the country still faces deep-rooted structural and institutional problems: arrears and indebtedness in the industrial sector, capital flight out of the country, lack of investment funds, social polarization and income diversification, and notorious multi-level corruption.

In the studies of post-communism, the contrast between the CEE states and Russia (and CIS generally) is typically examined within a transition paradigm of neo-classical economics. The policies of liberalization and democratization, or 'shock therapy', if implemented correctly and prudently, were supposed to transform formerly planned economies into modern, competitive market democracies and thus ensure their integration into the international economic system. Once domestic politico-economic restructuring is secured, foreign capital would direct funds into the new economies, promoting their growth and international competitiveness. The record of the CEE states in this process is the best demonstration that such policy approaches, authored mainly by the IMF, the World Bank and the EBRD, are feasible, workable and efficient. Accordingly, economic orthodoxy explains the failure of Russia and other 'lagging reformers' on the road to 'transition' in terms of government inefficiency, lack of political determination in introducing the policies of 'shock therapy' and producing social consensus on the reform course.

This chapter contests such 'transitology' explanations. Focusing on the divide between CEE economies and Russia, the chapter raises the following questions. What was the real role of Western capital in the economic restructuring of post-communist economies? Did Western financial interests differentiate between the sub-regions of post-communist, and can this explain the divergent outcomes of 'transition'? What role did national politico-economic and social factors play in mapping the future of post-communism? Finally, the chapter inquires into the type of capitalism that is emerging out of the former socialist terrain. Is the new system a replica of the Anglo-Saxon market-driven capitalism, as shock therapy initially envisaged? Can it be classified as an 'Eastern European' model of political economy, heavily influenced by the path-dependency on the command system? If so, could such a model represent essential politico-economic changes in both CEE and CIS economies, or do they differentiate significantly between sub-regions and countries?

Accordingly, the chapter is organized into three parts. The first section critically examines mainstream approaches to 'transition', and in particular, the role of international capital in the economic restructuring. It analyses the impact of foreign investment in Russia and CEE, demonstrating the discrepancy in western capital's engagement in the EU accession countries and Russia. The section reviews conflicting theories of the role of foreign investment in development, and points out that in both sub-regions of post-communism, the exposure to capital inflows has produced contradictory results. For Russia, a heavy reliance on foreign portfolio inflows in financing the budget deficit has resulted in the financial crisis of 1998, and the long-term deprivation of the productive sector. CEE, in contrast, typically has been attracting the bulk of strategic, long-term foreign direct investments (FDI) into the region. However, as this chapter demonstrates, despite the impressive presence of transnational capital in Eastern Europe, much of the initial promises of international integration through foreign assistance have mutated into divergent and place-specific, but ultimately destructive politico-economic outcomes.

Therefore, the second part of the chapter challenges mainstream neo-liberal approaches to post-communism, by revealing the diversity and attendant problems of inequality and social polarization across the post-Communist region. Here, the chapter concentrates on the dynamics of global capitalist transformations generally, and analyses their impact on the change in CEE and Russia. It provides a comparative analysis of the nexus between the transformed logic of global capital accumulation, and national politico-economic and social transformations in the countries of CEE and Russia. The third section continues this line of inquiry and addresses the issues of the genesis of capitalism in the post-communist region. It is argued that today, the pressures of global financial capitalism constitute a new phase of core-periphery contradictions in the social geography of capital accumulation. The chapter shows that there are two conflicting tendencies of the current wave of economic globalization – fragmentation and integration – that are shaping the future of the post-communism. Certain locales of post-communism, through socio-economic and political linkages to the core financial capital are being incorporated into the global economy. While the rest of the populations are thrown backwards to the position of either economic exploitation, or mere irrelevance.

'Transition' and the role of foreign capital in Central Eastern Europe and Russia

Despite the magnitude of recent financial upheavals in the emerging market economies, there has been no systematic attempt in the studies of 'transitions' to analyze the impact of the global political economy on change. From the perspectives of transitology, the impact of foreign economic factors is mediated by, and largely is regarded as secondary to, stable institutional architectures and domestic political stability (Robinson, 1998, pp.531-32). In these interpretations, it is often argued that in many respects, formerly planned economies already contained some market elements in their infrastructures. A whole series of economic institutions and mechanisms such as firms, prices, trade, banks existed in both socialism and capitalism. It is this resemblance that leads many to believe that by introducing new rules and procedures, a new regulatory regime for financial organizations, and recasting the functions of old institutions should be relatively straightforward. Such economic approaches tend to share the assumption that the success of transition is a matter of introducing, possibly by different means, and at different speeds, the right rules of the game and getting economic actors to behave accordingly (Pop, 2001). Thus, the scrupulous following of the main principles of the transition paradigm – liberalization, privatization and democratization, or what is known as the Washington consensus – was supposed to bring formerly socialist economies to greater freedom, and therefore economic growth and development. Indeed it seems, those countries that have been abiding by the new rules – Poland, Hungary, and the Czech Republic – have succeeded in transforming their economic systems; while Russia along with most of the CIS – countries with notoriously unreliable governments – have failed rather painfully.

For the prudent reformers of CEE, a vital factor securing transition progress has been the proximity to the European Union. As the IMF argues, the major reason for the greater determination and consistency with which the EU accession countries approached the structural reforms is explained by their underlying historical affinity to Western Europe and – with central planning introduced only in the late 1940s – a necessary understanding of the market-based economy. The resulting resolve to embrace the necessary structural change, and the positive incentive of joining the EU, accelerated the reform process and helped to prevent opposing coalitions from forming and obstructing it (IMF, 2002, p.119). In particular, proximity to Western Europe is typically associated with more favourable initial conditions: the imprint of central planning in CEE countries was relatively limited, while rapid reorientation of trade to more stable EU markets reduced these countries' exposure to external shocks caused by declining trade with the CMEA. The consequent favourable output performance was generally linked to more ambitious structural and institutional reforms, which in part are a result of moves toward accession to the European Union. Altogether, IMF empirical research suggests that the divergent performance of CEE states and Russia can be explained in terms of four main factors: difference in inherited economic structures; political developments – including civil strife and war in some countries in South-Eastern Europe and the CIS; reform strategies, and macroeconomic policies. But, IMF analysts admit, the close correlation between geographic location, initial conditions and policies complicates the assessment of the role each of these factors played in determining outcomes (IMF, 2002, p.91).

As most transitologists maintain, once domestic politico-economic restructuring is secured, the country would successfully compete for its share of global financial flows, investment and trade. Generally, the levels of foreign capital inflows measure a country's international economic ratings and investor confidence. In neo-classical growth theory, foreign investment is a powerful source of modernization. Foreign direct investment in particular is believed to have been the chief impetus determining the path of economic trajectories for the former socialist region. However, opponents of the economic orthodoxy, namely dependency theorists, argue that quite often the interests of transnational capital can cause a 'development of underdevelopment' in the host country. The negative effects of foreign capital inflows are primarily associated with portfolio flows. Short-term and speculative by nature, they have a great potential to de-stabilize the country's economic situation, transmitting financial contagion from other regions, provoking attacks on fragile national banking systems, currency and stock markets, thus ensuing an economic crisis. But strategic and long-term foreign investments can also have serious negative side-affects (see Table 7.1). The contradictory views on the role of foreign capital are reflected in conflicting theoretical positions, and are documented by empirical studies in emerging economies (King and Varadi, 2002, pp.5-7; Gowan, 1995 and 1996).

Table 7.1 The contradictory theoretical expectations of the impact of FDI on the host economy

	Dependency Theory	Modernization Theory/ Neoclassical Economics
Effect on the amount of investment capital	Sucks out capital that could be used for investment through: • repatriation of profits; • crowding out local borrowers	Adds investment capital through: • direct investment from foreign company; • providing access to western banks
Effects on labour productivity	Reduces labour productivity: • utilizes low value added labour; • eliminates local R&D capacity	Raises labour productivity through: • increasing skill levels via training and demonstration; • better utilization of labour through Western management techniques; • technology transfer; • driving inefficient firms out of business thereby freeing up resources for more efficient producers
Effects on level of competition	Reduces competition by: • preserving and/or creating monopolies and oligopolies; • too strong (and unfair) competition which kills domestic producers	Increases competition by: • creating new market actors
Effects on domestic productive capacity	Reduces domestic capacity by: • 'purchasing markets'; • substituting foreign suppliers for domestic suppliers	Increases domestic capacity through: • increasing demand for local suppliers • increasing demand by providing access to western markets; • increasing demand by creating high-paid jobs

Source: King and Varadi (2002)

In the countries of the former socialist bloc, foreign investment has a mixed history. Evidence most consistent with modernization view of foreign capital has been found mainly in the creation of small joint ventures in Central and Eastern

Table 7.2 Main recipients of FDI, 1992-1999

	1992-95		1996-99	
	US $ mln	% of GDP	US $ mln	% of GDP
CEE	21,091	0.5	50,558	3.3
Czech Republic	4,821	2.9	10,104	4.6
Estonia	647	3.9	1,050	5.2
Hungary	9,399	5.7	6,979	3.8
Poland	2,540	0.6	17,096	2.9
CIS	8,272	1.0	22,001	2.5
Azerbaijan	237	4.2	3,222	20.9
Kazakhstan	2,357	2.7	4,971	6.4
Russia	3,965	0.3	8,412	0.7
Turkmenistan	427	3.5	334	3.0

Source: World Bank (2002b, p.7).

Europe. Newly created businesses provide better income, create jobs and contribute to the economic growth. Also, new owners are keen to learn new methods of production and marketing, associating with 'Western' way of doing things and 'entrepreneurial' values. The effects of larger-scale strategic investments are more contradictory. The Visegrad countries have attracted the bulk of FDI inflows into the whole region (see Table 7.2). During the early transition years, Hungary has received most of the FDI inflows. Over the last four years, the Czech Republic has attracted the highest FDI per capita in the region, and it now has a larger stock than Hungary (Table 7.3). But newly created productive facilities are not evenly spread across recipient economies. In Hungary, for instance, greenfield investments usually locate in the developed western and central parts of the country, especially in the capital and along the Austrian border, thereby exacerbating regional inequalities. Moreover, transnational giants disrupt or weaken social and cultural cohesion of many CEE countries, typically representing a strong Americanizing influence on lifestyles. Shopping malls, fast food, and anti-union attitudes are often mentioned in this context (King and Varadi, 2002, pp.5-9). Generally across the region, some investment inflows aimed simply to control domestic or foreign markets. Once foreign investors had privatized firms, they were often shut down, or at least their production was significantly reduced, or foreign goods flooded their markets. Occasionally foreign investors bought up former state monopolies, creating new monopolistic structures (Eyal *et al*, 1997).

By and large, incoming foreign capital originated in Western Europe, a region already saturated with overproduction and facing historically high levels of structural unemployment, fiscal strain and social tensions. Any attempt by CEE companies to attain a significant share of the EU product markets was regarded highly undesirable by governments committed to deflationary economic management and fiscal retrenchment. At the same time, EC companies were striving to capture ex-Soviet markets from their previous suppliers in CEE. As Gowan (1995) argues, there was not a single West European productive sector that

Table 7.3 Growth and investment – the divided picture

| | Growth in Real GDP (%) | | | FDI ($ mln) | | |
	2000	2001	2002*	2000	2001	2002*
CEE and the Baltic states						
Croatia	3.7	4.1	3.5	827	470	1,090
Czech Republic	2.9	3.6	3.5	4,477	4,482	7,000
Estonia	6.9	5.4	4.0	324	350	300
Hungary	5.2	3.8	4.0	1,107	2,204	1,502
Latvia	6.6	7.6	5.0	398	300	250
Lithuania	3.9	5.7	3.5	375	450	545
Poland	4.0	1.1	1.5	8,171	6,502	7,000
Slovak Republic	2.2	3.3	3.5	2,058	1,500	3,500
Slovenia	4.6	3.0	3.0	110	338	131
CIS						
Armenia	6.0	9.6	6.5	104	92	80
Azerbaijan	11.1	9.9	8.5	117	314	1,307
Belarus	5.8	3.0	3.0	90	84	146
Georgia	2.0	4.5	3.0	152	100	150
Kazakhstan	9.6	13.2	7.6	1,245	2,400	2,500
Kyrgyzia	5.1	5.3	5.0	100	60	100
Moldova	2.1	4.5	3.5	100	60	235
Russia	8.3	5.0	3.5	-347	2,000	4000
Tajikistan	8.3	10.2	6.0	22	9	200
Turkmenistan	17.6	12.0	8.0	131	130	150
Ukraine	5.9	9.1	4.0	594	531	700
Uzbekistan	4.0	4.5	2.0	73	71	150

* EBRD forecast

Source: *Financial Times*, 17 May 2002

would welcome strong exporting in high-value added products from CEE. Yet, the initial planning of the new industrial and agricultural forces in the East was to be left largely to Western operators.

Different in character and long-term interests, foreign investment differentiated tangibly between resource-rich Russia and the relatively scarce resource-wise, but more developed in terms of infrastructure, economies of Eastern Europe. In Russia, Western investment experience has been less than satisfactory. Russia's fate is greatly affected by quite objective constraints of economic geography: (a) the severity of Russia's climate; (b) the vastness of the country; and (c) the predominance across this bi-continent of expensive land transport over cheap sea transport. Together, these factors ensure that in most areas of the Russian economy the intrinsic and irreducible costs of infrastructure are two to three times as expensive as elsewhere in the world. Western oil companies have lost around $10 billion in the 1990s, while Western direct investment in Russia has been only a fraction of investment in countries like Hungary, Poland, and the Czech Republic ($10 billion for Russia versus $20 billion in Poland and $16 billion in Hungary). In Central and Eastern Europe, FDI equals 4.6 per cent of GDP versus 1.6 per cent in Russia (Lynch 2002, pp.36-37).

Equally weighty are Russia's institutional and structural problems. Given Russia's low standards of corporate governance and poor legal system, the country was unable to attract foreign strategic investors. Due to their vast natural resources, in Russia and a few other CIS countries, the primary sector accounts for the largest share of inward FDI. Without significant assets ready for Western purchases, but offering instead oil and gas related blue chips through secondary circulation, Russia had to rely on debt financing and portfolio flows that do not depend on growth performance and infrastructural conditions. Instead, the country's relatively lucrative securities market has been accommodating most of the portfolio flows into the region, which in many ways have contributed to the financial upheaval of August 1998. Today, being most unlikely to finish with EU accession, Russia and the CIS must seek new forms of international economic cooperation (*Financial Times*, 17 May 2002).

In absolute terms, however, even the champion transition economies of CEE have received little FDI, without macroeconomic significance. The shock therapy vision of FDI bringing advanced technology into production processes in the post-communist region and thereby generating economic growth, presupposes that FDI is mainly production seeking. However, world economic history confirms that the precondition for large-scale FDI is domestic economic growth, not the other way around; and empirical studies of FDI in CEE have confirmed this premise. The bulk of the flow into the Visegrad countries has gone into the food, cigarettes, chocolate, soft drinks and alcohol sectors, consumer durables and the service sector (see Wagner, 2001; Abel and Darvas, 2001). This demonstrates that in the former communist countries FDI is principally 'market seeking'. FDI in the manufacturing sector has overwhelmingly meant one or two big deals in the host country's car industry. More than half of Poland's and Czechoslovakia's industrial FDI went into a single car industry project: Volkswagen's subsidiary Skoda in the Czech Republic, and Fiat's project in Poland (Gowan, 1995, pp.42-44). In the near future, Toyota Motor and PSA Peugeot Citroen are planning a new assembly plant in the Czech Republic. According to the plans, the assembly plant would employ 3,000 people and create another 7,000 indirect jobs (*Financial Times*, 17 May 2002).

The presence of transnational giants in CEE may be impressive, but as critics observe, much of this capital is going into the 'wrong' areas. Although generally the flow of 'greenfield' FDI into the region has been insignificant, the number of state enterprises purchased through FDI has been very large. The overwhelming bulk of privatizations of medium and large firms in Hungary and Poland have gone to foreign buyers and private investment funds. In telecommunications, power generation equipment, chemicals, glass, cement and pharmaceuticals, Western multinationals have sought control of strategic sectors at minimal cost and without serious plans for significant new investment. In line with this drive, the big Western players moving into Eastern Europe have typically tried to require governments to provide them with monopolistic control of the local market.[1] In Hungary, for instance, foreign investment is primarily in low-wage, low value-added, labour. Clearly, 'specializing' in low skilled cheap labour is not the way to 'catch up' with the West, given that most of the profits are in retail in the West European or North American country of final sale. Furthermore, with their privatization programmes more advanced, Hungary and Poland now have few big-ticket state assets left to sell. In both countries, capital inflows have dropped sharply in recent years, though they remain high by the standards of other countries (King and Varadi, 2002, p.11; *Financial Times*, 17 May 2002).

Therefore, while some types of FDI may benefit the host country and aid in the transition to a market economy, the overall impact of foreign capital inflows is highly controversial. Some, mainly small and medium-size joint ventures, have given workers reasonable wages and job security. The dominant trends, however, have been to sanctify individualized ownership at the expense of social equity, to pursue inappropriate loan policies, and to facilitate a corrupt bargain between owning and political classes at the expense of workers. Industrial workers across the former socialist bloc have fallen to near the bottom of the economic and social scale, there is still no effective middle class, and class boundaries are further solidified (Kideckel, 2002, p.115). The experiment of US-led globalist transition was predicated on the assumption that transnational capital flows are the primary engine of growth and development. The Russian crisis of 1998, and the less reported, but equally difficult experience of EU accession countries, show that such a belief is an overstatement of what transnational markets actually do. Transnational capital differentiates carefully between economic sectors, countries and regions, thereby aggravating politico-economic differences of post-Communism. It is plausible that FDI has been beneficial for Hungary and Central Europe, but damaging elsewhere in the post-Communist world (such as Russia and Ukraine). For instance, some multinationals have made massive investments in Hungary (e.g. pharmaceuticals) to produce drugs to sell in the eastern markets of the former USSR. These Hungarian based firms, if they are able to 'purchase' Russian and CIS markets, might result in the development for Hungary and France, but underdevelopment for Russia (King and Varadi, 2002, p.16).

Transnational capital has not moved to Eastern Europe on the scale expected, and local landscapes have been transformed only in narrow zones close to the present EU border. The manufacturing corridor along the highway between Vienna and Budapest remains the largest; Hungary and the Czech Republic by virtue of their early opening to the West, remain by far the biggest recipients of such flows (on a per capita basis). Even here, investment in manufacturing had largely dried up by 2001 (see Table 7.3). New flows in the banking, insurance and telecom sectors bring jobs and incomes for well-educated young people in the capital cities, but this will not be sufficient to sustain economic growth rates if growth declines in the West. This is not to say that FDI was unimportant, only to emphasize that it is highly selective and, in this region, most states east of the line Budapest-Warsaw have been *de facto* excluded. Left to its own devices, capital works by selection of place rather than by the lifting up of space (Kalb, 2002, pp.326-31).

Thus, in both sub-regions of post-communism – the seemingly more successful states of CEE, and the less fortunate CIS – the exposure to foreign capital influence, either in the form of portfolio investments or FDI, has produced contradictory results. The productive sectors of the real economy, which have not been picked up by Western purchasers, have deteriorated as the capital funds were diverted into speculative financing (Russia), or into a trade/services pattern of growth (CEE). Societies have been polarized, as those with ready access to the financial markets, Western capital and post-Communist elite networks rapidly became the new propertied class, while the rest of the population had to confront the hurdles of the new system without any support from the 'retreated' states. It appears that the initial promises of economic integration through foreign assistance and domestic economic restructuring that greeted the collapse of Communist regimes, have mutated into divergent and place-specific, but ultimately destructive politico-economic outcomes.

Beyond transitology: global capitalist transformations and post-communism

Orthodox economists explain the politico-economic and social contrast between CEE and the CIS by giving Central European states, Poland in particular, a high grade for applying the policies of 'shock therapy', and finding the Russian government at fault in a whole series of policy failures. Researchers of path-dependency dig deeper and point to crucial differences in the capacities of governments and the nature of the respective post-communist economies. Institutional economists, for instance, argue that the ex-Soviet economy was more monopolistic than the more fragmented economies of CEE, which turned price liberalization into an invitation for self-enrichment on the part of producers. In Central Europe, observers point to the long history of attempts to decentralize economies in Poland and Hungary, rendering these economies better prepared to respond to market signals and competitive pressures. Sociologists emphasize the relative power of an organized civil society in preventing perverse outcomes. Economic geographers note that Bohemia, Silesia and West Danubia are zones on the doorstep of the capitalist heartlands of the EU. Maybe if Russia had bordered on Germany, then Russian monopolistic practices would have been interrupted by the subsidized exports of German firms, which would have allowed avoiding many of the notorious problems of the country's restructuring. Russian failure in 1998 was a failure of the Yeltsin administration as well as of the Western advice and aid. But more than anything else, it might have been a failure of space (Kalb, 2002, p.328).

The disagreements about market reforms and the future of post-communist region are bound to last as long as the policy debate on 'transitions' is dominated by those who mistake the triumph of *capitalism* for the triumph of the *market*. Modern capitalist economies cannot be reduced to only one of their constitutive parts: markets are but one of a multiplicity of coexisting mechanisms in modern capitalism (Boyer, 1996, p.110). Capitalism evolves through numerous political-economic structures and agencies, societal institutions within the nation-state, through their (inter)-dependence and relations at local, regional and global levels. In the casino capitalism of today, it is not merely the external institutional environment of the decentralized credit system that challenges the ability of post-communist states to prevent imposing major limits on the prospects of economic and political reform (Hausner *et al*, 1995).

In the immediate period following the collapse of the Berlin Wall, the different states of the region had different reform trajectories. But as a general tendency, the main result of the immediate transition and the effect of global forces has been to reduce the function of the state by transferring its economic functions to private enterprises and its welfare functions to the market or the emerging civil society. The process came about via reforms from within, demands from western donors, and the demise of state resources carried out under the guise of privatization (Sampson, 2002, p.301). However, the path-dependency on the socialist system renders the conjuncture between the global and national politico-economic transformations inherently problematic. Often invisible remnants of previous economic, political and, crucially, societal orders still shape expectations and patterns of conduct (Hausner *et al*, 1995, pp.4-13). As a result, the actual transformations in post-communist states deviate significantly from the pathways set out by neo-liberal designers trying to erect textbook models of capitalism and democracy on what they regarded as a *tabula rasa*.

'Transition' is increasingly recognized as teleological, ethnocentrically triumphalist and disrespectful of cross-national variation (Kidelkel, 2002, p.115). In more recent analyses of post-Communism, the concept of transition, though it has not disappeared completely, has been increasingly replaced by less teleological terms such as 'transformation' and 'consolidation' (Robinson, 1998). This latter notion, with its geopolitical connotations, evokes complex processes with uncertain outcomes. It has been used especially to empathize the laborious importation of public structures and political practices from the Western democracies (Giordano and Kostova, 2002, p.74). The process of transfer of institutions and norms, which involves national governments, the IFIs and their economists is in fact shaped by struggles between elite groups both within the state, and between a transition country and the core structures of finance capitalism. The formation of capitalism is also influenced by the attitudes and acceptance of the new ideology by the society. Despite the common past, in different post-Communist countries similar conflicts are played out differently (Hausner *et al*, 1995, pp.4-13, 29).

Notwithstanding the alleged uniformity of globalizing tendencies, contemporary capitalist development is inherently contradictory and crisis-ridden. In the age of virtual telecommunications, information economy and accelerated capital flows, it is the interests of the global financial capital that play a leading role in shaping human geographical environment. In this process, various elements of social infrastructure meld together, forming distinctive kinds of 'human resource complexes'. In moulding the 'raw materials' for re-producing new social geographies, financial capital has to confront human resource complexes that are deeply sensitive to nuances in cultural, racial, ethnic, religious and linguistic history. The qualities of these initial 'raw materials' can be readily discernible in the results of socio-economic, political and cultural transformations (Harvey, 1999, pp.399-403).

The IT revolution, the rise of post-Fordism and flexible organization of economic activity in the core capitalist countries was paralleled by attempts of emerging economies and developing states to mobilize industrialization and adopt production orders that were previously the leading edge of growth in the developed economies. In most cases, these attempts were undertaken within the constraints of monetarism-inspired policy packages and under the influences of heightened international financial flows. As a result of these two developments – the advance of neo-liberal model of globalization on a world scale, and domestic neoclassical economic restructuring - by the end of the 1990s, emerging markets had effectively been turned into an export-oriented periphery to the world leading states, supplying low-wage consumer products and cheap natural resources to the countries of the core.

In the era of globalizing financial market, this way of shaping their relationship with the world system produced significant flaws in the countries' socio-economic spheres. It has become a cliché to blame the hardships of 'transition' on the laws of primitive accumulation: protagonists of neo-liberal capitalism insist that once this stage is passed, the post-communist countries will evolve into mature, Western-style capitalist democracies (Yavlinsky, 1998; Novodvorskaya, 2000). Such views forget, however, that the genesis of capitalism in the West was not directed by conscious design; its processes for selecting technologies and organizational forms were governed more by routine and competition than by rational choice. The merchants and bankers of the epoch of primitive accumulation could possibly have had no pretensions to power: they developed their businesses in the shadow and under the protection of a thoroughly non-bourgeois state (Stark, 1995, p.71; Burbach *et al*, 1997, p.134). Today, on the contrary, the distortion towards exporting activities in the allocation of both financial (direct investments, the infrastructure created to serve the exporting areas and sectors, etc.) and human resources (orientation on training and education in accordance with the needs of integration into the world capitalist market, etc.) is a characteristic of most post-communist societies. Generally, the 'democratic system' in Western Europe has been established and subjectively internalized for over centuries. In Eastern Europe, in contrast, it is largely alien, if not unwelcome, the outcome of a more or less opportunistic strategy to find favour with the winners of the Cold War (Elster *et al*, 1997).

Similarly, the application of an overly Western definition of civil society on post-communist landscapes has led to an unmistakably heightened level of incivility. In eighteenth and nineteenth century Europe, indeed, civil society was the battle cry and self-understanding of the rising urban bourgeoisie *vis-à-vis* autocratic rulers. The condition of late twentieth century post-communist citizens, with the possible exception of the intelligentsia, hardly resembled the situation of the historical European urban bourgeoisie. Blue-collar factory workers in mono-industrial peripheral regions, single mothers in provincial towns or ex-collective farm workers can hardly be compared to the classical burger family in Koenigsberg after Napoleon's invasion. Nor do huge geographic tracts on the Eurasian plains enmeshed in centrally administered continental divisions of labour resemble the social constitution of dense urban networks in West and Central Europe, with their long-established practices of local rule and civic autonomy. Civil society in Siberia and Central Asia could only become an item for luxury consumption. It has enabled local networks of well-educated citizens in the main urban centres to form NGOs and do 'good work', for example, in the professionalization of social policy or economic consultancy, even helping the state to open up for civic engagement and expand democratic competence. But among the rural population, amid small town industrial workers, the less-educated, women and children, it has done much less than it promised. It has also done much less than governing elites and global institutions have been willing to concede (Kalb, 2002, p.319).

Was it entirely a question of the unjustified application of a Western concept on non-western populations and regions? Closer inspection of the record and social function of civil society in CEE has shown that its revitalization in the 1980s and 1990s was not an arbitrary imposition by the West, but that it had strong local roots. At the same time, it was clear to most observers that civil society as a notion in Central European discourse was wedded even more firmly to monetarism than was the case in the West (Kalb, 2002, p.320). The role played by global financial capital in producing highly conflictual and divergent types of post-communist political economies, cannot be overlooked. The West has urged that those who managed to accumulate money-capital under Communism should form the core of the new domestic capitalist class (Gowan, 1995, 1996). But those people inevitably appear to be currency speculators, black marketeers, or corrupt government officials and tycoons in the import-export sectors, the latter particularly true for Russia. In 1992, when the state price of oil in Russia was 1 per cent of the world market price, domestic prices of other commodities were about 10 per cent of world prices. Managers of state companies bought oil, metals, and other commodities from the state enterprises they controlled on their private accounts, acquired export licenses and quotas from corrupt officials, arranged political protection for themselves, and then sold the commodities abroad at world prices. The total export rents were no less than $24 billion in the peak year of 1992, or 30 per cent of GDP, since the exchange rate was very low that year. The resulting private revenues were accumulated abroad, leading to massive capital flight. In 2001, Russia's capital account was still dominated by a big outflow of $26.8 billion (Åslund and Dmitriev, 1999; *Financial Times*, 17 May 2002). Clearly, entrepreneurial spirits do exist, but of a somewhat criminal kind. What made things worse was a neglect of the proliferation of crime and theft by many Western advisory bodies. In effect, American and European economic experts legitimized the criminalization of the economy: *The Economist* (9 July 1994), for example, has encouraged the Russian government to legitimize capital accumulated illicitly in the early years of the reform process and to guarantee property rights.

Thus, whilst capitalist spirits did develop inside social formations, the latter, regardless of the international pressure and control, have retained a nationally and/or regionally specific configuration of social forces and form of state. Local elites depend on incoming flows of money, technology, military assistance and legitimating ideologies from advanced capitalist countries, but at the same time, they still possess an autonomous local base of political and social power. It is the way state elites and the dominant classes maintain and reproduce their own social control through specific liaisons with agents of transnational capital, or with state elites in advanced economies, that is central in pulling the post-communist region into an uneven, dependent pattern of capitalist development. The impact of the market economy plunged millions into poverty. Post-communist regimes, increasingly constrained by international forces, have curtailed state redistribution, restored privileges to churches and other bodies, promoted private education, and generally contributed to a climate in which many citizens feel excluded from their national society, which they perceive to be institutionalizing unfamiliar inequalities (Hann, 2002, p.93). Contrary to expectations, the transition to a market economy resulted in a loss of jobs and sharp declines in industrial output. Economic collapse coupled with civil unrest has caused the escalation of poverty. Barring Poland and Hungary, all other post-communist states recorded steep increases in poverty. Some estimates indicate that between 1989-94, as many as 75 million people fell into the poverty trap in CEE (Atal, 1999, p.24).

The post-communist region is the only part of the world where poverty rates increased during 1990-98 (Table 7.4). Poverty and inequality counts have risen so drastically that anyone who speaks about 'the success of transition in Central Europe' is either a cynic or unable to look beyond macro issues of institutional design. Superficially, the poverty lines distributions and Gini coefficients come close to nominal West European poverty scores. However, while the shape of the curves may be comparable, the absolute levels are not. With largely similar price levels, the UNDP poverty line amounts to only one quarter of the actual poverty lines used by Western European governments, such as the Netherlands and Germany. Median incomes in Central Europe do not exceed some 25 per cent of median incomes in Western Europe. Therefore, local measures for the social minimum applied by CEE governments, based on a basket of necessary monthly purchases per household and thus taking into account actual price levels, give a more realistic picture of experienced material deprivation. In Poland in 1989, some 14.8 per cent of households fell below that line; in 1997, it was 47 per cent (Tarkowska, 2000). Bulgaria in 1997, after the introduction of the currency board, peaked to 80 per cent of households falling below a social minimum of DM 111 per month; measures for inequality in Romania were steeper than anywhere else in Europe, expect in the CIS (Kalb, 2002, pp.327-31). In the CIS, the increases in inequality have been unprecedented. In Armenia, Russia, Tajikistan and Ukraine, the level of inequality (measured by Gini coefficients) has nearly doubled (World Bank, 2002b, pp.8-9). It is also important to realize that unlike in the countries of the Third World, in the countries of former socialism, poverty has impacted on those who are actually employed. The poor of post-Communism are educated; in fact, poverty is greater among those who are more educated, and they are employed. Such a profile challenges the traditional theory on poverty: 'educate the poor, generate employment' (Atal, 1999, pp.26-27).

These results of 'transition' led many to contest the dominant neo-liberal market paradigm of reforms. Some critics argue that the region's problem is not too slow a

Table 7.4 Average poverty rates, 1990 and 1998 (%)

	Population living on less than $1 a day	
	1990	1998
Eastern Europe and Central Asia	1.5	5.1
East Asia and Pacific	28.2	15.3
Latin America and the Caribbean	16.8	15.6
Middle East and North Africa	2.4	1.9
South Asia	43.8	40.0
Sub-Saharan Africa	47.0	46.4
Total	20.0	17.1

Source: World Bank (2002b, p.8).

movement to capitalism, but too fast; not too little capitalism, but too much. Thus, Kideckel (2002, pp.115-16) suggests, rather than 'post-socialist', the new system may be better understood as a 'neo-capitalist' system that reworks basic capitalist principles in new, even more non-egalitarian ways than the Western model that it was supposed to replicate. The formerly Communist countries are caught up in a system, whose basic characteristics are capitalist, but clearly not of the American, nor as some say, European, variety. The new principles of property and governance appear to be the same, but the conditions and identities of the working classes are shaped by their rapidly diminishing access to resources – material, social and symbolic – in neo-capitalist society.

Far from large-scale capital transfer leading to an export-led industrial renaissance, the actual experience of Central Europe has been large-scale deindustrialization. Available stream of capital has been barely sufficed to save a fraction of the industrial infrastructure from devastation as a consequence of high interest rates, the severing of contacts with Eastern neighbours, and oligopolistic competition from the West. The real engine of growth in CEE seems to have been the booming of small services in retail, repair and maintenance, leisure, tourism, health, consultancy and real estate, together with the repatriation of incomes from migrant labour in the West. It is not an exaggeration to say that CEE has partly returned to a pre-industrial social structure, with very few areas enjoying access to solid export-based earnings. Even the new American-type malls around CEE cities, with huge investments from the West and generating direly needed employment for young local workers, are entirely dependent on a projected growth of incomes that may in the end not be realistic (Kalb, 2002, pp.326-27). The fragmented and highly contradictory nature of the post-communist political economy in the context of global financial accumulation regime is without a doubt. While national socio-economic factors constitute a potentially powerful bloc of forces that could facilitate the countries' integration into the world economy, it is the position of the core financial capital interests that ultimately determine whether such integration is indeed viable. And, as the next section shows, in most cases the verdict would not be in favour of the contenders.

The new periphery in global financial capitalism: fragmentation and integration

Within the discernible pattern of dependent regional development, there can be identified many historical, structural and stochastic factors which together ensure that the countries formerly united under administrative system, are unlikely to converge into some single 'Eastern European' or 'post-communist' model of capitalism. The region is undergoing a plurality of transitions in a dual sense: across the countries, and within any given country in different domains: economic, political, and social (Stark, 1995, p.70). The variations in the state/society problematic are vital to understanding how and why civil society and its elements feature in determining the success or failure of a 'transition'.

Here, again, the striking contrast between the decade of reforms in Russia and CEE comes into focus. The collapse of 'real socialism' did herald a rebirth of civil society in countries where it had been eradicated by the party-state. But, as Cox (1999) argues, it is the manner in which the gap between the retreated party-state and the problematic evolution of civil society traditions and institutions is being filled by various forces that ultimately determines the fate of the former Communist bloc members.[2] In both cases, the politico-economic and social space in which civil society could develop was expanded. But whether or not the opportunity was realized has been 'a challenge to human agency' (Cox, 1999, pp.8-9).

On this, illuminating views come from the historical sociology and anthropology. In Russia, quite in line with the long tradition of the country's radical changes, the 1991 push towards capitalism came from the top. Historically, each attempt to construct capitalism in Russia was accompanied by the retained system of values inherent in the pre-industrial society, and regimes of 'primary accumulation' of Russian capital tended to take the form of 'primary' stealing of the state (Kagarlitsky, 1999). Starting in the eighteenth century, Peter I and other Russian rulers strove to impose elements of Western civilization on the Russia, but the spiritual and cultural fabric of the people was largely untouched; and the mass mentality of Russians remains anti-market. The orientation towards collectivism, rather than individualism, was paralleled by the rejection of the institution of private property. It is fascinating to see that on the one hand, the interplay of national imperialism, carelessness and passivity, along with the Soviet-style slovenliness and unaccountability, had figured as a crucial impediment to the doings of romantic western-educated reformers. And yet on the other, it is this comparative weakness of individualism in Russia that has allowed mutual aid, kin networks and the extended family to persist to a degree unknown in many western, and particularly Anglo-Saxon, societies (Gray, 1998). Two institutions central to the Russian society – the extended family and a plot of land – are the most deeply entrenched rudiments that simultaneously help Russians cope with economic crises, and thwart the ideas of market rationality and individualistic logic from becoming popular. Throughout the CIS, earnings from such plots account for 40-70 per cent of total household earnings. Access to connections and informal networks and an ability to pay are key to finding a job and getting ahead. This has led to highly unequal outcomes (World Bank, 2002b, p.xiv).

The erosion of state authority and the eruption of a whole new layer of country's new rich, with big money but very few values, frustrated the majority of Russians. The consumer consolations of the new market economy are inadequate and not available to all, while the sordid aspects of the new system (e.g. prostitution, drug abuse, AIDS, crime) go uncontrolled. Some of those who grumbled most in the old days now share the nostalgia of the less articulate, for an age when they had fewer and less secure rights in a legal sense, yet their needs were more adequately fulfilled than is the case a decade later. And they often bring a moral dimension into their comments, regretting the shrinking of the public sector and articulating a strongly held sense that the new regimes do not respect entitlement to which they had become accustomed under socialism (Hann, 2002, pp.10-11). Another source of the volatility is the new elite itself. As in many 'newly developing states', the Russian ruling echelons have become divided into two groups. Both rely on corruption and access to state authority to ensure their control over resources and property. But they are divided by a fundamentally different approach to the use of this property. On the one side there is a bureaucratic bourgeoisie, only weakly linked to the West, lacking entrepreneurial dynamism, but striving for certain stability, for a social order that would guarantee them control over the use of property. Counterposed to these people is a group of bankers and speculators, a national version of comprador bourgeoisie with a lumpen-criminal psychology. All the Eastern European reforms were based on one or another formula for compromise between these two groups. But it was only in Russia that the lumpen-comprador group triumphed completely (Burbach *et al*, 1997). The decisive factor to help this layer succeed in the transfer of wealth and power has been the role of international financial institutions and policy advisors. As it was mentioned earlier, when the erosion of state authority and the consequent absence of effective economic regulation led to the proliferation of mafia control over economic activity, corrupt penetration of the state, and the forging of international criminal links, apologists for liberal economics showed their preference for crime over state regulation. Again, they could view it with equanimity as a probably necessary stage of primary accumulation (Cox, 1999, pp.22-23).

The post-1989 socio-political developments in the CEE states took a slightly different path. Political regimes in the countries of Eastern Europe, imposed by the Red Army and dominated by the USSR, were never fully legitimate (Boswell and Chase-Dunn, 2000, p.146). Hence, opposition movements there developed openly, and civil society played a significantly larger role in founding of the new regimes.[3] In these countries, the introduction of democratic traditions was not only 'announced' and encouraged by western politicians and media; importantly, it was welcomed and supported by local citizens. New independent organizations of protest grew into the political space that was opened by the disruption and uncertainty of political authority. In addition, and this is where mainstream and critical views on transition coincide, it is plausible that it was easier for these forces to develop within the CEE context, as these states have long sought to be identified with the 'Greater Europe'.

Indeed, in some countries of CEE, market-oriented attempts to reform were first undertaken back in the mid-1960s, and the slogan of 'combining planned economy with market instruments' became very popular. Most of these attempts to create a hybrid of the two systems failed despite the optimistic views of the West that saw in it a 'genuine rapprochement between socialism and capitalism' (Lavigne, 1999, p.38). Still, for the CEE states being in the Soviet bloc meant being forcibly wrenched out of a European model of life, and the post-communist period in these states has come as a rediscovery of 'normal times'. Such times have been variously identified, but their European province is beyond doubt. Countries with established historical memories of pre-communist 'golden pasts', often re-enforced by memories of the pre-communist and communist-era struggles for national survival, are thought to be more likely to look beyond the short-term costs of market transition to the future of national revival (Horowitz, 2001, p.227). Hence, the transition to 'western' institutions and values came as a relative success not because westernization and modernization are universally one and the same, but because the history and traditions of the CEE countries have always been those of European peoples. For them history has not ended with the fall of communism, it has been resumed after a half-century's interruption (Gray, 1998).

In this way, indeed, the shared national identities offer a plausible explanation for the widespread civilian support of market reforms; and the radical change of 1989-91 in Eastern Europe appears to be as much a political ambition of these countries' new leaders as it was a grass-roots rejection of state socialist ideology and a nationalist reaction to Soviet domination. The importance of socio-geographical proximity to Western European societies is confirmed by the EBRD's survey of foreign investors' assessment criteria of the quality of labour in 'transition' economies. The results of the postal survey of investors' preferences suggest that there is 'a certain hierarchy of factors in taking locational decisions, with geographic, cultural aspects coming first and subsequently wage and regulatory issues being considered' (EBRD, 2000).[4]

Public participation and support in politico-economic restructuring was fundamental to the CEE countries' reform progress. Under the dominance of finance interests, the leading forces for the formation of public opinion and civil society elements – political advisors, journalists, experts and others who Gramsci would have called the 'organic intellectuals' of marketization – are unavoidably associated with the interests of big capital. The winners of post-communism are bank managers, managers of investment funds, experts in the Ministry of Finance, IMF and World Bank advisors, and experts working for foreign and international financial agencies. Their power is a form of cultural capital; it is a function of their capacity to appropriate the sacred knowledge of the workings of the capitalist system. Managing budget deficits, negotiating international loans, setting exchange rates and the amount of money in circulation, they claim to know how to manipulate these economic technologies to produce a healthy economy and rising living standards. Their capacity to press and defend this claim results in substantial power, and is reflected in their exceptionally high salaries (Eyal *et al*, 1997).

Across the whole of the former socialist bloc, there emerged a large minority of those who could hope to become the new propertied class. But while the new capitalists in CEE states have come to see Western powers and institutions as their champions and future protectors through incorporation of western institutions; such linkage has been much weaker in the case of aspiring capitalists in Russia. Although it has become the most easily penetrated country, Russia remains much less structurally open to real western influence than CEE countries. Once this is appreciated, as Gowan (1995) points out, it is possible to grasp the obsession on the part of the OECD governments with Yeltsin. As one review has acutely put it, 'if post-communism in Central Europe is capitalism without capitalists, then in Russia it is "capitalists without capitalism"' (Eyal *et al*, 1998). Indeed, the configuration of post-communism in East Central Europe was largely determined by the fact that the 'revolutions' of 1989 came about as the technocracy, in alliance with dissent intellectuals, defeated the ruling bureaucratic estate and took power in its place. In Russia, however, the technocracy and the dissident intelligentsia were much weaker to begin with, and they had to wait until 1991 when, rather than defeating the old ruling estate, they compromised with it.

In order to understand how contemporary global tendencies impact upon the formation of capitalist structures in the formerly socialist terrain, it is necessary to note that the current wave of globalization contains three overwhelming tendencies. First, it erodes the cohesion and coherence of national states, except a few core ones. Second, it is characterized by sharply increasing levels of inequality and disparities of power between the core and the peripheries, between national states but also within each of them. Third, it generally comes to receiving territories in a highly uneven bindle of components- capital, goods, information and people (Kalb, 2002, p.318). These global forces tend operate in two ways: they bring about both fragmentation and integration. Fragmentation – along class, ethnic, regional or social lines – tends to occur in areas outside zones of capital accumulation and political decision-making. Fragmentation in the former Second and Third worlds has largely taken the form of ethnic or class polarization, often linked to regional secession movements, and is invariably associated with local corruption as either precipitant cause or result. Polities have become smaller, peripheral areas less controllable, and mafia formations emerge to control border traffic between the more integrated and less integrated border areas and between these areas and the EU. This mixture of economic difference, weak central authority and ethnic border zones creates the foundation for the kind of ethnic discontent, crime and paramilitary banditry we see in the western Balkans along the border of Albania, Macedonia, Kosovo and Serbia, as well as in the Caucasus.

Integration rewards those groups who can establish relations with representatives of Western capital. Integration occurs in those zones or among those groups who have been brought into the circles of accumulation and central decision-making. The integrated areas are those where the telephones work, where an internet café is close by, where the roads are well-paved, where young people have not all emigrated. For those groups unable to articulate with the West – the non-computer-literate, non-Anglophone, traditional working/peasant populations in the provinces – the choices seem more limited: wait for the state to provide welfare benefits, affiliate with a local leader's party, or join a band of violent entrepreneurs selling commodities any way they can (Sampson, 2002, pp.302-304). Poland represents perhaps the most striking example of how these contradictory tendencies work. It took Poland thirteen years of painstaking economic, diplomatic and legal efforts to come to the verge of EU membership, the triumphant final chapter of its post-Cold war reunion with the West. Yet today, the prevailing mood among most Poles is one of exhaustion, apathy and frustration. The year 2001 has seen a marked coarsening of political discourse with the election to parliament, for the first time, of radical Eurosceptic parties. September 11, and Russia's subsequent rapprochement with the US, have diminished Poland's geopolitical standing by weakening its claim to be an indispensable eastern ally of USA and the EU. Falling economic growth has exposed gaping holes in Polish public finance, industrial competitiveness and corporate governance; unemployment has soared to 20 per cent. Poland has turned from 'Europe's tiger into its hippopotamus' (*Financial Times*, 17 June 2002).

Therefore, rather than being framed around the one-dimensional formula of 'transition', post-communist politico-economic development is better comprehended in terms of shifts in a structure of 'dual dependency' in which economic exploitation and political domination by both the USSR and the western capitalist countries have taken different forms over time (Boswell and Case-Dunn, 2000, pp.129-130). All semi-peripheral countries are trying to find a profitable niche in the global market. Central and Eastern Europe's previous position between Soviet imperialism and dependence on foreign financial capital is being replaced by an even greater degree of penetration by direct investment from global mega-corporations.[5] Neo-liberal economic doctrine treats massive and rapid privatization by foreign strategic investors as a clear possibility for a donor country (or company) to spread risks internationally, and for the recipient to become a competitive player in the global economy. But FDI raises the dependence on foreign capital, narrows the channels for domestic economic regulation, widens the opportunities for capital speculations, and depresses domestic producers.

In parts of Eastern Europe, shock therapy policies produced a slump that matches that of the Great Depression of the 1930s (Kolodko 2001). In most of the CIS countries, the slump is many times larger (see Table 7.5). Yet, Western politico-economic actors effectively rejected all the roles Sachs – the principle intellectual mentor of shock therapy – delegated to them except those involving the imposition of constraints and pressure with one significant exception, Polish debt cancellation. Otherwise, debt cancellation was off the menu, as were macroeconomic grants and the radical opening of the EU market. Instead, Western state subsidies for exports were in, arbitrary protectionist actions were in, subsidies for FDI for their own firms were in (Gowan 1995). With economic growth in CEE resumed, the EU had to accept the enlargement as an inevitable, though protracted, process. Still, the demonstration of the success in economic transition was by no means enough to qualify for an entry into the European club. The EU's 15 member states are in no way united in 'how, or even whether, to enlarge the Union.

Governments are snared in internal debates over which polices to admit, how to spread agricultural subsidies and development aid, how to cope with the influx of cheap labour from Eastern Europe' (*Washington Post*, 12 August 2001). Gunter Verheugen, EU enlargement commissioner, warned recently that the window for

Table 7.5 The transition recession

	Consecutive years of output decline	Cumulative output decline (%)	Real GDP, 2000 (1990=100)
CEE	3.8	22.6	106.5
Czech Republic	3	12	99
Estonia	5	35	85
Hungary	4	15	109
Latvia	6	51	61
Lithuania	5	44	67
Poland	2	6	112
Romania	3	21	144
Slovak Republic	4	23	82
Slovenia	3	14	105
CIS	6.5	50.5	62.7
Armenia	4	63	67
Azerbaijan	6	60	55
Belarus	6	35	88
Georgia	5	78	29
Kazakhstan	6	41	90
Kyrgyzia	6	50	66
Moldova	7	63	35
Russia	7	40	64
Tajikistan	7	50	48
Ukraine	10	59	43
Uzbekistan	6	18	95
Output decline during the Great Depression, 1930-34			
France	3	11	
Germany	3	16	
UK	2	6	
USA	4	27	

Source: World Bank (2002b, p.5)

expansion was closing amid a rise in extreme-right rhetoric. Enlargement barely figures as a popular issue in most member states, but it could enter voters' sights as a negative when the financial issues reach the negotiating table in the end of 2002 (*Financial Times*, 17 June 2002).

Unable and unwilling to fully assimilate the entire Eastern expanse, transnational capital is instead trying to establish its strong points in the region, raising certain areas to the level of the 'civilized world.' This coincides with the ambitions of the local elites. If the large resource-rich countries like Russia are doomed to the role of the periphery of the West, certain regions may reach the level of semi-periphery, with a chance of eventual inclusion in the western community of wealthy. In order to create suitable conditions for this, the states or regions concerned need to separate themselves from their less favoured neighbours using state borders, visas and customs duties. At the same time, they need to thwart all efforts to redistribute funds to the advantage of less developed regions. Burbah *et al* (1997) insist that it is this process, rather than nationalist outbursts, that is the primary cause of the disintegration of all the eastern European federations. The collapse of the USSR created favourable conditions for what the authors call a '*Kuwaitization*' of the Baltic republics. In Yugoslavia, it was Slovenia that became 'Kuwaitized'. And after the disintegration of Czechoslovakia, the Czech Republic attained a privileged economic status compared to impoverished Slovakia. In Russia, resource-rich regions such as Yakutia or Tatarstan may become new Kuwaits. Interestingly, drawing on this general picture of the post-communist region, Burbah *et al* conclude that in Eastern Europe, dependent capitalism is evolving according to a Latin American scenario, while in Russia the pattern is more akin to that in Africa.

Enquiring into the future of the region, there is a strong likelihood that in the next twenty years, the bifurcation process will intensify, and most of the successor states to the socialist bloc are to experience downward mobility in the international hierarchy of politico-economic interests. A few of them might succeed in becoming incorporated into an expanded core region centred in the EU. This is certainly true of the former East Germany, very likely for the parts of Czech Republic, Hungary and even Poland and Slovenia (Boswell and Chase-Dunn, 2000, p.129). Russia, by contrast, has clearly rejected the Western model of democracy and a market economy. But that does not mean that it is not developing. The anarcho-capitalism left over from the Yeltsin's era does have a window of opportunity to evolve into something akin to the highly successful state-led capitalism that generated the rapid economic development of Russia in the last decades of the tsarist regime (Gray, 1998, pp.152-65). But that, needless to say, depends on the ability and will of the country's political leadership to strengthen state authority and rebuild Russia's national ideology, as well as on the skill to mobilize economic resources and turn from being a predominantly export-oriented appendix to the world economy into a more domestically oriented, mixed type of the economic system. What is clear so far, is that an administratively strong and interventionist state – one that protects Russian industry and directs resources from profitable (resource-based) sectors to unprofitable but vital sectors and regions – is an essential prerequisite to Russian welfare, as the typical costs of production will not normally be assumed by private investors with free access to the world's generally more attractive investment possibilities (Lynch, 2002, p.39).

Overall, the on-going process of capitalist development in the former socialist terrain may be characterized by what Hoogvelt (2001) termed 'involution of capitalism'. Through a multifaceted process of dependency on the dominant fraction of capital, certain locales (countries, cities or regions) of the post-communism, through socio-economic and political linkages between new capitalist elites and sometimes even middle layers are being incorporated into the global economy. While the rest of the populations are thrown backwards to the position of either economic exploitation, or simple irrelevance – eg Romania, Bulgaria, certainly Belarus and even Ukraine. In this new kind of core-periphery relationship, costly exercises of military power by the capitalist centre are not necessary (though, of course, Kosovo confirms that these measures are still on the agenda). Rather, the structural power and financial capital pressures, conveyed through numerous international organizations to the contender territories, constitute a new phase of imperialist contradictions in the social geography of capital accumulation.

Conclusion

Sitting in the auditoriums of business schools in Sophia or Warsaw, or walking the streets of Budapest or Prague, and certainly going shopping in Berlin, it is easy to fall for the wisdom of 'The Market'. Yet, driving some fifty miles away from Moscow it is equally easy to feel nostalgic for the times of Soviet stability and faith. There hardly could have been a better portrayal of how the capitalist system works and fails to work than the contrasting outcomes of the decade of post-Communist reconstruction. The irony of the present moment is that the collapse of state socialism has coincided with the time when capitalism has reached the stage where maximizing economic efficiency leads to undermining the bases of the very society that requires maximum efficiency as a principle of its existence (Kagarlitsky, 1999, pp.32-35).

Through the flow of foreign capital, open foreign exchange markets and domestic economic liberalization post-communist countries are increasingly integrated into the global political economy. For most of them, the decade of 'transition' was a roller-coaster ride. Moscow has earned a reputation of the second most expensive city in the world, whereas thousands of Russians were paid in toilet rolls and army boots for their work. Prague and Budapest have turned into the new Meccas of Eastern Europe luring tourists and businessmen with low costs and reasonable service, whereas neighbours are killing each other in the former Yugoslavia. Previously united under the Communist rule, the ex-members of the Soviet empire are coming face to face with the dramatic controversies of the new capitalist way of life, and learn their tough lessons. The most important of them – as this chapter has attempted to show – is the notion that free markets are not synonymous with the virtues of free democracy, and crucially, the very notion of competitive free markets needs to be placed in the context of the transnational oligopolies that dominate world trade and commerce. The now legion of writings on 'transition' are predominantly economy-focused; and in this, they are critically flawed. Former citizens of the USSR and their East European neighbours, perhaps more vividly than people in the core capitalist countries, are coming to recognize that markets are primarily social, rather than technical institutions, and that G-7 governments are quite likely to prefer order to political freedom if the alternatives involve the sacrifice of creating market societies in the east: there is too much at stake for the interests of the core capital (Gill and Cheru, 1997, p.163).

Furthermore, the already discernible divergent paths of the post-communist development support the notion that in a theory of transformative change the new comes from reshaping existing resources, rather than from the new itself. The comprehensive blueprints for all-encompassing institutional change suffer from an inadequate comparison of socialism and capitalism (Stark, 1995, pp.70-71). Misled by the obviously superior performance of capitalist institutions, observers and key participants start to believe that these institutions can be replicated by thoroughly following the demands of the theoretically equipped and experienced international financial experts. Indeed, it seems, the governments of most of the Central European countries have been remarkably more successful in implementing the reform packages, and managed not only to re-gain the economic growth, but also to stay out of the drama of the world financial debacle of the late 1990s. Russia, in contrast, appears to have been phenomenally persistent in abusing the requirements of the IMF and foreign economic experts, and paid the high price for her mistakes in the summer of 1998.

This line of logic drives the still dominant orthodox theorizing of the transition cases. However, the pertinent comparative lesson of a decade of transformation in the post-communist societies is that the failure of socialism rested precisely in an attempt to organize all economic processes according to a grand design. This chapter has tried to demonstrate the perils of parsimonious economistic approaches to analyzing post-communism. It called for a deeper political-economic understanding of modern capitalist development, and in particular, for a critical examination of the role of global financial capital in shaping the future of the post-Communist Europe. Mainstream transitology needs to be challenged by the scholarship in economic geography, political economy, and, especially, development theory. The latter is no way a call for narrow-minded identifying of the post-communist states with developing economies of the Third World; indeed, it was precisely this approach that had inspired the 'one-size fits all' structural adjustments packaged to the former Soviet bloc members in the early 1990s. Rather, a wider interdisciplinary framework would reveal the present social, economic and geopolitical contradictions of post-Communism that are vital for shaping the future of the region.

Notes

1   Gowan expands on the original study by Parker (1994).
2   Some of them take the form of exclusionary populism: various forms of extreme-right political movements and xenophobic racism. Some of them originate in the covert world of complex congeries of underground activities, some carried out secretly in the name of states, some criminal. The collapse of state authority also

unleashed sub-national forces of ethnic nationalism that became vehicles for garnering the residues of economic and political power (Cox, 1999, p.13).

3 In Poland, Solidarsnosc as a trade union became a rallying point for a broad based opposition to the communist regime and the Catholic Church had long stood as an alternative pole of loyalty to the state. According to Cox (1999), the current scholarly interest in civil society very largely originated in observation of the popular movements in Poland, Czechoslovakia, Hungary and the GDR, which toppled the communist regimes in these countries after the USSR had signalled it would not, or could not, support them any longer.

4 'How do foreign investors assess the quality of labour in transition economies? Results from a postal survey', Produced by the Office of Chief Economist at the EBRD, available through www.ebrd.org/english/public/index.htm; a fuller version is presented in the *Transition Report* (2000).

5 The 1993 Copenhagen Summit agreed on the basic criteria that the Association countries had to satisfy to be eligible for EU membership. In the economic context it called for 'the existence of a functioning market economy as well as the capacity to cope with competitive pressure and market forces within the Union.' In addition, Membership requires 'the ability to take on the obligations of membership, including adherence to the aims of political, economic and monetary union'. The EU calls for an orderly liberalization of capital movements that should be completed before accession. In terms of the economic conditions for accession, inability to abolish capital controls would be interpreted as inability to cope with competitive pressure and market forces within the Union. There are no precise demands on how and in which order this liberalization should take place. However, some indications can be derived from the Europe Agreements, the so-called Association Partnerships as well as from the regular Progress Reports issued by the Commission. Although the Europe Agreements differ slightly in how capital movements are treated, all of them include the obligation that foreign payments should be liberalized early on (Article VIII liberalization in the IMF's terminology), as should capital movements relating to the establishment of companies and self-employed professionals, including the acquisition of real estate needed for such establishment.

Bibliography

Abel, I. and Darvas, Z. (2001), 'Relative resistance to currency crisis: the case of Hungary, comparisons with the Czech Republic and Poland', in D. Daspugta, M. Uzan and D Wilson, (eds), *Capital flows without crisis?* London: Routledge, pp.111-30

Abelin, A. (1996), *Long-term economic growth strategy*, Tokyo: Economic Planning Agency, Working paper 47

Amman, R. and Cooper, J. (eds), (1982), *Industrial innovation in the Soviet Union*, New Haven: Yale University Press

Åslund, A. (1989), *Gorbachev's struggle for economic reform*, London: Pinter

Åslund, A. (1995), *How Russia became a market economy*, Washington: Brookings

Åslund, A. (2002), *Building capitalism. The transformation of the former Soviet bloc*, Cambridge: Cambridge University Press

Åslund, A. and Dmitriev, M. (1999), 'Economic reform versus rent seeking', in A. Åslund and M. Olcott (eds) *Russia after communism*, Washington, DC: Carnegie Endowment for International Peace, pp. 91-130

Astapovich, A. and Grigor'ev, L. (1993), 'Inostrannie investitsii v Rossii: problemy i resheniya', *Mirovaya ekonomika i mezhdunarodnie otnosheniya*, (5), pp.16-29

Atal, A. (1999), *Poverty in transition and transition in poverty*, New York: UNESCO

Bates, R.H. (2001), *Prosperity and violence. The political economy of development*, New York: W.W. Norton

Baylis, T.A. (1994), *The West and Eastern Europe. Economic statecraft and political change*, Westport: Praeger

Bednazh, S. (2000), 'Ukraine and the EU: comparative perspectives', unpublished paper

Belyaev, N. and Chichkanov, V. (1992), 'Russia's foreign economic strategy', *International Affairs*, (2), pp.39-46

Berengaut, J., De Vrijer, E., Elborgh-Woytek, K., Lewis, M. and Lissovolik, B. (2002), 'An interim assessment of Ukrainian output developments 2000-2001', *IMF Working Paper* WP/02/97

Berliner, J. (1976), *The innovation decision in Soviet industry*, Cambridge, MA: MIT Press

Blanchard, O., Dornbusch, R., Krugman, P., Layard, R. and Summers, L. (1991), *Reform in Eastern Europe*, Cambridge, MA: MIT Press

Blanchard, O., Boycko, M., Dabrowski, M., Dornbusch, R., Layard, R. and Shleifer, A. (1993), *Post-communist reform. Pain and progress*, Cambridge, MA: MIT Press

Blasi, J., M. Kroumova and D. Kruse (1997), *Kremlin Capitalism. Privatizing the Russian Economy*, Ithaca: Cornell University Press

BOFIT (Bank of Finland Institute for Economies in Transition) (1997a), *Russian and Baltic Economies - the week in review*, (48), e-mail version (http://www.bof.fi/bofit)

BOFIT (1997b), *Russian and Baltic Economics - the week in review*, (49), e-mail version (http://www.bof.fi/bofit)

BOFIT (1997c), *Russian and Baltic Economics - the week in review*, (51-52), e-mail version (http://www.bof.fi/bofit)

BOFIT (1998a), *Russian economy. The month in review*, (2)

BOFIT (1998b), *Russian economy. The month in review*, (3)

BOFIT (1998c), *Russian economy. The month in review*, (6)

BOFIT (1999), *Russian economy. The month in review*, (2)

BOFIT (2000), *Russian economy. The month in review*, (5)

BOFIT (2003) *Russian economy. The month in review*, (7/8)

Bogdankevich, S. (2002), 'Trudnosti i perspektivy razvitia demokratii v Belarusi', http://www.ucpb.org/rus/showart.shtml?art=198

Bogomolov, O. (1992), 'The collapse of the communist empire: an avenue to European civilization', in M. Keren and G. Ofer (eds), *Trials of transition. Economic reform in the former Soviet bloc*, Boulder: Westview, pp.27-38

Böhle, D. (2000), 'Internationalisation: an issue neglected in the path-dependency approach to post-communist transformation', in M. Dobry (ed.), *Democratic and capitalist transitions in Eastern Europe. Lessons for the social sciences*, Dordrecht: Kluwer Academic Publishers, pp.235-61

Bojcun, M. (1985), *The working class and the national question in Ukraine, 1880-1920*, unpublished PhD dissertation, York University

Bojcun, M. (1999), 'The Ukrainian economy since independence', *Working Papers in Ukrainian Studies* (1), http:// www.unl.ac.uk/ukrainecentre

Borzunova, O. (2000), 'Vsemirnaya Torgovaya Organizatsiya i tamozhennoye regulirovaniye. Pravovye problemy prisoyedineniya Rossii k VTO', http://www.akdi.ru/econom/iam/av7.htm

Boswell, T. and Chase-Dunn, C. (2000), *The spiral of capitalism and socialism*, Boulder: Lynne Rienner

Boyer, R. (1996), 'State and market. A new engagement for the 21st century', in R. Boyer and D. Drache (eds) *States against markets*, New York: Routledge, pp.84-116

Bunce, V. (1985), 'The empire strikes back: the evolution of the Eastern bloc from Soviet asset to Soviet liability', *International Organization*, 39 (1), pp.1-46

Burakovsky, I. and Biletsky, V. (1999), *Ukraine's way to the European Union*, Kiev: Freidrich Ebert Stiftung

Burawoy, M. and K. Verdery (eds), (1999), *Uncertain transition. Ethnographies of change in the postsocialist world*, Lanham: Rowman and Littlefield

Burbah, R., Kagarlitsky, B. and Nunez, O. (1997), *Globalization and its discontents*, London: Pluto Press

Cagan, P. (1956), 'Monetary dynamics of hyperinflation', in M. Friedman, (ed.), *Studies in the quantity theory of money*, Chicago: Chicago University Press, pp.47-85

Chase Dunn, C. (1989), *Global formation: structures of the world-economy*, London: Blackwell

Chubais, A. and M. Vishnevskaya (1993), 'Main issues of privatization in Russia', in A.Åslund and R. Layard (eds), *Changing the economic system in Russia*, London: Pinter, pp. 89-99

Chossudovsky, M. (1998) *The globalisation of poverty: impacts of the IMF and World Bank reforms*, London: Zed Books

Collins, S. and Rodrik, D. (1991), *Eastern Europe and the Soviet Union in the world economy*, Washington, DC: Institute for International Economics

Considine, J. and Kerr, W. (2002), *The Russian oil economy*, Cheltenham: Edward Elgar

Conway, P. (1995), *Currency proliferation: the monetary legacy of the Soviet Union*, Princeton: Princeton University, Department of Economics, International Finance Section.

Cook, L. (1994), *The Soviet social contract and why it failed: welfare policy and workers' politics from Brezhnev to Yeltsin*, Cambridge, MA: Harvard University Press

Cox, R. (1999), 'Civil society at the turn of the millennium: prospects for an alternative World Order', *Review of International Studies*, 25 (1), pp. 3-28

CPCFPU (2001), *Report 21-27 April 2001*, Kiev: Centre for Peace, Conversion and Foreign Policy of Ukraine

Crystal, J. (1990), *Oil and politics in the gulf: rulers and merchants in Kuwait and Qatar,* Cambridge: Cambridge University Press

Demetriades, P. and Luintel, K. (2001) 'Financial restraints in the South Korean miracle', *Journal of Development Economics,* 64 (2): 459-79

Denizer, C., Desai, R. and Gueorguiev, N. (2000), 'Financial liberalization and financial repression in formerly socialist economiesi, *Financ A Uver,* 50 (1), 17-39

Dienes, L. (1985), 'The energy system and economic imbalances in the USSR', *Soviet Economy,* 1 (4), pp.340-72

Dietz, R. (1991), 'The role of western capital in the transition to the market - a system's theoretical perspective', in L. Csaba (ed.), *Systemic change and stabilization in Eastern Europe,* Aldershot: Dartmouth, pp.103-23

Dyker, D. (1999), 'Foreign direct investment in transition countries – a global perspective', in D. Dyker (ed.), *Foreign direct investment and technology transfer in the former Soviet Union,* Cheltenham: Edward Elgar, pp.8-26

Dyker, D. (2001), 'Technology exchange and the foreign business sector in Russia', *Research Policy,* 30 (5), pp.851-88

Eatwell, J., Ellman, M., Karlsson, M., Mario Nuti, D. and Shapiro, J. (1995), *Transformation and integration. Shaping the future of Central and Eastern Europe,* London: IPPR

EBRD (European Bank for Reconstruction and Development) (1995) *Transition report 1995,* London: European Bank for Reconstruction and Development

EBRD, (1997), *Transition report 1997,* London: European Bank for Reconstruction and Development

EBRD (1998), *Transition report 1998,* London: European Bank for Reconstruction and Development

EBRD (2002), *Transition report,* London: European Bank for Reconstruction and Development

EIU (1991), *USSR. Country profile 1991-1992,* London: Economist Intelligence Unit

Elster, J., Offe, C. and Preuss, U. with Boenker, F., Gottling, U. and Rueb, F. (1998), *Institutional design in post-communist societies,* Cambridge: Cambridge University Press

Esanov, A., Raiser, M., and Buiter, W. (2001), 'Nature's blessing or nature's curse: the political economy of transition in resource-based economies', *European Bank for Reconstruction and Development Working Paper,* (65)

EU (2001), *Country Strategy Paper 2002-2006: National Indicative Programme 2002-2003 Ukraine,* Brussels: European Union Commission

Evangelista, M. (1996), 'Stalin's revenge: institutional barriers to internationalization in the Soviet Union', in R. Keohane and H. Milner (eds), *Internationalization and domestic politics,* Cambridge: Cambridge University Press, pp.159-85

Eyal, G. and Szelenyi, I. (1998), *Making capitalism without capitalists,* New York: Verso

Eyal, G., Szelenyi, I. and Townsley, E. (1997), 'The theory of post-communist managerialism', *New Left Review,* 222, pp. 60-92

Eyal, J. (1992), 'Military relations', in A. Pravda (ed.), *The end of the outer empire. Soviet-East European relations in transition,* London: Sage, pp.34-72

Faminskii, I. (ed.), (1993), *Rossiya: vneshekonomicheskie svyazi v usloviyakh perekhoda k rynku,* Moscow: Mezhdunarodnie otnosheniya

Fel'zenbaum, V. (1994), 'Inostrannie investitsii v Rossii', *Voprosy ekonomiki,* (8), pp.10-24

Fieleke, N. (1992), 'The liberalization of trade and payments', in D. Kennett and M. Lieberman (eds), *The road to capitalism. Economic transformation in Eastern Europe and the Former Soviet Union,* Fort Worth, TX: The Dryden Press, pp.266-81

Filipenko A. (1997), 'Zovnishnoekonomichni vidnosyny Ukrayiny', in T. Stepankova, P. Dudkiewicz and M. Ghosh (eds), *Ukrayina na Perekhidnomu Etapi,* Kyiv: Akademiya, pp.151-55

Filtzer, D. (1992), *Soviet workers and destalinisation*, Cambridge: Cambridge University Press

Fish, M.S. (1995), *Democracy from scratch. Opposition and regime in the new Russian revolution*, Princeton: Princeton University Press

Fish, M.S. (1998), 'The determinants of economic reform in the post-communist world', *East European Politics and Societies*, 12 (1), pp.31-78

Frieden, J. and Rogowski, R. (1996), 'The impact of the international economy on national policies an analytical overview', in R. Keohane and H. Milner (eds), *Internationalization and domestic politics*, Cambridge: Cambridge University Press, pp.25-47

Fry, M. (1995), *Money, interest and banking in economic development*, Baltimore: The Johns Hopkins University Press

Gaddy, C. (2002), 'Has Russia entered a period of sustainable economic growth?', in A. Kuchins (ed.), *Russia after the fall*, Washington, DC: Carnegie Endowment for International Peace, pp.125-44

Gaddy, C. and Ickes, B. (1998), 'Russia's virtual economy', *Foreign* Affairs, 77 (5), pp.53-67

Gaidar, Y. (1999), *Days of defeat and victory*, Seattle: University of Washington Press

Gerschenkron, A. (1962), *Economic backwardness in historical perspective*, Cambridge, MA: Harvard University Press

Gerschenkron, A. (1970), *Europe in the Russian mirror. Four lectures in economic history*, Cambridge: Cambridge University Press

Giovannini, A. and De Melo, M. (1993), 'Government revenue from financial repression', *American Economic Review*, 83 (4), pp.953-63

Godin, Y. (2001), *Rossia i Belorussia na puti edineniya,* Moscow: Mezhdunarodnye otnosheniya

Goskomstat (2000), *Rossiiskii statisticheskii ezhegodnik*, Moscow: Goskomstat

Goskomstat (2001), *Rossiiskii statisticheskii ezhegodnik*, Moscow: Goskomstat

Goskomstat SSSR (1987), *SSSR v tsifrakh v 1987 godu*, Moscow: Finansy i Statistika

Gowan, P. (1995), 'Neo-liberal theory and practice for Eastern Europe", *New Left Review*, 213, 3-60

Gowan, P. (1996) 'Eastern Europe, Western power and neo-liberalism', *New Left Review*, 216, 129-40

Gowan, P. (1999), *The global gamble. Washington's Faustian bid for world dominance*, London: Verso

Granovetter, M. (1985), 'Economic action and social structure: the problem of embeddedness', *American Journal of Sociology*, 91 (3), pp.481-501

Gray, J. (1998), *False dawn. The delusions of global capitalism*, London: Granta Books

Grigor'yan, I. (1997), 'Transnatsional'nie korporatsii v Rossii', *Svobodnaya mysl'*, (2), pp. 14-27

Gustafson, T. (1989), *Crisis amid plenty. The politics of Soviet energy under Brezhnev and Gorbachev*, Princeton, NJ: Princeton University Press

Halchynsky, A. (1999), *Ukrayina: postup u maibutnie*, Kiev: Osnovy

Hann, C. (2002), 'Farewell to the socialist "other"', in C. Hann (ed), *Postsocialism. Ideas, Ideologies and practices in Eurasia*, London: Routledge, pp.1-11

Hanson, P. (2003), 'The Russian economic recovery: do four years of growth tell us that the fundamentals have changed?', *Europe-Asia Studies*, 55 (3), pp.365-82

Hart-Landsberg, M. and Burkett, P. (1998), 'This is no alternative: the Asian crisis and the crisis of development theory', mimeo

Harvey, D. (1999), *The limits to capital*, London: Verso

Hausner, J., Jessop, B. and Nielsen, K. (eds) (1995), *Strategic choice and path-dependency in post-socialism*, Cheltenham: Edward Elgar

Hellman, J. (1998), 'Winners take all. The politics of partial reform in postcommunist transitions', *World Politics*, 50 (2), pp.203-34

Henderson, K. and N. Robinson (1997), *Post-communist politics*, London: Prentice Hall

Hewitt, E. (1988), *Reforming the Soviet economy. Equality versus efficiency*, Washington, DC: Brookings Institution

Hewett, E. with Gaddy, C. (1992), *Open for business. Russia's return to the global economy*, Washington, DC: Brookings Institution

Hoffman, E. and Laird, R. (1985), *Technocratic socialism. The Soviet Union in the advanced industrial era*, Durham, NC: Duke University Press

Hoogvelt, A. (2001) *Globalisation and the postcolonial world. The new political economy of development*, Basingstoke: Palgrave

Illarionov, A. (1998), 'Kak byl' organizavan Rossiiskii finansovyi krizis', *Voprosy ekonomik*i, (11), pp.21-43

IMF (1999), *Ukraine: recent economic developments Country Report 99/42*, Washington, DC: IMF

IMF (2000a), *World economic outlook 2000*, Washington, DC: IMF

IMF (2000b), *Russian Federation. Selected Issues. Country Report 00/150* Washington DC: IMF

IMF (2001), *Ukraine. Statistical Appendix. Country Report 1/28*, Washington DC: IMF

IMF (2002), *Republic of Belarus: Selected issues*. IMF Country Report no.02/22, Washington DC: IMF

IMF, World Bank, Organization for Economic Co-Operation and Development, European Bank for Reconstruction and Development (1990), *The economy of the USSR. Summary and recommendations*, Washington, DC: World Bank

IMF, World Bank, Organization for Economic Co-Operation and Development, European Bank for Reconstruction and Development (1991a), *A study of the Soviet economy. Volume 1*, Paris: Organization for Economic Co-Operation and Development

IMF, World Bank, Organization for Economic Co-Operation and Development, European Bank for Reconstruction and Development (1991b), *A study of the Soviet economy. Volume 2*, Paris: Organization for Economic Co-Operation and Development

IMF, World Bank, Organization for Economic Co-Operation and Development, European Bank for Reconstruction and Development (1991c), *A study of the Soviet economy. Volume 3*, Paris: Organization for Economic Co-Operation and Development

Ishiyama, J. (2002), 'Neopatrimonialism and the prospects for democratization in the Central Asian republics', in S.N. Cummings (ed.), *Power and change in Central Asia*, London: Routledge, pp.42-58

Johnson, J. (1998), 'Russia's emerging financial groups', *Post-Soviet Affairs*, 13 (4), pp. 335-365

Johnson, S. and Kroll, H. (1991), 'Managerial strategies for spontaneous privatization', *Soviet Economy*, 7 (4), pp.281-316

Jones Loung, P. and Weinthal, E. (2001), 'Prelude to the resource curse. Explaining oil and gas development strategies in the Soviet successor states and beyond', *Comparative Political Studies*, 34 (4),. 367-99

Kagarlitsky, B. (1999), *New realism, new barbarism*, London: Pluto Press

Kalb, D. (2002), 'Afterword. Globalism and postsocialist prospects', in C. Hann (ed), *Ideas, ideologies and practices in Eurasia*, London: Routledge, pp.317-34

Karavayev, V. (1992), 'Russia's foreign economic strategy in the 1990s', *International Affairs*, (8), pp.10-17

Kideckel, D. (2002), 'The unmaking of an East-Central European working class', in C. Hann (ed), *Postsocialism. Ideas, Ideologies and practices in Eurasia*, London: Routledge, pp.114-32

King, L. and Varadi, B. (2002), 'Beyond Manichean economics: foreign direct investment and growth in the transition from socialism', *Communist and Post-Communist Studies*, 35 (1), pp.1-21

Kolodko, G. (2001), 'Globalization and catching-up: from recession to growth in transition economies', *Communist and Post-Communist Studies* 34, (2), pp.279-322

Korhonen, I. (1998), 'The sustainability of Russian fiscal policy', *Review of Economies in Transition*, (1), pp. 5-12

Kornai, J. (1986), 'The soft budget constraint', *Kyklos*, 39 (1), pp.3-30

Kornai, J. (1992), *The socialist system. The political economy of communism*, Oxford: Clarendon Press

Kotkin, S. (2001), *Armageddon averted. The Soviet collapse 1970-2000*, Oxford: Oxford University Press

Kriukov, V. (2001), 'Ownership rights, hierarchical bargaining and globalization in the oil sector', in K. Segbers (ed.), *Explaining post-Soviet patchworks. Volume 2. Pathways from the past to the global*, Aldershot: Ashgate, pp.170-92

Kuchma, L. (2000), *Poslannia Prezydenta Ukrayiny do Verkhovnoyi Rady*, Kiev: Administration of the President of Ukraine

Kuvaldin, V. (1998), 'Prezidentstvo v kontekste rossiiskoi transformatsii', in L. Shevtsova (ed.) *Rossiya politicheskaya*, Moscow: Carnegie Endowment for International Peace, pp. 20-60

Kuzin, D. (1993), 'Rossiiskaya ekonomika na mirovom rynke: problema konkurentosposobnosti', *Obshchestvo i ekonomika*, (3), pp.32-44

Kuznetsov, A. (1994), *Foreign investment in contemporary Russia. Managing capital entry*, Basingstoke: Macmillan

Lankes H.P, and Stern, N. (1998), 'Capital Flows to Eastern Europe and the Former Soviet Union', *EBRD Working Papers*, (27), pp.1-6

Lavigne, M. (1990), *International political economy and socialism*, Cambridge: Cambridge University Press

Lavigne, M. (1999), *The economics of transition. From socialist economy to market economy*, Basingstoke: Macmillan, 2nd edition

Lazarev, V. and Gregory, P. (2003), 'Commissars and cars: a case study in the political economy of dictatorship', *Journal of Comparative Economics*, 31 (1), pp.1-19

Ledeneva, A. (1998), *Russia's economy of favours*, Cambridge: Cambridge University Press

Ledeneva, A. (2001), 'Networks in Russia: global and local implications', in K. Segbers (ed.), *Explaining post-Soviet patchworks. Volume 2. Pathways from the past to the global*, Aldershot: Ashgate, pp.59-77

Lenin, V. (1915), 'Socialism and war', in (1975), *The Lenin anthology*, R.C. Tucker (ed.), New York: W.W. Norton, pp.183-95

Lenin, V. (1916), 'Imperialism: the highest stage of capitalism', in V. Lenin (1968), *Selected works*, Moscow Progress Publishers, pp.169-262

Linz, J.J. and Stepan, A. (1996), *Problems of democratic transition and consolidation. Southern Europe, South America, and post-communist Europe*, Baltimore: The Johns Hopkins University Press

Lisovskaya, N. and Korosteleva, J. (2002), 'Belarusian economic policies from official and opposition Perspectives', in Korostelava, E.A., Lawson, C., and Marsh, R., (eds), *Contemporary Belarus: between democracy and dictatorship*, London: RoutledgeCurzon, pp.137-51

Lockwood, D. (2000), *The destruction of the Soviet Union. A study in globalization*, Basingstoke: Macmillan

Lushin, A. and Oppenheimer, P. (2001), 'External trade and payments', in B. Granville and P. Oppenheimer (eds), *Russia's post-communist economy*, Oxford: Oxford University Press, pp.261-300

L'vov, D.S. (2001), 'Rossiya i sovremennii mir', in *Postsotsialisticheskie strani v usloviyakh globalizatsii. Sbornik materialov mezhdunarodnoi nauchnoi konferentsii*, Moscow: IMEPI RAN, pp.16-35

Lynch, A. (2002), 'Roots of Russia's economic dilemmas: liberal economics and illiberal geography', *Europe-Asia Studies*, 54 (1), pp.36-37

Macmillan, C. (1993), 'The role of foreign direct investment in the transition from planned to market economies', *Transnational Corporations*, 2 (3), pp.97-119

McKinnon, R. (1992), 'Taxation, money, and credit in a liberalizing socialist economy', in C. Clague and G. Rausser (eds), *The emergence of market economies in Eastern Europe*, Oxford; Blackwell

McKinnon, R. (1993), *The order of economic liberalization*, Baltimore: Johns Hopkins University Press, 2nd edition

Ministerstvo Innostrannykh Del RB (1997), *Prognoz Vstuplenoya Respubliki Belarus vo Vsemirnuyu Torgobuyu Organizatsiyu. Sluzhebnaya zapiska*, Minsk: Belosusskii Dom Pechati

Ministerstvo Innostrannykh Del RB (1999), *Nekotorye Problemy po Prisoyedineniyu v VTO. Sluzhebnaya zapiska*, Minsk: Belosusskii Dom Pechati

Ministerstvo Innostrannyh Del RB (2000), *Natsional'naya Programma Razvitiya Eksporta na 2000-2005 gody*, Minsk: Belosusskii Dom Pechati

Murrell, P. (1992), 'Conservative political philosophy and the strategy of economic transition', *East European Politics and Societies*, 6 (1), pp.3-16

Novodvorskaya, V. (2000) *Dialogi A. Panikin i V. Novodvorskaya*, Moscow: Solidarnost'

OECD (Organization for Economic Co-operation and Development) (1992), *Bulgaria. An economic assessment*, Paris: OECD

OECD (1999), *Post-Uruguay Round Tariff Regime. Achievements and outlook*, Paris: OECD

Oesterreichische Nationalbank (2000) *Focus on Transition*, (1), Vienna: Oesterreichische Nationalbank

Olson, M. (2000), *Power and prosperity. Outgrowing communist and capitalist dictatorships*, New York: Basic Books

Pashkov, M. (2000), Commentary with no title in *Rozvytok ta rozshyrennia Ye.S. pid chas holuvannia Frantsii. Perspektyvy dlia Ukrainy*, Kiev: Atlantic Council of Ukraine

Pleines, H. (1999), 'Crime and corruption in the Russian oil industry', in D. Lane (ed.), *The political economy of Russian oil*, Lanham: Rowan & Littlefield, pp.97-110

Pop, L. (2001), 'From naïve communism to "popular capitalism" in Eastern Europe? A case of selective participation in the global market place', paper to the PSA Annual Conference, Manchester, April 2001

Popov, V. (2000) *The political economy of growth in Russia*, Washington, DC: Center for Strategic and International Studies, PONARS working paper series 17

Popov, V. (2001), 'Russia: inconsistent shock therapy with weakening institutions', in G. Cornia and V. Popov (eds), *Transitions and institutions. The experience of gradual and late reformers*, Oxford: Oxford University Press, pp.29-54

Robinson, N. (1994), 'From coup to coup to ...? The post-communist experience in Russia, 1991-1993', *Coexistence*, 31 (4), pp. 295-308

Robinson, N. (1995), *Ideology and the collapse of the Soviet Union*, Cheltenham: Edward Elgar

Robinson, N. (1998), 'Corporate interests and the politics of transition in Russia, 1991-1994', in J. Gary Hopps and D. Iatridis (eds), *The socioeconomic impact of privatization*, Westport, CT: Praeger, pp. 169-83

Robinson, N. (1999), 'The global economy, reform and crisis in Russia', *Review of International Political Economy*, 6 (4), pp.531-64

Robinson, N. (2000), 'The presidency: the politics of institutional chaos', in N. Robinson (ed.), *Institutions and Change in Russian Politics*, Basingstoke: Macmillan, pp.11-40

Robinson, N. (2002), *Russia. A state of uncertainty*, London: Routledge

Rohach O. and Shnyrkov O. (1999), *Transnatsionalizatsiya svitovoho hospodarstva ta perekhidni ekonomiky*, Kiev: Kyivskiy Universytet

Roland, G. (2000), *Transition and economics. Politics, markets, and firms*, Cambridge, MA: MIT Press

Ross, M.L. (2001), 'Does oil hinder democracy?', *World Politics*, 53 (3), pp.325-61

RTR-Vesti (2002), 'Neurozhai-plokho, urozhai-eshche khuzhe' http://www.akdi.ru/econom/new/20-09.htm

Ruatava, J. (2002), *The role of oil prices and the real exchange rate in Russia's economy*, Helsinki: Bank of Finland Institute for Economies in Transition Discussion Papers, (3)

Rusakevich, I. (2002), 'Monetarnaya politika v Respublike Belarus' *Belaruskaya economika: ot rynka k planu*, 1, Minsk: Center for Social and Economic Research, Institute for Management and Privatization, (http://ipm.by/pdf/Book/1-05.pdf)

Russian Government (1992), 'Medium-term programme of the economic reforms of the Russian Government', *Russian Economic Trends*, 1 (3), pp.43-71

Rutland, P. (1993), The politics of economic stagnation. The role of local party organs in economic management, Cambridge: Cambridge University Press

Sachs, J. (1993), 'Western financial assistance and Russia's reforms', in S. Islam and M. Mandelbaum (eds), *Making markets*, New York: Council for Foreign Relations Press, pp.143-75

Sampson, S. (2002), 'Beyond transition. Rethinking elite configurations in the Balkans', in C. Hann (ed), *Postsocialism. Ideas, Ideologies and practices in Eurasia*, London: Routledge, pp.297-316

Shmelev, N. and Popov, V. (1989), *Na perelome: ekonomicheskaia perestroika v SSSR*, Moscow: Novosti

Schumpeter, J. (1961), *The theory of economic development: an inquiry into profit, capital, credit, interest and the business cycle*, New York: Oxford University Press

Schumpeter, J. (1991), 'The crisis of the tax state', in R. Swedberg (ed.), *Joseph A. Schumpeter. The economics and sociology of capitalism*, Princeton: Princeton University Press, pp.99-140

Sergeev, A. (2001), 'Fighting for labor rights in a transitional economy', in H. Isham with N. Shklyar (eds), *Russia's fate through Russian eyes. Voices of the new generation*, Boulder: Westview, pp.114-25

Shambayati, H. (1994), 'The rentier state, interest groups and the paradox of autonomy. State and business in Turkey and Iran', *Comparative Politics*, 26 (3), pp.307-31

Shaw, E.S. (1973) *Financial deepening in economic development*, New York: Oxford University Press

Silitski, V. (2002), 'Political economy of Belarus-Russia integration', in V. Bulhakau (ed.), *Belarus-Russia integration*, Minsk: Encyclopedix, pp.222-69

Smith, A. (1992), 'Economic relations', in A. Pravda (ed.), *The end of the outer empire. Soviet-East European relations in transition*, London: Sage, pp.73-93

Solnick, S. (1997), *Stealing the state. Control and collapse in Soviet institutions*, Cambridge, MA: Harvard University Press

Stalin, J. (1924), 'Ob osnovakh Leninizma', in Stalin, J.V. (1952), *Voprosy Leninizma*, Moscow: Gospolitizdat, 11th edition, pp. 1-80

Stark, D. (1995), 'Not by design. The myth of designer capitalism in Eastern Europe', in J. Hausner et al (eds), *Strategic choice and path-dependency in post-socialism*, Cheltenham: Edward Elgar, pp.67-83

Stark, D. and Bruszt, L. (1998), *Postsocialist pathways. Transforming politics and property rights in East Central Europe*, Cambridge: Cambridge University Press

Statkomitet SNG (2000), *Statisticheskii ezhegodnik '99*, Moscow: Interstate Statistical Committee of the Commonwealth of Independent States

Statkomitet SNG (2002), *Sodruzhestvo Nezavisimikh Gosudarstv v 2001 godu*, Moscow: Interstate Statistical Committee of the Commonwealth of Independent States

Stone, R.W. (2002), *Lending credibility. The International Monetary Fund and the post-communist transition*, Princeton: Princeton University Press

Suraska, W. (1998), *How the Soviet Union disappeared. An essay on the causes of dissolution*, Durham, NC: Duke University Press

Tarkowska, E. (2000), 'An underclass without ethnicity: the poverty of Polish women and agricultural laborers', in R. Emigh and I. Szelenyi (eds), *Poverty, ethnicity and gender in Eastern Europe during the market transition*, Westport: Praeger, pp.83-122

Tompson, W. (2002), 'Putin's challenge: the politics of structural reform in Russia', *Europe-Asia Studies*, 54 (6), pp.933-57

Treisman, D. (1998), 'Fighting inflation in a transitional regime. Russia's anomalous stabilization', *World Politics*, 50 (4), pp. 235-265

Triulzi, U. (2000), 'The Partnership and Co-operation Agreement: a new Marshall Plan? Paper delivered to the European Commission Stagiaire Conference 'A New Iron Curtain? EU-Russia Relations in Focus', Brussels, 26 June 2000.

UCIPR (2000), *Research Update*, 6 (191)

UN (1999), *World Economic and Social Survey 1999*, New York: United Nations

UNDP (1999), *Human Development Report*, New York: Oxford University Press

UNDP (2001), *Human Development Report*, New York: Oxford University Press

Urban, M. (1985), 'Conceptualizing political power in the USSR: patterns of binding and bonding', *Studies in Comparative Communism*, 18 (4), pp.207-226

Urban, M. (1994), 'State, property, and political society in postcommunist Russia: in search of a political center', in C. Saivetz and A. Jones (eds), *In search of pluralism. Soviet and post-Soviet politics*, Boulder: Westview, pp.125-150

Urinson, Ya. (1994), 'Investitsionnii klimat v Rossii i privlechenie inostrannikh investitsii', *Voprosy ekonomiki*, (8), pp. 4-9

van Selm, B. (1997), *The economics of Soviet break-up*, London: Routledge

von Zon, H. (2000), *The political economy of independent Ukraine*, Basingstoke: Macmillan

Wagner, N. (2001), 'Poland's experience with capital flows in the 1990s', in D. Daspugta, M. Uzan and D. Wilson, (eds), *Capital flows without crisis?* London: Routledge, pp. 83-110

Watson, J. (1996), 'Foreign investment in the Russian oil industry', *Europe-Asia Studies*, 48 (3), pp.429-456

Wedel, J. (1998), *Collision and collusion. The strange case of western aid to eastern Europe 1989-1998*, New York: St Martin's Press

Woodruff, D. (1999), *Money unmade. Barter and the fate of Russian capitalism*, Ithaca, NY: Cornell University Press

World Bank (1997), *World economic indicators*, Washington DC: World Bank

World Bank (2002a), *World development report 2002*, New York: Oxford University Press

World Bank (2002b), *Transition: ten years*, Washington DC: World Bank.

World Bank (2002c), *World development indicators*, Washington DC: World Bank

WTO (1994), *The results of the Uruguay Round of Multilateral Trade Negotiations. Legal texts*, Geneva: GATT Secretariat

WTO (1995a), *Accession of Ukraine. Agriculture*, WT/ACC/UKR/17, 23 November

WTO (1995b), *Accession of the Russian Federation. Questions and replies*, WT/ACC/RUS/2, 2 June

WTO (1995c), *Accession of Ukraine. Questions and replies*, WT/ACC/UKR/5, 5 October

WTO (1996a), *Accession of the Russian Federation. Additional questions and replies*, WT/ACC/RUS/9/Add.2, 30 May

WTO (1996b), *Accession of Ukraine. Additional questions and replies*, WT/ACC/UKR/25, 8 May

WTO (1996c), *Accession of Russia. Additional questions and replies*, WT/ACC/RUS/9, 23 April

WTO (1996d), *Accession of the Russian Federation. Additional questions and replies*, WT/ACC/RUS/9/Add.1, 30 May

WTO (1996e), *Accession of Russia. Information on non-tariff measures on products*, WT/SPEC/RUS/2 of 30 August

WTO (1997a), *Accession of Ukraine. Additional questions and replies*, WTO/ACC/UKR/25/Add.1, 7 April

WTO (1997b), *Accession of Ukraine. Additional questions and replies*, WT/ACC/UKR/22/Add.2, 21 March

WTO (1997c), *Accession of Russia. Additional questions and replies*, WT/ACC/RUS/17 of 11 March

WTO (1997d), *Accession of Russia. Information on subsidies system*, WT/ACC/RUS/22, 24 November

WTO (1998), *Subsidies. United States*, G/SCM/N/38/USA, 19 November

WTO (1999), *Subsidies. European Communities*, G/SCM/N/48/EEC, 12 November

WTO (2000a), *Replies to questionnaire on import licensing procedures. United States*, G/LIC/N/3/USA/3, 9 November

WTO (2000b), *Replies to questionnaire on import licensing procedures. Singapore*, G/LIC/N/3/SGP/3, 1 December

WTO (2001a), *Replies to questionnaire on import licensing procedures. Turkey*, G/LIC/N/1/TUR/3/Add.1, 21 September

WTO (2001b), *Replies to questionnaire on import licensing procedures. European Communities*, G/LIC/N/3/EEC/4, 17 October

WTO (2001c), *Subsidies. Brazil*, G/SCM/N/60/BRA, 8 January

Yates, D.A. (1996), *The rentier state in Africa: oil rent dependency and neo-colonialism in the Republic of Gabon*, Trenton: Africa World Press

Yavlinsky, G. (1998), 'Russia's' phony capitalism', *Foreign Affairs*, 77 (3), pp.67-79

Yeltsin, B. (1994), *Zapiski prezidenta*, Moscow: Ogonyok

Zaiko, L. (2002), 'Mesto bezdeistvia – Belarus', *Belaruskaya gazeta* 25 (341)

Index